Tell Me
Everything

Tell Me Everything

A MEMOIR

Minka Kelly

Henry Holt and Company

New York

Henry Holt and Company
Publishers since 1866
120 Broadway
New York, New York 10271
www.henryholt.com

Photograph insert credits: Page 8, top two photographs, courtesy of Zach Gilford.
Page 8, bottom photograph of Minka Kelly by Jeffrey Reiner.
All other photographs are from the author's personal collection.

Library of Congress Cataloging-in-Publication Data is available.

ISBN: 9781250852069

Our books may be purchased in bulk for promotional, educational, or business use.
Please contact your local bookseller or the Macmillan Corporate and
Premium Sales Department at (800) 221-7945, extension 5442, or by e-mail at
MacmillanSpecialMarkets@macmillan.com.

First Edition 2023

Designed by Meryl Sussman Levavi

Printed in the United States of America

1   3   5   7   9   10   8   6   4   2

This work is a memoir. The names of some individuals have been
changed to respect their privacy.

To all the wounded inner children out there,
looking for protection and healing. I see you.

Contents

Author's Note

This is a work of nonfiction, based on my memories, journals, and conversations with people from that time in my life. To protect the privacy of certain individuals, some names have been changed. As we all know, memory is fallible, but this narrative recounts as truthfully as possible the way I remember things and the way they felt. That said, this narrative tells my experience from the point of view of a scared and traumatized child. As a result, while the depiction of some family members are accurate as to how they felt in the moment, in the years since, my understanding of the frailties of the human condition has softened my perspective. Now, I can see the love that had been offered, even if I didn't see it at the time.

Tell Me
Everything

Prologue

THE BIG EYE

The low-slung stucco building squats along a frontage road off Interstate 25 in Albuquerque, solitary, as if the nearby storefronts and fast-food joints are deliberately keeping their distance. Without the cloak of nighttime, the Big Eye looks even dumpier, the huge leering eyeball and neon letters spelling out ADULT VIDEO tired under the harsh southwestern sun.

The parking lot sparkles with oil drippings and crushed glass. Sad little weeds peek through the pitted asphalt. It's the kind of place I'd never have noticed if my boyfriend hadn't tricked me into coming here last Saturday night, promising we were going to see *Men in Black* at the multiplex. I was pissed at the time about Rudy's bait and switch, but today I'm glad. I finally have a plan. I take a deep breath and get out of the car.

The storefront is crammed with porn-watching cubicles, adult toys, and DVDs. The back half of the building features a pair of peep show stages with individual booths for customers to watch live girls perform for tokens and tips. The Madonna video *Open*

Your Heart features a similar peep show, but it's a shiny and sterile version of this armpit. Still, I've made up my mind. Being a coin-operated girl can't be that bad.

I hand the manager the ID card I've obtained with a friend's documents, *Lydia Gonzalez, twenty-two*, holding my breath, waiting for her to call me out on the obvious mismatch between the girl pictured on the driver's license and me. She turns the card over, nugget-size rings concealing stumpy fingers, barely glancing at it.

I don't look anything like the real dark-haired, dark-eyed Lydia Gonzalez, though my lips are lined dusky, eyelids heavy with black liquid eyeliner, eyebrows plucked to thin pinstripes. Maybe I look close enough. Girls here seem interchangeable. I'm seventeen and frightened, but the manager doesn't notice, just gives me the once-over to make sure my tits are big enough to hold attention.

"Start Tuesday? Shift is nine to midnight."

Perfect. I'll go to high school during the day and come here in the evening. I feel queasy, afraid I might be crossing a threshold, the one that lured my mother down a rabbit hole, but I'm desperate.

I'm basically on my own since Mom signed my custody over to Rudy's father last year. She and the man who raised me were running from the cops and I've been fending for myself since. Rudy is turning into an asshole and even his father knows it's time for me to move on. "You're too good for my son, mija," he tells me. "Save up for first and last and I'll cosign an apartment for you, okay?"

But where will I go?

I've been earning minimum wage at the Check 'n Go, yet at this rate it's going to take months to set aside enough for a place of my own. Plus, my middle-aged boss keeps hitting on me. I turned down his advances last week and he fired me. This peep show, I decide, is going to be my get-out-of-jail-free card. Six months, I promise, and I'll have enough to break free.

◇◇

Three nights later, when I enter the back half of the building where the live action goes down, ready for my first shift, the smell slams into me. It's as if the whole place has been doused with undiluted Clorox. The fumes make me cough, every breath a reminder of how squalid the Big Eye is. The lighting is harsh, the industrial carpet matted and piebald. I've already washed my hands three times since I arrived and resolve never to use the toilet.

The peep show is built in the shape of a large rectangle split in half by the dressing room. On one side is a stage fronted by half a dozen little booths for customers to watch what happens on that stage. An identical layout is on the other side. Two girls work the adjoining stages at once, dancing to music that thumps loudly from the overhead speakers like a migraine.

Backstage in front of a vanity to get ready, I put my clothes on a chair to provide a barrier between my butt and the seat. I'm nervous but determined. My hand shakes and I smear my lipstick but fix it up before anyone notices.

I'm wearing a long-sleeve, white stretchy lace top that ties at my sternum, showing off a lacy bra that I adjust, making sure it pushes up my boobs. The matching lace pants with bell bottoms sink low on my hips, accentuating the G-string. I didn't have to shop for stripper costumes for this job. I have three or four of Mom's, passed down to me from the time I was young as if they're some kind of inheritance. Call it weird or disorienting nostalgia, but as I filled out, she loved having me dress up in her old getups. In some ways, they *are* my inheritance, the only source of power she has to share with me. My mother's looks and her ability to attract men are the only security she's ever known. Whether she meant to convey that particular message, it's the one I've learned.

This outfit is my favorite of hers. I've even taken her stage name, "Frankie." I didn't tell her about this job when we talked on the phone a few days ago, though. I don't want to know what she'd think about this choice. It would break her heart to think of me in her world.

All my life, my mom tells me I can be anything I want, to dream big, the world's my oyster, but she frames my future choices in gauzy terms with no instructions on how to get there. She doesn't tell me to focus on school or to create a path to whatever I might desire. I don't even know what my options are. Clearly, if she knew how to make a better life, she would have done so herself.

Now, looking back, I just wish once in a while she'd compliment me on my resourcefulness, intelligence, or resilience. I'd like her to see me as someone with potential, but the only praise she gives me is the one she considers the highest compliment: "You're so beautiful."

If this is my only source of power, I'd better learn to use it.

◇◇

Like other peep shows, the platform where I'll be dancing is separated by glass from the small private booths where the customers are. That glass barrier is one of the reasons I considered the job in the first place; it'll keep me apart and isolated. Customers won't be able to touch me. Frankly, after being with Rudy, I'm starting to think that all men should be held behind glass.

Here, I'll be able to close my eyes and dance the hours away pretending I'm not doing this, imagining I'm somewhere else. It'll be like the customers don't even exist.

Next to me at the makeup table, Tina, my coworker, is also getting ready.

"Hey," I say, looking for an ally or some guidance. I'm tired of feeling so damn alone.

Tina ignores me, putting on fake eyelashes and picking a selection of Ani DiFranco tunes for our set. Okay, I guess I'm on my own here, too.

And then it's nine o'clock. Showtime.

∞

I'm tense, waiting for my first client. When he inserts a token, a red light will come on over my stage and the divider that keeps me hidden from view will rise. The only way I'll earn money is if a client slips a tip into my slot, so I have to be alluring and give him a taste of something soft he can't have. The peep show doesn't pay us for appearing.

The music throbs, Ani DiFranco pouring out her pain in a staccato voice with finger-plucked strings, but so far, no takers. I try to get comfortable on the cafeteria-style chair, picking at my fingernails and pushing up my boobs again, thinking I might need to pee. I want to get the first one over with.

On Tina's side of the stage, things are ramping up. Her red light is lit like a lurid Christmas tree. The customers all seem to want Tina.

My light will come on soon, I tell myself.

I hear Tina moaning, loud and carnal. Everyone in the shop, even at the very front, can hear her. She knows how to put on a show. Later, I'll learn that she plays with herself and uses sex toys in her act. I'm glad I didn't figure that out this first night; it might have scared me away.

I wipe the sweat from my palms and recross my legs.

∞

Finally, my red light flicks on.

Here we go! My heart pounds against my rib cage as I stand to dance. The divider rises and I face a man wearing a soiled backward ball cap and what appear to be unbuttoned jeans. Everything about him, particularly his facial features—unshaven, wan, and tired—is more hyperreal than I imagined. I thought we'd be more distanced from each other, that I could trick myself into believing he wasn't really there. This feels as if we're in the same room, alone together. It's too intimate. I think about running for the exit.

He stares at me expectantly, waiting for me to show him my body. He's looking for me to turn him on, to get him heated enough that he'll lose his inhibitions, pull his dick out, and jerk off. This man's face will stay with me the rest of my life, the way he stares, believing I'm about to give him tacit permission to abandon himself to the urge. I'm not sure how to do this.

Though I'm cold and want to cover up, I sway my hips and wave my arms, trying to guess at what he wants to see. If I hope to make money tonight, I'll need to seduce him into wanting more time with me and stuffing bills into my slot to get it. I've watched porn with Rudy and try to mimic the facial expressions, opening my mouth, licking my lips. How soon am I supposed to take my clothes off? How much do I remove?

Dancing for this man, I feel bewildered. It's like being sober with someone who's drunk. You're lucid and present and the other person is on another planet. He's consumed with desire, not even aware I'm really here. Plus, I'm not practiced at these moves, and unlike at a strip club, there's no other dancer to watch. I can't see Tina.

As I dance and try to lure him in, I remove myself from the room as much as I can, steal myself away from my body, try to blot out my consciousness. I make myself numb, repeating in my mind that this peep show is not really similar to what Mom had to do. No lap dances here, no touching. It's safer, here. Really.

Tina's boisterous moaning, though, combined with this man's unnerving stare, waiting for me to turn him on, tells me something different.

Finally, I'm starting to get into the moves. I feel a rhythm, I'm swaying my hips, though I'm pretty certain I'm not doing it right.

I look at him and move toward his window to let him know I see him. I'm ready to be what he needs me to be, ready to leave my sense of self behind, ready to show him my body.

I reach up to undo the knot holding my flimsy top in place, inserting my fingers into the twisted strands to release them, when the divider between us slams shut. I'm flooded with relief. Oh, thank God! I don't have to go through with it. I've been given a reprieve.

And then regret smacks me hard across the face. He didn't put in another token. I've lost my first client.

Meanwhile, the noise from Tina's half of the room rises in volume. How many fake orgasms can she have?

I wait for another client. I'm resilient and hardworking. I can learn to do this. But my bulb doesn't light.

∞

When I leave at midnight, pulling on a hoodie and sweats, Tina's counting a stack of bills. I haven't earned a buck.

Making money here is possible. I know it. The night I was here with Rudy, we stood in one of the booths as he fed in tokens. I leaned against the back wall, trying to make myself small, wishing we were at the movies like he promised. When the door opened and the dancer appeared, though, she surprised me. She seemed friendly. I think she could tell I was nervous because she focused on me, ignoring Rudy. She seemed to say, "I see you. It's okay."

Maybe it was refreshing to see a girl in the room. In this line of work, you see dirtbag after dirtbag, some of them licking the glass, no one cleaning it between tongues, and spend three hours watching guys jerk off. Their heads bob woodpecker-like with their percussive hand motions. It's a struggle to get that image out of your head. But I don't know any of that yet. Only that the woman on the other side of the glass dances and strips a little, nothing too raunchy. I like the soft way she looks at me, protective and caring.

Soon, though, I stop watching her because my vision zeroes in on the fanned-out pile of hundreds she's displayed on a chair. Easily a thousand bucks. She made that in one night?

I can do what she's doing. I can learn.

Still, it's her eyes more than anything I take from that night, how kind and gentle, maybe even welcoming, they are. Those eyes ask the very question I've spent a lifetime trying to answer:

What are you doing here, sweet girl?

Part I

Family pathology rolls from generation to generation like a fire in the woods taking down everything in its path until one person, in one generation, has the courage to turn and face the flames. That person brings peace to his ancestors and spares the children that follow.

—TERRY REAL

CHAPTER ONE

Mom's Beloved "Bag Lady" Sketch

"Oh baby, I have something special in store for you!" Mom gushed. She hugged her arms close to her chest as if she needed to keep the joy from bursting through her entire body, like it was a current of energy that pulsed through her, not always under the influence of her control.

Tonight, she was thrilled about the Top Ramen she was making for dinner as well as the evening that would follow. It wasn't exactly Bring Your Daughter to Work night, but that's what it was about to become. When I stood next to her, it was like standing beside a redwood tree, she was so sinuous and graceful, her head up in the clouds. Now she squatted to my height and wrapped me in a hug.

I was seven and often tagged along with her to Crazy Girls on La Brea, just south of Sunset Boulevard, a few blocks from Hollywood's tourist zone in the shadows of florid neon and half-acre billboards. Tonight, she wanted to show me her new act and I was excited to go. It sure beat the usual routine of being dropped off with neighbors or people I didn't know, falling asleep on a stranger's couch until Mom came to pick me up well after midnight.

"I'm going to put an egg in your ramen, just how you like it!" she said, checking on the noodles on the hot plate and opening the minifridge.

Her enthusiasm was always dialed up to ten and she found childlike eagerness for the smallest goodness. "Oh baby, this is going to be so much fun!" was her most common refrain, and usually she was right. A trip to the movies meant ordering absolutely everything at the concession stand: Red Vines, popcorn, Slurpees, hot dogs, M&M's. When she had money, a Target foray was a chance to indulge in new T-shirts, jeans, and toys, or maybe sneakers from Payless, whatever my heart desired. She loved to say yes to everything, was like a two-year-old who could mine from even the most mundane activity an extravagant level of glee.

At thirty-one, she was really just an oversized kid. And I was her favorite playmate.

We lived in the storage room of an apartment complex where we'd once had our own unit, a cut-rate offer bestowed on us by the landlady when Mom ran out of money to pay rent. There was barely enough room to walk between the mattress and the wall in the 125-square-foot box, but as she shimmied and pranced around the room, the Christmas lights she'd put up to make the place feel homey reflected in her tousled, done-up hair. I beamed.

She fixed dinner between daubs of makeup, turning to make faces at herself in the mirror. Singing and dancing, she flung the hem of her silk robe into the air, filling our tiny place with her bright mood. I was certain magic dust floated around her.

Making someone else feel good was Mom's superpower and I could see the pleasure on her face now, her eyes as effervescent as a just-opened bottle of 7 Up as she planned our night. Tonight, she would share with me a part of her work that made her particularly joyful, certain that her delight would be mine as well.

We ate our ramen on the full-size mattress on the floor, then packed up my My Little Pony backpack with coloring books and crayons. She took me by the hand as we walked the few blocks to the club. At school, I'd learned about crosswalk safety and was trying to get her to follow the program.

"A crosswalk? Why would we walk all the way over there? Let's run. Ready, set, go!"

Hand in hand, we darted across La Brea, our laughter rising into the night.

◇◇

"Here comes Mo!"

The minute we walked into Crazy Girls, the cheer that followed her everywhere rose up from those inside.

Everyone loved Maureen, who brought the party wherever she went. She called people "sweetie" and "baby," asked about each one individually as if they were her closest friend, gave each her full attention. If you didn't like your nose, say, she'd make a point of telling you how beautiful your nose was, lavishing you and your nose with praise. Her attention was a beam of warm light, making you feel as if you were the most important person in the world. This was her true talent. Clients, bartenders, dancers, janitors, the DJ—everyone was happy to see Mo.

Making our way through the club, its interior darker than the night outside, our eyes adjusted as she greeted and air-kissed the DJ and bartenders. Then we settled in the backstage dressing room where the dancers were getting ready. All young women in their twenties and early thirties like my mom, they doted on me, showering me with kisses and compliments.

"How gorgeous you are!"

"You've gotten so big."

"You're a beaut, Mink!"

I delighted in the attention, even if I blanched a tiny bit at the smell of beer or vodka on their breath. They were giddy, enthusiastic, and likely drunk.

◇◇

I loved the women backstage. They called themselves "girls" and laughed and gossiped. The room reeked of makeup and Victoria's Secret lotion mixed with spilled whiskey and stale cigarette smoke. Still, they seemed powerful, confident, so sure of themselves. Occasionally, one would stumble back from her act and proffer one of the long-stemmed red roses she'd been given by a client. "For you, Mink," she'd say.

After they hugged me, I'd find glitter in my hair, stuck on my sweatshirt and face.

By the end of the night, I knew Mom, like the rest of them, would walk away with an impressively thick rolled-up wad of cash, and the next day, I'd get to do something nice with her because of it—maybe a barbecue by the pool in the apartment complex. I knew the world they lived in was seedy, but I figured it must be worth it.

I also knew Mom was different from the others who worked here. The rest seemed content to come in and do their shifts, but Mom gave it her all and was the creative force behind the acts. She choreographed dances for the other women based on her favorite musicals, like *West Side Story*. (One skit was a riff on the Officer Krupke song and she'd erupt with laughter every time at the final line: "Gee, Officer Krupke, Krup you!")

To my eyes, she was unique, creative, gorgeous. I adored her.

◇◇

This night, for the first time, she was going to let me watch her perform what she referred to as her "Bag Lady" sketch.

While the women around me powdered their faces, painted

their lips, and primped their hair, I settled into my usual spot near my mother's mirror with my coloring book, before I noticed one of the dancers pulling Mom aside, talking in a whisper.

"You really think this is a good idea?" She jerked her head in my direction.

I pretended I couldn't hear.

Mom's hiss was low and deadly. "Don't tell me how to raise my daughter! I know what I'm doing." I smiled to myself. That dancer should have known better.

Mom walked over to me and pulled me close—"My baby! Come here!"—and smothered me in kisses so the woman could see just how much I was loved.

As Mom got ready for her act, the girls kept an eye on me, then one escorted me to where I could get a clear view of the stage and still remain hidden. I'd seen Mom getting ready and knew the trick she was about to play.

◇◇

Disco lights in the main room bounced off the mirrored walls, multiplying the colorful beams into an endless, whirling kaleidoscope. It was near ten, well past my bedtime but the height of the evening rush at Crazy Girls. By now the sparse crowd had filled in and pulsing music with a heavy bass line made the floor rumble. I felt a rush, curled into myself at the backstage door, hiding behind the dancer who'd led me there.

I'd been in this room many times but had never been allowed to watch when the show came on, until now. This was going to be my mom's big moment.

I craned from backstage to see the crowd. Forty or fifty people, mostly men, filled the space, many clumped at little tables with pitchers of beer in front of them. A few sat in the back enjoying lap dances, girls rippling in front of them, the men's hands hovering an inch over the girls' backsides, sticking bills into G-strings, laughing. Topless cocktail waitresses and a handful of other dancers filled out the crowd.

On the main stage, a topless woman in a G-string twirled around a shiny pole like an acrobat. I was wondering how she kept from getting dizzy, going around in circles like that, when a bag lady burst into the club's side door as if she'd stumbled in by mistake. She was layered in sweaters and an overcoat, wrapped in scarves, and carrying what seemed to be her sole belongings in stained sacks. A knit hat was pulled low, covering part of her face, her hair shoved inside.

"Well, hello there! Who's having the party?"

The men put down their drinks and swiveled their heads. The room fell silent.

The bag lady looked around, drunk or lost. She walked between the tables, picking up a customer's drink. She tasted it, approved, and set it back down on the table as the customer recoiled. She picked up another's drink, spat it out, and tossed the glass. The strippers looked at her, then at each other, unsure of what was happening; they were all in on the ruse.

"Ma'am. Can we help you?" the DJ asked over the PA system.

"Me?" she shouted back. "I don't need any damn help!" She continued hobbling toward the stage. "Oh honey, you're sexy!" she said to one of the girls giving a lap dance. "Hey, I can dance, too!" she called out as she got closer to the stage. "Let me up there."

She climbed onto the raised platform as the men hissed. "Isn't there a bouncer here?" someone cried from the audience.

The woman strutted across the stage, awkward at first, but soon her movements became smooth. Layer by layer, she shed the rags. The men went from scowling to rapt.

The DJ cued up Led Zeppelin's "Since I've Been Loving You." At that moment, my mother pulled off the huge wrap that encircled her head and shoulders, then shook out her mane of long blond hair. The timbre in the room changed dramatically.

Hoots and claps thundered. "Oh baby!" someone cried.

All eyes were on Mo. They loved it.

The music dialed up a notch and Mom twirled and shimmied with abandon, peeling layer after layer, revealing a stunning, statuesque woman in a golden bra and G-string.

Crumpled bills pooled around her feet. I was excited, not just to see her surprise the room, but because their howls meant she'd get good tips. It meant crayons, coloring books, and groceries.

∞

I felt a tug at my sleeve. "Come on, honey." The dancer who'd brought me from the dressing room was at my side, pulling me away. "That's enough for now. Let's go."

I understood it was my mom who'd timed my exit, but it didn't matter. I already knew what would happen next. The golden bra would fly off, and soon she'd be gyrating her hips in a stranger's face. I'd stolen glimpses of the lap dancers and seen yet others walking around the club topless. Even then, I recognized Crazy Girls as a place where women took off their clothes for men. In her way, Mom was trying to protect me, and for a long time I let her think she had.

I wasn't proud of Mom's work, but at seven, I wasn't exactly embarrassed by it, either, mostly because there was no one to be embarrassed in front of. Outside of school, I was often the only kid in a crowd of adults.

I now know that a kid's calibration for what's normal is determined by whatever she grows up with. If your dad's a drug dealer and your mom works in the sex industry, that's just your regular life. For me, this was it—Crazy Girls was life as usual.

∞

Backstage, I buried myself in my coloring book, the loud music and applause fading into background noise. I was happy. Mom had tricked them all. She hadn't just done a predictable strip routine but had blended her creativity and acting skills to develop something novel and unexpected, delighting the crowd. Every sign of appreciation from the audience translated into cash in our pockets, the ability to buy cereal and Hamburger Helper. If Mom did really well, at the end of the week she'd treat the two of us to new shoes.

∞

Still, I didn't understand how she made fistfuls of money and yet there was never enough for rent. I wanted our old apartment back. Then, we'd had a proper living room and space to stretch out, we weren't confined to the cramped box we lived in now. But I didn't tell her that. She went to a lot of trouble to brighten up our small storage space. For her sake, I pretended it was enough.

∞

After her first show, I got tired and Mom made a little nest of blankets for me in a corner of the dressing room. As sleepiness overtook me, I remembered the cheers Mom's act had garnered. She used to be a Vegas showgirl; I'd seen the pictures. She was so glamorous then. But that was before me and single parenthood. This club, I knew even then, was a step down from the dazzling life she'd envisioned, but still, the men had applauded and enjoyed her act. They'd tossed money at her feet. That was a kind of success, wasn't it?

I fell asleep, pressing my nose into the folds of my Cabbage Patch doll, comforted by the smell of vanilla and baby powder. I wanted all the stink of whiskey, stale cigarettes, and perfume to go away. The deeper I breathed in my doll, the more I imagined a different life, one in which we had our old apartment back and I didn't fall asleep way past my bedtime on a school night in the back of a strip club.

∞

Sunlight streamed through the sliding glass door and hit me square in the eye. Looking around, I didn't know where I was. The apartment was as drab and neglected as a crappy hotel room. The coarse stinky couch where I'd slept had left my cheek raw. The shag carpet smelled as if the previous owner had a cat who wasn't good at using the litter box. Had Mom brought me here last night?

I found my backpack by my feet, digging out the spare toothbrush I carried for nights when I wouldn't be going home. In the bathroom, I washed my face and finger-combed my hair, then headed to the kitchen to see if I could rustle up something for breakfast or pack a lunch for school. This wasn't the first time I'd found myself in this situation. I was used to fending for myself.

I went to a fridge with a broken handle and pulled at the corner to find a box of baking soda, a sticky bottle of teriyaki sauce, and a six-pack of beer. Good thing I'd tucked a few packs of string cheese in my backpack yesterday. I ate one and tried to figure out how I was going to get to school.

I loved school and I didn't want to be late. My teacher said I was good at math and reading. Playing tetherball at recess was my favorite. I'd been tardy almost every day recently, though, and was humiliated by it. The school really prized timeliness.

The door to the apartment's only bedroom was opened a crack, so first I knocked. When no one answered, I slowly pushed it open.

Mom was passed out on the bed, wrapped only in the stink of cigarettes and booze, her hair a blond mop unraveled across the bed. A guy with long dark hair sat upright next to her, a sheet covering his lap.

I went to her side. "Mommy." I pulled at her arm, but she didn't move. The guy just watched, a curious but disengaged bystander.

Mom had a thing for these gaunt, long-haired dudes. She'd said something last night at the club about this one, that he was from some rock band. She'd told me to be cool, that he was a good one. I still gave him the side-eye.

I pushed Mom's shoulders, getting a bit rough. "Come on. I have to go to school. Please get up."

"Okay, baby," she said, but she didn't move or open her eyes.

I tried again but she was like a block of concrete.

The long-haired guy lifted his eyebrows. "Give me a minute to get dressed. I'll take you."

◇◇

From the living room where I tugged at the Velcro of my sneakers and zipped my backpack, I heard him calling a cab. A few minutes later he appeared in worn jeans, a torn T-shirt, and flip-flops. He put on sunglasses, the cool kind prescribed by a doctor or bought at a boutique, not picked from a bin at the convenience store, to dim the shock of the bright morning light, then grabbed a wallet. "Ready?"

As we climbed into the cab at the curb, he asked, "What school you go to?"

I told him Laurel Elementary.

He gave directions to the driver, then rested his head against the seat back as if it weighed too much for his neck, and the cab made consecutive right turns through a part of Hollywood I didn't know well. When we crossed La Brea, then over to Fairfax into more familiar terrain, I relaxed, confident now he was really taking me to my school.

He looked out the side window without a word. I didn't ask if Mom was going to get me after school, or who he was, or if he'd make sure she was okay, though I thought of all those questions. I didn't ask about how much drugs she did last night and how long she'd be feeling badly afterward. I just wanted to get to school and pretend I lived a life like Josh, the son of our landlady.

Josh's mom made him breakfast, checked his homework, sat down to meals with him. They played board games and did jigsaw puzzles. The landlady was a single mom, too, but their way of being together was different.

As we turned onto North Hayworth and pulled up in front of my school, I gathered my backpack and scooched toward the door.

"What's your name?" the long-haired guy asked.

"Minka," I said, getting out.

"Nice to meet you, Minka," he said, not just to break the silence. I think he really wanted to know my name.

∞

Mom picked me up after school that day in her chauffeur's outfit—one of her side gigs was driving a limo—and I didn't know until she appeared that I'd been holding my breath for hours, afraid she might not come. But she always came, I scolded myself, even if she was usually late. The after-school caregivers were used to waiting around for her. Maybe I worried too much.

Mom's tux looked incredible on her, though it was just a normal tux. She made everything she wore look special. She opened the back door of the sleek black car with a flourish, bowing a bit as if I was one of her clients and she was an old-fashioned servant. I slid in.

She was still feeling the effects from last night; I could see it in the tightness of her jaw and the way she kept her eyes hidden behind dark glasses. Whenever she dropped me at school or picked me up with the limo, I didn't want the other kids to see, a feat she made easy by never coming to the school gate and avoiding the other parents and my teachers entirely.

It was as if she had split personalities: Among people she felt comfortable with, she was all touchy-feely and sweet, chitchatting, getting close. But with those who might judge her, she retreated and stayed hidden. She was the most skittish at my school. When the boys from my class or their fathers got a peek at her, though, they stared, slack-jawed.

"How was your day, Boo?" She tried to make conversation as we drove home, but I could tell it was a struggle. Mom had two speeds: hyperexcited and ready to party, or tuned out and bleak. Today, she was in Mode Two, but I could tell she was making the effort for me. I always appreciated it.

Back in our little storage space, I searched for the makings of a snack, stepping around the mattress to the minifridge, trying to maneuver around her while Mom touched up her makeup at a tabletop vanity mirror, ready to continue her limo shift. Next to her, on the counter, sat a glass mirror with skinny rows of white powder.

"What's that?" I pointed at the traces, knowing I was putting her on the spot.

"Just powder for my face." She pulled out her Coty Airspun loose face powder and patted her cheeks to demonstrate. The difference was obvious, though. The powder that spilled from the container was the creamy peach of her skin, while the other was chalky white, not to mention completely different textures. She didn't touch her makeup brush anywhere near the white stuff.

I was an observant child, noting every shift in her, an amateur meteorologist trying to get a bead on the change from high pressure to low. When she was being all secretive, like now, I recognized her fidgety energy and edgy mood swings. It was on me to manage those moods and make sure I didn't upset her. If she was stressed out—or, like today, exhausted from too much partying—she could become unpredictable. I needed to be careful. Almost anything could set her off.

Her anger, when it came, was like a sudden thunderstorm, taking us both by surprise. She didn't mean to hurt me at those times; still, I'd grown feelers acutely sensitive to her moods. My question about the powder was my way of letting her know I wanted her attention. I hoped she'd see what she was doing and decide to prize me instead of the drugs. But the powder always won.

◇◇

"Ladies and gentlemen! Welcome to the stage the vivacious bombshell, five-foot-eleven inches, big-bosomed lady, Frankie!"

When Mom heard the DJ say her name, she looked up from where she was doing a line of blow behind me, thinking I wouldn't see it from where I sat backstage with my math homework, and ran out toward the stage.

We were back at Crazy Girls on a Friday night and Mom was flying so high, I worried she'd tumble and fall off the stage, toppled by her high heels. This time it wouldn't be an act.

I tried to focus on my schoolwork and forget where I was, but it was hard. I worried about her and didn't know how to help.

◇◇

"Wake up, baby." She nudged me some hours later. I'd fallen asleep in the corner. "Look what I made!" She rained ones with the occasional fives, tens, and twenties all over me. I smiled. She was ecstatic whenever she had an especially good night.

"Wanna get some groceries?"

The club had just closed, the main room cleared out, and a janitor was taking out the trash. The other girls had already left. Mom's eyes were lit with sparkles of mischief. She wasn't ready for the night to end.

When she was flush with cash like this, Mom liked to spend it. Fast. In that mood, she'd let me pick out things I liked. I nodded and got up.

By the time we got to the Ralph's on Sunset I was fully awake, and we took over the deserted grocery store like it was an amusement park reserved for us alone. Wearing short shorts that revealed half her butt cheeks, and a shortie, cut-off T-shirt, she pushed the cart and I rode in it as if on a Tilt-A-Whirl, squealing as she whipped me around the end caps, getting mildly strange looks from the man washing the floor and the high school kids stocking the shelves. This was Hollywood at three in the morning; it took more than me and Mom to draw serious attention.

When we passed items we needed, I pitched them into the cart and she gave me points for each successful toss. One point for a case of Top Ramen or a box of Stroganoff Hamburger Helper. Two points for milk, regular and chocolate, small enough to fit in our minifridge, or a box of Cap'n Crunch. I'd lose points if I reached for a bottle of 409 or Lysol wipes.

"Can we get these?" I picked up a package of Oreos.

"Whatever your heart desires, baby."

I flung them in, too, but grew nervous as we headed to the checkout. How many times had we done this and overshot the mark? I'd have to surrender my cookies to the checker if there wasn't enough to cover the tab.

Tonight, though, there was enough. I was forty points to the good, with Oreos and chocolate milk to boot.

◇◇

The next morning Mom slept so deeply, I had to bend close to her face to make sure she was breathing. The Opium perfume she'd put on the night before mixed with her sweat for a rancid tang; her makeup stained the pillowcase. It was a Saturday morning. I wouldn't have to fight her about getting me to school, but I was stuck here with nothing to do.

I tiptoed around our little space, careful not to wake her. I wanted her to be rested. She'd still be groggy and not much fun when she finally got up, but at least she wouldn't be mad if I let her sleep. I crammed fistfuls of Cap'n Crunch in my mouth then found one of the cinnamon honey buns she bought at 7-Eleven in her purse, wedged among crumples of bills. Even after our epic shopping trip last night, there was still cash left.

For the rest of the morning I stayed outside, drawing hopscotch boxes on the sidewalk. I dug in the dirt looking for buried treasure, then followed a line of ants swarming an apple core. I used my magnifying glass to burn holes in leaves. She was still passed out by lunchtime and I knocked on the door of the landlady's apartment. Norma would know I was hungry.

Watching Norma make lunch for me and her son, Josh, I was

rapt. I studied the way she laid out the slices of Wonder Bread on the counter, layering bologna with Velveeta cheese, spreading mayo, then lining up the edges and slicing off the crusts. She cut carrot sticks and poured us each a glass of milk.

Josh was a year younger and we weren't really friends. Sometimes he came around to play, but I had plenty of friends at school. I didn't need another friend. I needed a full-time mom who trimmed the crusts off my sandwiches and didn't sleep through the best part of the day. After we finished lunch, Norma gave us four Oreos on a sparkling white plate. It was all so dreamy and homelike.

I went home in the afternoon to check on Mom—still breathing, still sleeping—then invented games for myself and talked quietly to my Cabbage Patch doll.

Being with Mom could be great sometimes, the way she injected playfulness into everything we did. When she finally got up, she'd take me to Jack in the Box for deep-fried Monster Tacos we'd dip in ranch dressing, just like she'd taught me. We'd laugh and have fun again.

Often, I thought I had the best mom in the world. Other times, though, I wanted something more normal, whatever that meant.

Waiting for her to get up, I got hungry and opened the package of Oreos, grateful I'd been able to keep them last night. I thought again with envy of Josh. He got to have a regular mom who did regular things. He got to have both his mom and Oreos, too.

CHAPTER TWO

How We Got Here

We all like to think magic sparked in the air between our parents when they met, that the glimmers of love that united them became so intense and golden that they exploded into new life, that our parents had intentionally tried to conceive their special, beloved child.

It's a nice thought, but that's not my story.

∞

My parents met in the fall of 1979 at the Record Plant Recording Studios on Sycamore, just south of Santa Monica and east of La Brea, a nondescript building that might have passed itself off as an accounting firm were it not for the scores of long-haired musicians lugging guitars and basses through its halls day and night. Rod Stewart was the big name at the time, but the studio hosted other musical artists in the late '70s/early '80s, including Bruce Springsteen, Tears for Fears, Chicago, REO Speedwagon, Heart, Whitesnake, Billy Idol, and Mötley Crüe.

My father, Rick Dufay, a French guitarist and songwriter with long, curly dark hair and a goatee, was in the studio one evening working on a solo album with his producer and best friend, Jack Douglas. Jack was known for producing artists like John Lennon and Yoko Ono, Patti Smith, Cheap Trick, and Aerosmith; he later became my godfather. When Rick got frustrated with the way the project was coming together, Jack threw him out of the room. Waiting in the hall, eating peanuts, he watched my mom slink by in a pink catsuit. He was dumbstruck by her beauty and wanted to meet her.

Rick looked at the unshelled peanuts in his hand. He tried to smile as he lobbed one at her, landing it with precision in her teased hair. In no time, they were chatting. At the time, Rick was twenty-eight and soon to replace Brad Whitford backing up Steven Tyler of Aerosmith. He was cocky and charismatic. He made her laugh and she beamed a hundred-watt smile at him. In no time, they moved in together.

Soon, though, Rick was packing to go on the road with Aerosmith—all his hard work as a musician was about to pay off. And besides, they weren't really a couple in a committed sort of way. They'd just hooked up and taken it day by day. Or, more to the point, night by night.

∞

When my mom realized she was pregnant, she didn't say a word to Rick but made the two-hour drive to San Diego to seek her mother's advice. I grew up hearing stories of my grandmother Renee, who was the sun, moon, and stars to her. They spent every moment they could with each other, acting more like sisters than mother and daughter. By this time, Mom had been a showgirl in Vegas and a part-time model. She'd dreamed of being an actor but had little success other than the occasional callback where the producer just wanted to stare at her tits. Career wise, she was adrift. Life wise, she was equally lost. She'd already had three abortions. She didn't want to have another one.

Though her mother was only one rung up the ladder from mere survival, still pulling shifts as a waitress at Denny's, Renee suggested the two of them raise the baby together. The way my mother told me the story, they both decided that Mom wouldn't have to be a single mother if Renee was involved; they'd be in the child-rearing trenches together.

With a plan in place, Mom told Rick about the pregnancy. He tried to talk her out of it, telling her he'd pay for an abortion, but she was determined. Becoming a father was the last thing he needed. He was about to begin one of the most heady stages of his life. He'd been working years for this moment, having played in garage bands, written hundreds of songs, picked strings until his fingers bled. Fatherhood would mess up his dreams.

Rick drove to the nearest bank branch and withdrew a couple thousand dollars to give to Mom to start her new life. Mom told Rick he was off the hook, saying the decision was hers alone. With that, Rick drove away, unsure of what he'd just done but certain about his future. The tour's charter plane was leaving the next day for his once-in-a-lifetime break. He wasn't going to miss it for anything.

◇◇

Was my mom's plan a solid one? Would it have worked out the way she and Renee hoped? I'll never know and neither would my mom because a few months into her pregnancy, her mother died abruptly from a brain aneurysm, leaving Mom pregnant and alone, with no source of income.

Throughout my childhood, my mother showed me pictures of her mother and cried. Sometimes, she'd call out for her mother. "I need you so badly, Mommy."

Something in her shattered with her mother's death. Sometimes, I'd see glimpses of the bright-eyed, spunky young woman she used to be and wonder where she'd gone. I never found a sufficient answer.

◇◇

With her mother dead and no partner to help her raise the coming child, Mom needed to find a source of security. Experience had taught her that safety comes to women through good looks and the protection of a man. She went to work to find a benefactor. I still don't know how she met David, but he became The One.

Tall, powerfully built, with long black hair, high cheekbones, piercing dark eyes, and dark skin, David was Mexican with an indigenous phenotype and wore that identity with a deep sense of pride. He dressed in black jeans and black T-shirts with the neck cut out, and sometimes wore a cowboy hat or bandana to cover his receding hairline. He was the consummate alpha male, confident and striking. He and my mom made quite the couple. He had a child from a previous relationship, Little David, and though David occasionally spent time with his young son, he didn't seem all that engaged. For whatever reason, David latched on to the idea of becoming *my* father. He took my mom to her obstetrician appointments, and when she went into labor, David and his extended family were by her side for my birth in the summer of 1980. From day one, my mother referred to him as my dad.

I did, too.

◇◇

Mom, David, and I lived together in little apartments, and then big fancy houses in the Hollywood Hills when David's career was going well. Throughout my childhood, their relationship was rocky, as if scripted from the lyrics of U2's hit "With or Without You." They broke up and got together, got violent with each other, locked each other out of the house, and found themselves trapped inside a twisted dynamic neither could fully escape. I simply thought that was what relationships looked like.

Sometimes Mom and I moved away to escape David, usually moving in with Mom's best friend, Claudia. Other times, we moved back to rejoin him. Regardless of the state of their relationship, David treated me as if I were his daughter and loved me adoringly.

◇◇

When I was three, Rick was onstage at The Forum in Los Angeles performing with Aerosmith when he was pelted continuously with Tic Tacs. "Shit's always hitting you when you're onstage, but this was new," he told me later when I asked about my childhood.

Initially, he didn't make the connection with the peanut bombardment that had marked my parents' first meeting. Mom was duplicating that encounter with whatever was close at hand.

When the show wrapped, his security guard approached Rick. "I've got a couple of broads here. One of them wants to know if you want to meet your daughter."

He realized it had been Mo throwing the Tic Tacs.

"Oh Jesus. Either of them carrying anything that looks like a summons?" Rick was certain he was about to be sued for child support.

"No man, she's with another girl who's just as tall, and gorgeous."

"Get her number and tell her I'll call."

◇◇

Rick had been performing with Aerosmith almost four years and the tour grind had become exhausting. Rick called Mom a few days later and arranged to come over to meet me. We were living with Claudia at the time. I was so young, I don't remember the meeting, but Rick said I was curled up on the bed out of shyness, my hair forming a corona around me.

"Minka, there's someone I'd like you to meet," Mom said.

I lifted my head and looked at him. As Rick remembers it, I had these huge doe eyes, and my hair flailed in every direction. "Is that my real dad?" I asked.

"Yes," Mom answered.

I put my head back down, not sure what to make of this guy.

Rick softened in that instant and began to recalibrate. Mom looked great and now that she had a kid, she seemed to have changed a bit, had matured. *I like this*, he thought. *Let's give it another shot.*

To hear Rick tell it, he fell in love with Mom at that time and really tried to make the relationship work. "I was off the drugs and I took you and your mom on the road," he told me. "You were great. Steven loved you, of course. You seemed comfortable with whatever was going down. I could bring you anywhere. Quiet. I liked to think you were just happy to be with your dad."

◇◇

Rick was always the peacemaker in the group, the mediator, often not in his own self-interest, a quality I came to love about him. He suggested to Tyler that Brad Whitford, Rick's predecessor, return and reunite with the band. Rick made the suggestion knowing that Whitford's return would end his own run with Aerosmith. He was right. When Whitford finally made his comeback, Rick bowed out and watched from a distance as the band went on without him.

By then, Rick was ready for a quieter life and the timing was perfect. Mom was on the outs with David, so Rick moved us all to New York City, first to the Esplanade Hotel on the Upper West Side and then out to Sneden's Landing, across the Hudson from Tarrytown.

Later, we moved to the West Side by the park on Seventy-second Street. In no time, though, Rick relapsed and the two of them were caught again in a sticky web of drugs and all-nighters.

"Maureen was always into drugs," Rick said, "and the using for both of us just got worse and worse. I loved it in New York, but Maureen didn't fit in there. I worked hard to try to make it work, but we ended up doing drugs more than anything else."

Rick thought that maybe, back in L.A., they'd clean up their act. So he moved his little family back to the West Coast.

Returning to Hollywood and Claudia's apartment on Fountain, though, was like adding kerosene to their already fiery lifestyle. Soon, Rick and Mom were out until all hours. One night, Rick told me, they left me with a makeup artist friend.

"I didn't know she was a full-blown junkie," Rick explained.

When Mom and Rick came home, flashing EMT lights lit up the street. The babysitter had overdosed.

◇◇

For a length of time, we all lived with Claudia in L.A. in one of those U-shaped complexes with a pool in the middle.

Mom and Claudia were having a pool party one summer day and were pretty wasted. Rick was off somewhere else. I couldn't swim yet but rested on a flimsy air mattress in the middle of the pool, enjoying the splashes of water on my sun-warmed skin as the adults drank beer, passed joints, and laughed poolside. The motion of the water beneath me made me sleepy and I closed my eyes for a few minutes. When I opened them, the adults had all gone back inside and left me alone.

The sun was dipping low and I was getting chilled. It was time to call it a day. I paddled to the side of the pool and grabbed the edge to pull myself closer to the deck. I must have yanked too hard because suddenly the float flipped over and dumped me in the water. I don't remember much about what happened next, only trying to get to the side and failing, sinking deeper and deeper, the sunlight fading, darkness closing in.

Mom loved to tell this story because from her standpoint, it illustrated her love of me, and the lengths to which she was willing to go to ensure my well-being. In her telling, she looked out the apartment window and saw my floatie upside down. She panicked and ran out of the apartment, screaming, and jumped into the pool fully clothed, making her way from the shallow end to the deep end to pull me out.

She dragged me onto the cement deck, where I sputtered. Everyone from the party gathered around as she crumpled in tears and cried over me when I started to breathe on my own. She never asked herself why I'd been left alone in a pool when I couldn't swim. Instead, she bragged that my near drowning had caused no harm whatsoever. After all, I'd gotten back in the water the next day, ever the fearless little girl.

◇◇

The relationship between Mom and Rick during this time was growing increasingly tense. Mom was off partying most of the time and Rick was at loose ends. He didn't know what he was doing with either his career or his life. Mom, meanwhile, was hooking up with other guys, leaving Claudia and Rick to do all the parenting. Rick started spiraling.

The situation came to a head when my godfather, Jack Douglas, the guy who'd been with Rick when he first met Mom, called Rick out.

"What are you doing, man? You've lost your balls. You don't know who you are anymore."

Rick didn't have an answer.

"They'll survive," Jack said. "But you've got to get your shit together because you are not going to be any good to this kid if you stay here and go down this rabbit hole. I've arranged a ticket for you at LAX. You need to get back to New York where you know yourself."

◇◇

When Mom came home at six the next morning, Rick was waiting for her.

"Listen," he said. "This isn't working out. Not for any of us. I need to go back to New York and get myself settled." Rick had lived most of his life in New York, having moved there from Paris when he was young. It was where he felt most at home.

"Oh. Okay. Great."

Mom was working as a limo driver at the time, and she drove Rick to the airport. A Paul Young song came on the radio: "Every Time You Go Away." When Rick heard the lyrics, he realized what he was doing and started to cry, his heart broken. It was a tearful goodbye.

Just an hour later when the plane was over Arizona, though, he felt as if ten thousand pounds had been lifted off his chest. He landed in New York, determined to get clean and start fresh.

Two weeks later, Mom called to ask when he was returning. She didn't realize he'd pulled the plug.

"I'm not coming back."

"Do you want us to come out, then?"

"Not really. We're done, Maureen. This is it. But you can send Minka out." He would have made space in his life, he told me. He loved me and missed me. But Mom wouldn't part with me.

"Okay, I'll send Minka," Mom said. Of course, she never did.

◇◇

After that, I didn't much notice that Rick was gone. My mom had an ever-changing stream of men in her life and they quickly took his place, primarily David. I knew Rick was my biological father, but David was the man who raised me. For my entire childhood, David was my "dad."

Over the years, though, Rick kept in touch with Mom. He called about once a year, and when he did, she asked if I wanted to talk to him. I always said no. As far as I was concerned, I had my dad in David. As complicated as David was, he was there for us. Plus, I was offended that Rick thought he could just call whenever he felt like it after leaving us.

Still, Rick continued to check up on me, asking how I was doing. Mom's answer was always the same. "Oh, she's in school and can't come to the phone now, but she's doing great."

As Rick put it later, from his perspective, "It was all bullshit."

CHAPTER THREE

Red Lobster

Piecing together the details of my childhood has been like putting together a jigsaw puzzle with half the pieces missing. I know there's a red barn in the left front, a pond in the middle distance, and storm clouds in the background, but figuring how these elements connect, and defining the border that keeps them in place, is nearly impossible. I've spoken with Rick, with my mother's friends, and with the people I knew as a child to fill in the blank spots. Still, the story comes together with jump cuts and a disrupted chronology.

Psychologists have long believed that humans are more likely to remember negative experiences over positive ones. This impulse, some argue, has evolutionary roots because it's more important for our survival to notice the lion in the undergrowth than the beautiful birds chirping in the trees. The fact that our youngest years tend to focus more on fraught memories is also due to evolution. Younger people, because they have a long and vague future in front of them, need to collect a lot of information and so they remember ample details about negative experiences to help manage their unclear futures.

I have no doubt there were times when my mother and I wrapped ourselves in joy and love, that I giggled with Rick and delighted in some small pleasure he showed me, that there were times when my adoration of David filled me with security and peace. But like those missing puzzle pieces, I can't fully see those moments. It's just the red barn, again and again. That pond. Those same damn threatening clouds.

◇◇

"Oh my goodness, Mink! This is going to be so special!"

Mom bubbled as Norma, the landlady who'd been letting us live in the storage room of her duplex, shouldered open the wide door to the two-car garage that faced the back alley, forcing it through a series of squeaks and moans. We'd entered from the side door off the backyard into the wood-sided garage that no one ever seemed to use. Norma and Mom had cooked up this idea.

Before Norma opened the big garage door, I'd held tight to Mom, certain the dank, pitch-black space was filled with hidden spiders. The place smelled like motor oil, rat poison, and Raid. But with the door open, a burst of fresh air chased away the staleness. Light filtered in.

"We're going to have so much more room!" Mom crowed.

Once again, we were scrambling for a place to live. This was right after my visit to Crazy Girls when I'd seen Mom strip for the first time. Up until then, we'd been living in Norma's storage room. Before that, we'd been staying with David. But like one wave following another, Mom and David had come to blows. He could be nasty and cruel, and whenever they got into a fight, she'd pack our things and tell him she could survive just fine without him, that son of a bitch, and we'd hightail it somewhere else.

For her sake, I wanted her to stay away from David. They only brought out the worst in each other. Still, I liked having him around. It was nice to have a father. He made me feel protected and safe, even though at times it was from him I needed protection. I seldom thought of Rick anymore and maybe that was simply a coping mechanism. I told myself that I had David as my father. That was enough. I didn't need Rick.

∞

Before we moved into the storage room and before our previous stay with David, we'd lived with Mom's best friend, Claudia. I'd liked that. Claudia actually got up in the mornings and made me breakfast and helped me get ready for school.

One day I slipped up, or maybe I was trying something out, and called Claudia "Mommy." I hadn't forgotten who my real mother was, I just wanted to cement my place in Claudia's heart. That way, if anything happened and Mom couldn't get it together to care for me, maybe then Claudia would take me in. In hindsight, I can see I hoped that word would endear me to her—David always loved it when I called him "Dad"—but Claudia looked as if I'd just slapped her. Her eyes filled as she crouched to my size.

"Now, Mink, you know Mo's your mother. I can be your auntie Claudia, but you need to use the word 'Mommy' only for your mom. A mother is something precious and special, and reserved for the one who brought you into this world. You understand?"

I nodded, but I didn't understand. Parents seemed interchangeable. Besides, Claudia did more of the mom things than my own mother did.

∞

"Wow, it's like having a house with a movable wall!" Mom said, standing in the dusty garage, our new home. Brackets on the walls hinted at the tools they'd once held, now just ghost images against the faded wood. The place smelled of gasoline and turpentine. Cans of old paint sat in one corner along with canisters of motor oil.

"Just like David's fancy-pants neighbors up in the Hills. We can leave the big door open for light and sunshine whenever we feel like it. And at night, just think, Boo: We can look at the stars!"

She called me Boo, short for Boobie, but I had to convince her to stop using that name because what kid wants to be called a boob? It's embarrassing.

"There's no bathroom," I said, my voice barely a whisper, afraid to disrupt the moment, knowing her mood could swing from euphoria to despair in a breath.

"Norma gave us a key. We can use her place when we need the bathroom. We just have to be quiet if she's sleeping." Mom gave Norma a side hug.

"Just look at all the room we'll have." Mom danced around, showing me where she'd put the bed and my dresser.

"What about making food?"

"Taco Bell's right down the street, and Jack in the Box. Won't that be great?"

Norma must have been some kind of special friend to be so accommodating. Apparently, she needed the storage room back and so, lucky us, we got the garage.

It was a funny kind of luck.

∞

Mom and I spent that Saturday afternoon moving our things and trying to turn the old garage into a home. I brought a broom and knocked at every corner, wanting to make sure there weren't creepy crawlies or scorpions that might bite me in the night. We ran an extension cord from the storage room to set up our little fridge and hot plate, plus a lamp, a TV, and a VCR. Mom piled extra blankets next to the bed in case it got cold at night. I set up my dresser in a corner behind the bed we shared, and tried to avoid stepping on the oil splotches on the concrete floor before we finally got a rug.

Mom kept touting the move as a step up, but I wasn't so sure. I held my tongue. I needed to show her I was a good sport and not make things harder.

Once we got settled, she made it as homey as she could. We *did* have more space and weren't falling over each other. With the door open, fresh air circulated and brought with it sunshine.

We kept the garage door open until we were ready to sleep. I think Mom knew I was scared about sleeping in the garage because she snuggled with me on the bed that first night and pointed out the scent of night-blooming jasmine from someone's backyard as she smoothed my hair. "We'll always know if a car's coming because of the crunch of gravel," she said. "We're safe and cozy. Snug as a bug in a rug."

"Are there bugs?"

"No, baby. Just you and me. Safe and sound."

"You sure?"

"I am."

She got out of bed to close the big door and the space grew way too dark. The sound of crickets scared me; I couldn't tell if they were inside or out. The roar of traffic nearby seemed louder than when we'd lived in the storage room, as if the garage walls were more porous somehow, less likely to keep out the scary things.

Soon, Mom began to snore. I looked at the rafters after my eyes adjusted to the dark, imagining a legion of spiders dropping down by scores of filaments, ready to pop into Mom's mouth with her next big inhale.

We'd read *Charlotte's Web* in school and though Charlotte was a good spider, I wasn't convinced the garage spiders would be so generous. Eventually, I fell asleep.

◇◇

We spent many nights and more than a few days in that garage, cuddling in bed, ordering pizza, and watching movies and musicals. *West Side Story* seemed to play on repeat, along with *Beetle-*

juice, Mary Poppins, Charlie and the Chocolate Factory. Eating in bed and watching movies was our favorite pastime.

This was a time when other kids my age were playing sports, learning an instrument, picking up a new language, engaging their brain in the world around them in order to determine what moved or inspired them. Looking back, I wish she'd encouraged my education and growth as a human rather than use me to keep her company when she had nothing to do.

Quickly, we settled in to a routine not unlike the one we'd had in the storage room. Mom slept until noon most days and I ate breakfast with Norma and Josh. I let myself quietly into their duplex in the night if I had to use the bathroom, and on those nights when I was tired and didn't want to disturb them, I peed on the back lawn. It was dark and no one could see.

◇◇

"Mink, I'm really sorry, but I have to go home." Mr. Morris, the man in charge of the after-school program, hunkered down at my height. All the other kids had been picked up hours ago. Twilight had faded and serious darkness prepared to fall. I was eight and in third grade.

"I'm going to call someone to get you, and they're going to take care of you, okay?"

I nodded, sitting on the front steps of the school facing Hayworth as streetlights blinkered on along the block. The traffic on Fairfax surged and ebbed. The evenings were getting cooler and I wished I had a sweatshirt. I kicked at the leaves by my feet with my scuffed sneakers.

It had been a great day at school. I loved being there because there was always a routine and order and I knew what to expect. I had friends. I was good at sports and played handball and tetherball at recess, beating almost everyone who dared challenge me. My teacher, Mrs. Sheridan, said I was smart, too. Quizzes and assignments came back with 97 and 98 on them and happy faces drawn in the margins. I sat up front in class and devoured everything Mrs. Sheridan said. If my life had been nothing but school, I would have been the happiest kid alive.

Every afternoon, though, the school day came to a close and there was always some complication or mess like this to deal with. I'd visited the homes of friends and noticed their lives were different. Their parents picked them up on time. They lived in proper apartments or houses. Kids had their own bedrooms and their moms sometimes cooked meals on a stove or in an oven, not on a hot plate.

Mr. Morris sat next to me, apologizing, letting me know how many people he'd called trying to find someone to take me, trying to avoid having to call the police.

"That's okay," I said. "It's not your fault."

◇◇

A month ago, Mom and I had moved out of the garage and were now living with David again in the Hollywood Hills, though they weren't a couple these days. I think he kept taking us in because he adored me and felt sorry for Mom. Plus, she could be fun at a party, and God knows, he liked to throw parties. Most nights, the music and drinking went on until the wee hours of the morning, people using drugs, dancing, laughing, fighting. Sometimes I'd stumble on couples having sex.

I wasn't completely sure of what happened during sex, but once I'd peeked around the room divider that shielded David's bedroom from where I often slept. He was lying on top of a girl who had her legs up in the air. I knew that was sex.

When kids at school speculated about what happened during sex, drawing stick figures to try to piece together what it entailed, I feigned ignorance. One girl said she was sure her parents didn't do that nasty thing, but they *did* like to wrestle a lot. I didn't correct her. I didn't want them to know what I knew.

David had a new girlfriend these days, Charmaine, and Little David was around a lot, too. I envied him. Little David's mother had gotten fed up with the way David treated her and moved out when Little David was a toddler. He was several years older than I was and still came over because his mom wanted him to have a relationship with his father. Little David was jealous of me because David showed me more attention than he did him. He wanted what I had: his father's love.

And I wanted what he had: a mother who'd broken free from this strange David-focused, messed-up life.

∞

When we stayed at David's, I mostly kept to myself, and spent hours exploring the Hollywood Hills. I'd get lost in the dense brush and climb the trails and ridgelines that separated Hollywood from the San Fernando Valley. I found wild anise and honeysuckle, delighting in the black-licorice-tasting plant and sucking sweetness out of the honeysuckles. I'd get lost and then found again, my shins scraped and my face dirty, making up stories about being an explorer.

Sometimes I'd visit my classmate who lived nearby. Her father was the guy who founded New York Seltzer, and their house included an amazing compound where he kept tigers and lions. Their house had been built around a three-story glass enclosure and I could sit and watch the huge cats and other exotic animals prowl along on tree branches. I envied her, too.

I wished the wild animals in my life were as easily contained. I wanted my mom to get away from David because they were too volatile around each other. She'd taunt and bait him until he'd explode. Or he'd mock her until she starting hitting him and screaming. In a curious way, the lions and tigers seemed so much more predictable.

Contrary to the way he treated my mom, David doted on me, taking me to garage sales and swap meets in his old Cadillac—I think it belonged to his dad—buying me records and a portable record player. He bought me a My Little Pony castle with a herd of My Little Ponies, my most treasured possession. Every morning, when I got up, he had Elton John playing throughout the house. He was a photographer and giant prints of recording artists he'd photographed covered the walls, Billy Idol the size of an elephant. David adored me and the warmth of his admiration made me stand taller and feel special.

Mom and David usually took turns picking me up after school, though Mom often strong-armed friends to take her place when it was her turn. She was always on the lookout for someone else to shoulder her responsibilities. David was the reliable one.

∞

The officers summoned to the school refrained from disrupting the neighborhood peace with their siren, but the red and blue emergency lights swiveled across the façade of the school and houses along Hayworth. Part of me was excited. I'd seen police chases on TV and wondered what it would be like to ride in a cop car. I expected an adventure. But then the smarter part of me kicked in. I should be afraid.

Mom and David were always on the watch for cops, peering out through the blinds to make sure they weren't being watched by some kind of narco detective. They had reasons to be afraid. Their cars were never properly registered, and certainly never insured. There were always warrants and expired licenses, drugs in the glove box or under the seat. I suspected David was dealing; one time, the house had been raided. The last thing I wanted tonight was for Mom or David to get into some kind of trouble because of me.

After the black-and-white came to a rest at the curb, two offi- cers hulked up the walkway, putting their hats in place. The sight of them intimidated me, guns bobbing in their holsters, batons swinging by their sides.

"Hi, Minka, I'm Officer Sanders." One officer crouched to talk to me while his partner spoke with Mr. Morris. "You're not in any trouble at all, I want you to know that."

I nodded.

"My partner and I are going to take good care of you until we can find your folks, okay?"

I went along with what he said and didn't let on that I was afraid. No one would ever see me worrying about anything if I had my way. Showing fear was the fastest way to mess things up.

"Can you tell us how to get to where you live?"

A bunch of turns were involved to get to David's place; I didn't think I could find it on my own. Plus, I knew that David's house was not in the zone for my school. Mom said I needed to keep our real address a secret from the school; they'd kick me out if they knew. I shook my head.

"Any idea where we might find your mom?"

I shrugged. "We used to live with Claudia." I pointed north. "A few blocks that way."

"Maybe we should go by there first and see if anyone's around. Sound good to you?"

◇◇

A few minutes later I sat in the cruiser, a cage between the front and back seats, the doors locked, feeling small and scared. The car smelled bad, like maybe someone had gotten sick in it some time ago.

The officers approached the apartment, hands on their guns

as if ready to apprehend a suspect. Would they kick in the door? They knocked and rang the doorbell but Claudia wasn't home. The officers spoke with one of her neighbors and then returned.

"I bet you're hungry," Officer Sanders said. "Let's get you a bite."

I wasn't hungry but I didn't want to contradict them.

They took me to the Red Lobster on Santa Monica in West Hollywood. Usually, when we ate out, it was burger joints, Del Taco, or Johnny Rockets. This was a step up and I wished I could enjoy it, but my stomach hurt.

When it came time to order, I asked for the fried shrimp. The officers kept trying to talk to me, but I wanted to hide. I looked down at my lap, wanting to be anywhere else. I wasn't afraid that my mom was missing or hurt or was not coming back for me; I was used to her forgetting me. Rather, what I felt was pure embarrassment. I knew the cops had better things to do with their time and I was mortified that they were having to babysit me. Knowing I was a burden pained me physically.

The food came and all I could do was sit there, looking at my lap, and cry.

"It's going to be okay. Let's not have any of those crocodile tears." One of the officers dabbed at my face with a napkin.

At the time, I thought his efforts to comfort me were sweet, until I learned later that "crocodile tears" referred to crying for attention. God, attention was the last thing I wanted! Shame covered me. I was humiliated to be a burden, unable to fully care for myself.

Eventually, I knew, David or my mom would get me. I kept picturing the moment when one of them would show up. If it was David, he'd be wearing his cowboy hat and sweep me into his arms, making a joke about the whole thing; then we could get back to normal. For now, though, the spotlight was on me and I'd have to let the night play out.

The officers paid the check, though I hadn't eaten a thing—

they'd nibbled on my fries to make me feel better and to entice me to eat—then got me an ice cream cone at Fosters Freeze and drove me to the station, where they set to work finding my mom.

◇◇

The station was pretty well empty, echoey and cold. Most of the day crew had gone home. The officers cast about for a place to put me. When I entered the dispatch room with a bunch of computer terminals, I lit up. I loved keyboards.

"You want to play on one?"

I did.

They pulled up a chair and put a phone book on it so I could reach the keyboard, where I busied myself typing in neon green letters against the black screen background, first my name, over and over again, then my birthday.

The station wasn't like what I'd seen on television. I expected people coming in wearing handcuffs, radio traffic, maybe officers staring at me. It was much quieter, and what little commotion did occur I blocked out. I'd developed a knack for being able to remove myself from almost any situation, and with the computer at my fingertips, I completely erased the sounds and fluorescent lighting of the station, content within my own mind.

When I got sick of typing my name, I worked on an acrostic poem, like I'd been taught in school, using the letters of MOMMY as each line's starting point. I would tell her about it when she got here and that might soften her up. She wasn't going to be happy about this situation.

> Most wonderful mother ever
> Other kids don't have it so good
> Maureen is so beautiful
> My mother always comes back for me
> Your Boo loves you the most!

The hours passed and I just kept typing. Eventually, I found a piece of old cardboard and drew pictures of houses and stick people. Finally, I rested my head on the desk, closing my eyes.

◇◇

"Where's my daughter? Where are you holding her?" It was late, ten or eleven, when Mom burst into the lobby. She'd clearly had a few drinks. She wore leopard print leggings with a gold lamé low-cut top showing lots of cleavage. Her hair was teased high—I could smell the hair spray across the room—and her makeup nearly as glittery as the necklace she wore. The officers rolled their eyes when they saw her.

I toppled from the phone book to run to her, ready to bury myself in her arms, but the two officers pulled her away before I could cross the room.

"We'll bring her back to you in a minute, Minka. Go work on your computer."

They escorted her into a glass-walled room where I could see the three of them, Mom gesturing wildly, pointing at me through the glass, clearly yelling though I couldn't hear what she said. Back at the computer terminal, I tapped out my name again and again, convinced that if I could get the letters to scroll out smooth and superfast—this time with absolutely no errors—I could get them to let her go.

◇◇

I kept my eyes on the screen, not wanting to know what was happening, but when I snuck a peak, I saw Mom open her pocketbook and pull out a wad of cash. She laid bill after bill on the table. Was she having to pay for my release?

"My baby! My poor baby!" Her acting was over the top when they let her out of the room. No wonder she never landed any roles. She cried over me, wailing as if she hadn't seen me in months. "What have they put you through?"

I just wanted her to be quiet and take me home.

"It's all David's fault," she called out to the room in general, though no one was listening. "It was his turn. I'm gonna kill that son of a bitch when I get ahold of him."

◇◇

A slick-looking dude sat behind the wheel of the Mercedes waiting at the curb. She put me in the back seat and told him to drive. He must have been her "date" for the night. She didn't introduce me, too busy railing to the guy about David's lack of consideration. She picked up the brick-like car phone in the center console and started punching numbers.

"David, you asshole," she bellowed. "It was your turn to pick up Mink. Four hundred bucks it cost me. They wouldn't give her to me until I cleared up a warrant."

I curled up and tried to tune her out.

"She's right here in the back seat. Where do you think she is?" She nudged me in the ribs with the big phone receiver. "Minka, your father wants to speak to you."

I had to hold the phone with two hands, it was so heavy. "Dad?"

David's voice was calm. "Minka, honey. You know I'd never forget about you, but it's all okay now. Your mom got the details wrong. It was her turn to get you. You all right, baby?"

"Yeah."

"Okay. I'm sorry this happened, but we'll just put it behind us, okay?"

"Okay."

"I'll see you later."

◇◇

Soon after, Mom left David again. This time, we moved in with one of Mom's other friends. We showed up like always: on someone's doorstep, unexpected, bags in hand.

Mom would tell the friend how she couldn't possibly manage without their help, and they'd inevitably open the door and let us in.

I was starting to see a pattern and I didn't like it. Moving from this friend's couch to this person's apartment, to a garage, back to David's—it was all taking a toll. Mom used to tell me it was just the two of us together against the world. We were the dynamic duo that could do anything. But Mom needed to be propped up by others, and I was starting to feel like an appendage that followed her wherever she went.

CHAPTER FOUR

It's a Jolly Rancher Life

How does a nine-year-old learn to parent herself when those in her life are unable to do so? She figures it out, one way or another, because what choice does she have? Kids are resilient and imaginative, coming up with ways to make sense of what's happening around them; that's the upside. Alas, it's taken me years to realize there's a downside, too. The harmful lessons sometimes picked up in the process of practicing that resiliency can take a lifetime to exorcise.

◇◇

"Minka, dinka, bottle of ink-a. Cork fell out and Minka Stinka!"

The kids at my new school took the playground rhyme to a different level, thinking it was funny. It wasn't. The phrase "Minka Stinka" echoed after me wherever I went, the kids giggling with pleasure at how clever they were.

I hated my name and wished I'd been named Lisa. I also wished Mom hadn't changed my school. It was bad enough she was gone and I was living somewhere else. Now I didn't have my friends, my favorite teacher, or my regular routine.

◇◇

A few weeks earlier, Mom had burst into the apartment where we'd been staying, blasting like a volcano that couldn't help erupting. She danced in a little circle in her thigh-high boots, jiggling as usual in tiny shorts that didn't cover her behind. Her yellow sequined halter top picked up the afternoon sun, shooting sparks around the dim room. She held a piece of paper high above her head and waved it like a flag. If she'd had confetti, she would have been tossing it every which way. I hadn't seen her this happy in forever.

I got up from the couch where I'd been watching cartoons. "What happened?"

"They chose me!" She squealed like the kid who'd won the golden ticket to the chocolate factory. "I have a job!"

She showed me the paper they'd given her, laying out the terms of engagement. "They're sending me to the Philippines! For a traveling lingerie show. Claudia's going, too. She'll sing and model some, but they want me to be the crown jewel of the show! Holy shit! Me!"

This was a change I welcomed. Before, Mom stayed in bed most days, unwashed, sleeping and eating candy. She kept a stash of black licorice, toffies, and gummies near her bedside and ate nothing most days but those sweets paired with her favorite drink: vodka mixed with rainbow sherbet and 7 Up in a sports bottle with a thick plastic straw. She still drove for the limo company on those few occasions when they called and she was in the mood to hustle. And when she got desperate for cash, she'd take a shift at Crazy Girls, but she did that less and less. Mostly, she stared at the walls and tried to make life go away, relying on friends to house and feed us.

Whatever caused her to be this happy must be a good thing. I was thrilled.

That is, until I realized the price I'd have to pay.

◇◇

We stood at the threshold of an apartment in the Valley sometime later, having left the neon billboards of Hollywood behind, along with artsy homes that nestled themselves in the creases of the hills. Now, flatness was all I could see. Smog rested its dingy brown paw on everything, from the overhead power lines to the miles of concrete that made up the San Fernando Valley. It was hot here. On the drive over, my T-shirt had stuck to my back. I tugged it to let in cooler air as we stood at the front door.

"Minka, this is Linette." Mom introduced me when a skinny woman with a quick smile opened the door. Mom had put my clothes and few toys in a trash bag when she'd packed her own suitcase, only I wasn't going with her.

Linette had agreed to take me for the six weeks Mom would be out of the country and working with Claudia. Was Mom paying Linette to house me? Was Linette a friend or distant cousin? No one explained anything. I didn't want to stay with Linette, didn't want to change schools, didn't want Mom to leave, but I knew better than to speak up. I couldn't do anything that might sully Mom's joy. Not now that she was getting herself out of bed in the mornings and dressing. She was finally brushing her teeth and combing her hair. She even sang along with Rickie Lee Jones's "Chuck E's in Love" on the radio in the car. If I followed the program, maybe she'd stay like this.

I nodded a shy hello at Linette, who showed me the layout of the apartment, fancy with a security gate outside, a marble entryway, and nice furniture. Her six-year-old daughter, Amy, wasn't home but would be soon. Amy's nanny picked her up and dropped her off from school every day. I'd share the nice bedroom Amy had all to herself, making a bed of blankets on the floor next to her canopied bed. Maybe I'd have a bedroom that special one day.

Linette cleared room in the entryway coat closet and I plopped my trash bag of clothes there. Mom held me tight for a moment and said I wouldn't even miss her.

"I'll write letters and call. It'll be like I'm not even gone at all."

Then the door shut and I was alone with Linette.

"You hungry, Minka?" she asked.

◇◇

I didn't realize how good I'd had it at Laurel Elementary, where I knew everyone and fit in. I'd never been one of the cool kids, but I'd found my place. Here, I didn't belong at all. Everyone looked at me funny. On the days when I had money for lunch, I'd go to a stall in the bathroom to eat, the door shut and my legs pulled up on the toilet seat so it looked empty. I didn't want anyone to know I had no friends to sit with at lunch.

◇◇

One day, school let out earlier than usual. When I punched the security code to get into the building and let myself into the apartment, the door to the master bedroom was open. I could hear a man's voice. I was used to coming home and finding men I didn't know with Mom, so I went to the kitchen to make a snack. Soon, they were making noises that let me know Linette wouldn't want me around.

I eased the front door shut, then hung out just beyond the security gate. A man exited Linette's apartment a little while later, tucking in his shirt. We eyed each other as he left. He didn't know to connect me to Linette's apartment, but still, I felt something creepy in his look.

I punched in the code again and let myself in, settling at the dining room table and pulling out my homework. Linette was just out of the shower, in a robe, her hair in a towel.

"Hi honey." There was an edge to her voice. Clearly, she was surprised to see me that early. "When did you get here?"

"Just a minute ago."

Her face relaxed.

I was pretty smart for a fourth grader; either that or nine-year-olds are smarter than we give them credit for. Either way, I figured it out. Linette didn't go to a regular job for one reason: her work came to her while Amy and I were at school.

"A package came for you today." Linette handed me a small FedEx box, a bunch of candy inside and a card from Mom with her beautiful handwriting.

"Hi my Boo. I'll be home from work in just a couple more weeks. We'll be together again so soon, I promise. I miss you and I love you with all my heart and soul. Love, Mommy."

I wanted to believe her, that she'd be back soon, that we'd move into a more normal life together, but she'd already been gone longer than she'd said. I wanted it to be me and her against the world again, to be a pair. The sting of betrayal blinded me. I couldn't picture our reunion. Hoping and believing in that promised moment hurt more than being punched. I knew I'd be disappointed again. I put the card away and did my homework.

◇◇

David was in and out of my life while I was staying with Linette. He'd pop up when he was making a lot of money and take me shopping. Once, he took me on a shopping spree at The Limited. The clothes seemed so fancy and nice; everything new! And then he was gone again. He was a larger-than-life, mystical creature, there one moment, gone the next.

He could be charming and charismatic—that was the David I

focused on. But more and more, I couldn't help but see the other side, the aspect of him my mom fought all the time, the asshole side. The narcissistic side.

⬦

I was staying with him one weekend when the party vibe was strong. He and his friends and his new girlfriend, Charmaine, were up all night drinking, doing drugs, dancing. I set up the Care Bears tent David had bought me in the quietest corner in the house and tried to sleep.

The minute I opened my eyes the next morning, I knew I had to get to work. It was my job to clean up after them. The house was modern with lots of black lacquer, minimalist. David liked it neat at all times. If he woke before I'd finished putting the house back together, there'd be trouble. Everything had to be immaculate.

This morning, the carpet was a mess from the night before, but I knew better than to wake him by turning on the vacuum. He'd taught me to sweep the carpet rather than vacuum for mornings just like this. I held the broom at an angle so that the bristles dug deep, then used small, quick strokes backward. It sounds ineffective but did a great job cleaning the carpet noiselessly and removed any reason for him to be mad at me. The few times he'd woken before I'd cleaned, I was in trouble. "What is this mess?" he'd yell, swatting me or grabbing my face. He didn't hurt me much at this age. At that time, he was still enamored with me.

⬦

David's real surname was Gonzalez and he claimed an Apache Indian heritage. When I was older, I heard him argue with his own mother about his ancestry. He claimed he was Native American and she corrected him.

"No, mijo, you're Mexican. *We're* Mexican." They argued in Spanglish.

"I'm an Apache Indian," he insisted.

As descendants of the indigenous people of this continent, many Mexicans are Native American, but his mother kept telling him he was simply Mexican. He liked his own story better and tried to correct the record by introducing himself to new people as David Jet-Black Horse.

I believe David genuinely loved me, but that's because I knew how to behave. I knew not to talk back, to do as I was told whether I liked it or not, to keep the house pristine, to have manners, and to not speak when the adults were speaking. I respected him out of fear. I'd learned these behaviors fast.

One day, he'd told me, "Go get me my phone book," and I sucked my teeth, making a sound of displeasure.

"What did you just say?" His timbre turned instantly dark.

"I didn't say anything."

"Come here," he ordered. "What was the sound you just made with your teeth?"

I made the sound again and he whacked me in the face so fast I didn't see it coming. Other times, he just cut to the chase. "Come here so I can smack you."

"I don't want to," I'd say, but I had to. I had to come close so he could hit me and then he'd tell me that he'd done so out of love. What made it especially hard was that, when he hit me, I wasn't allowed to cry.

Once, I was with him and his friends at a restaurant and I asked for something—money for the video arcade, or maybe I asked for my mom—and when he said no, I began to cry.

He reached under the table and pinched my thigh so hard, I wanted to scream but I knew I had to hold it in unless I wanted more pain.

"I'll give you something to cry about," he whispered.

He was always careful, though, not to leave marks. He used to brag about that.

◇◇

David had a way with the ladies and a conga line of women waited to get in his good graces. It's not that he often wooed them or was doting, though he did both in the early days of a relationship. David was a classic narcissist and Mom and the women like her were particularly vulnerable. Mom had low self-esteem and he made her feel cared for.

He replicated this pattern in all his relationships, I can see now as an adult. After he'd cemented a woman's dependence on him, he'd suddenly drop the charming mask. He'd take everything the woman had to offer—her kindness and nurturing, her love, her adoration, even her money—until he'd depleted any woman able to brave him for that long. The girlfriends were under his control by that point, and he told them how lucky they were to be with him. Usually, they believed him.

Charmaine was his main squeeze at this time. Gorgeous, long hair, and big, beautiful lips. She was so sassy and funny. I loved her makeup, earthy with this brown-tinted lipstick that had an opal sheen. She dressed in tight, high-waisted jeans and always looked stunning. She was one of my favorites.

◇◇

I was asleep at David's house when I heard a noise, an erratic banging sound, almost like someone was hammering a nail but with less frequent thuds. I'd heard David and Charmaine fighting earlier, calling each other names and cursing, so I'd put a pillow over my head and tried to go back to sleep. The banging got louder, more insistent. I left my tent to have a look.

When I got to the living room, David was holding Charmaine

by the throat, pinning her against the wall, her feet six inches off the floor. He stood in the half-light, his face eerily calm. Charmaine wore a brown fringed suede jacket. Maybe they'd just gotten home from somewhere, or she'd been putting on her jacket to leave. I remember the fringe the most because it swayed back and forth in a rhythm that makes me sick to this day.

David spoke in the creepy whisper-like voice he used when he was really angry. "Who do you think you are?" The words slipped through his clenched teeth as he slammed her head against the wall. I winced with the force of it. "You want to get smart with me again?" His tone was menacing. Another slam. Disrespecting him was the ultimate offense.

Charmaine's face was a mask of terror, mascara smeared below her wide, bulging eyes. She couldn't breathe and was about to pass out. Every time he slammed her head, she shuddered and seemed to grow a little smaller.

I wanted to scream "Stop it!" but my mouth had turned to cotton. I wanted to rush to him and pull his hands away from her, but then *I'd* become the focus of his anger. For my own protection, I had to stay out of it.

I crept back to my tent and put the pillow over my head, feeling like a coward for not coming to her rescue. Charmaine had always been good to me and I'd abandoned her. I tried to sleep, telling myself that he couldn't possibly kill her.

Could he?

∞

This degree of violence didn't shock me. There was always an air of danger with David, and he made the threat of his viciousness clear at every moment. He walked around with his chest puffed out like, "I am the king and you *will* respect me." Once he laid into one of his friends for cursing in front of me. "You don't speak that way in front of my daughter!" he threatened.

I thought, *Oh really?* It was a nice performance, but David used way worse language around me all the time, not to mention hit me. This guy had simply sworn, but that wasn't the point. It was up to David and David alone as to when I'd be subjected to bad language or rough treatment. He had to be the one in charge.

That moment with Charmaine wasn't the first time I saw him get rough with a woman, my mother included. To be fair, Mom could dish it out, too—with David and with her friends. She'd scratch, slap, punch, pull hair, kick. Sometimes she'd whale on me.

The next morning, Charmaine and I made breakfast together. Her eyes were puffy and her throat bruised. When she spoke, her voice was raspy.

"I'm sorry," I whispered as I peeled the potatoes, afraid to look at her. She waved her hands to brush my words away. Later, when I walked through the living room, I noticed scuffs of brown from her suede jacket marring the paint. The drywall was cracked above it.

◇◇

Mom was true to her word and care packages arrived regularly. And in a way, she was right: Though I missed my old school and friends, I didn't really miss her all that much. It was a relief, sometimes, that she was gone.

◇◇

A few days later I was back at Linette's when she surprised me with a pair of Nike sneakers. All the kids at school wore Nikes and I only had the cheap knockoffs from Payless. She must have seen me looking at pictures in a magazine or read my mind. Somehow she knew I was having trouble at the new school and that these sneakers with purple swooshes on a white leather background might ease my transition. I could have kissed her.

One drawback of this living situation was that Mom hadn't set up an account with the school cafeteria and hadn't left lunch money for me. I didn't want to ask Linette for cash. I couldn't. She'd already been so kind.

◇◇

Every morning, I walked to the bus stop on my way to school, passing a convenience store, not quite a 7-Eleven, just one of the liquor stores that dotted the neighborhood. Once a week or so, I went into the store to buy a Coke or to have a look around. When the clerk wasn't watching, I crept to the candy aisle and dumped an entire box of Jolly Ranchers into my backpack. I knew how to be sneaky and quiet, how to not take up space and to make myself small so no one would notice me.

I grabbed a Coca-Cola from the fridge and paid for the drink, or told the clerk I hadn't found what I was looking for but thank you, walking out with all thirty-six sticks of the candy.

Once I got to school, I peddled the candy to classmates for a quarter each. Apple and Watermelon were the favorites. Soon I became known as the girl with the candy more so than Minka Stinka. That eased my way to making friends, along with the new purple swoosh Nikes.

I was tired of eating in the bathroom stall and, unless the cafeteria was serving pizza, I wasn't interested in their offerings. Besides, I hated the whole cafeteria scene, everyone aware of who got to eat with whom, establishing the social hierarchy of the school.

With the funds from my Jolly Rancher sales, I bought two tacos on my way home from school, eating in the anonymity of Taco Bell. There, no one cared who you were sitting with. I was learning to fend for myself.

CHAPTER FIVE

Here, There, and Everywhere

The last two years of elementary school don't unspool in my memory in a clear-cut order because there was no order, just bits of remembered moments, everything jumbled in a chronology I'm not even sure is correct. What I see now is that the coping mechanisms I developed to outlive these circumstances served me as a child. As an adult, though, they've slammed into whatever structures I've tried to build with potential life mates, eliciting cracks and fractures in the fragile web of trust I long to construct. Even as I try to craft a healthy and safe container in which love and tenderness might bloom, that old wrecking ball of learned behaviors keeps crashing into whatever I try to build, raising dust that clings to my hair and hurts my eyes, splintering my efforts to smithereens.

If I'd had a more normal childhood, perhaps I'd be able to straighten out this chronology by examining mementos gathered from this time—beach glass found walking the shores of Santa Monica with a classmate, say, or an acorn kept in a drawer as a reminder from a hike with Mom in Griffith Park. But I have no such mementos, no tangible objects to help me tell the tale, only half-remembered names, faces of people kind enough to take me in when my mother was nowhere to be found, people who gave my body, if not my heart and spirit, sanctuary. And the crisp imprint of those who made my daily life far worse than it needed to be.

Mom left me with these strangers because her earlier efforts of relying on family to care for me had not ended well. When I was about six, she asked her sister Coleen in Oregon to house me for a while. Though I enjoyed the traditional family dynamic in her house, it was completely foreign to me. We sat to eat dinner together as a family each night—so novel!—but the fact I hadn't yet been taught table manners quickly became apparent. One night, I used my own spoon to scoop up a serving of peas from the communal bowl, ignoring the designated serving spoon right in front of me. Coleen was furious and decided my punishment would be to finish the entire bowl of peas. The amount of peas seemed enormous. I sat at that table into the wee hours, all the lights in the house extinguished save for a small lamp nearby; everyone else had gone to bed. I wasn't allowed to move from the table until that bowl of peas was done. Finishing it took me nearly the entire night. After that, I hated peas for decades. Only until a few years ago have I enjoyed them again.

David was supposed to be coming to get me, to keep me for a while. That's what Linette believed, too. She'd asked me to pack my things that morning and gave me a nice royal blue Adidas duffel so I wouldn't have to move with trash bags again.

Mom had been gone far longer than the six weeks she'd promised. I didn't know where she was now, when she'd be coming back, or what she was doing. All I knew was that months had passed. My best guess was that she'd found other work after the Philippines and had been sent elsewhere. Stripping, lingerie shows, or the kind of bedroom work that Linette did? Whatever it was, I didn't understand why she had to be away to do her work. Couldn't she be here, with me?

Still, she called and wrote all the time, and talked with Linette to make sure I was okay. I wrote back, too. Our letters kept us connected and reminded me that she hadn't forgotten me. She had been the one to tell me I'd be leaving Linette's today to stay with David until she got back. She'd made all the arrangements.

See, I'd consoled myself, she *did* love me. She was caring for me from afar, and as long as I knew I was loved, what more did I need?

◇◇

That afternoon, the hours passed and David didn't arrive. I was flopped on my belly watching *Chip 'n Dale: Rescue Rangers* in the living room, Linette's daughter, Amy, sitting on my lower back braiding my hair, when Linette answered the phone. My ears pricked up.

"I can't do that." Her voice was a knot of frustration as she paced the kitchen, tied in place by the phone cord. "I have to go out of town tomorrow. Two o'clock flight." She lowered her voice. "I can't keep doing this."

Sometime later, Linette sat on the sofa next to where I sprawled.

"Honey." Her voice was tentative. She didn't want to have this conversation any more than I did. "Your dad can't pick you up. But another friend of your mom's is going to come get you. Isabel. You'll like her. She has two daughters, Marina and Serena. You'll fit right in. It's only until your mom gets back."

"Okay." I kept my eyes fixed on the glowing screen, afraid to look at her. "Thank you." I used my manners.

The same flood of shame I'd felt when the police officers took me to Red Lobster crested inside. I hated that I was a burden to carry. I didn't want Linette to see me cry—she was so nice and this wasn't her fault. I stared at the two animated chipmunks cavorting on the screen as Amy undid my hair and started a new braid. I didn't push her off.

A new darkness crawled up my chest and tightened my throat. No one was coming for me. When I'd been left before, it was because something had simply gone wrong with the details of a plan. Mom's or David's schedule didn't align, or they didn't have their shit together.

This was different. It was me. I wasn't good enough or important enough or special enough for them to pay attention to. This was a whole new feeling. There was something wrong with me.

◇◇

By the time I added my duffel bag to the trunk of Isabel's Nissan Maxima, darkness had fallen and car headlights flashed past us like the strobe at Crazy Girls, turning our little clump of humanity at the curb into a headlining act for just a second before darkness swallowed us up again. The Valley smelled of exhaust and freshly poured tar as I hugged Linette and Amy goodbye, holding them tighter than I intended. Living with them hadn't been perfect, but we'd gotten along and I'd loved playing school with Amy.

"I'll be the teacher and you can be the student," I'd say, and she always went along with my suggestion; this was the advantage of being the older kid. To make our classroom as realistic as possible, I stole markers, construction paper, glitter, adhesive stars, and wide-ruled paper from school. I almost got away with stealing a pair of silver rings to hold big presentation boards in place—I was going to duplicate that teaching aid at home—but the teacher caught me. When I left school that day, I wasn't overly abashed at having been apprehended. My biggest thought was *Damn, she took my rings.*

The school year ended soon after and then summer was upon us. Maybe that's why Linette needed me gone. Without school to babysit me a few hours each day, and with Amy cared for by her nanny, I was in the way.

I was a castaway, about to be taken in by another unknown woman because no one else wanted me, not even Linette.

As we stood under the mercury vapor streetlights, I realized for the first time how special it was that Linette and Amy had welcomed me and made me feel at home. Linette had seen me in a way most adults didn't, knowing that a pair of Nikes would make my life easier. And Amy was so excited whenever I came home from school, genuinely glad to see me. Unlike with David and Mom, where I seldom felt like my presence mattered, I was visible to Linette and Amy.

Saying goodbye, I kept my eyes dry, but my lower lip trembled. I wiped my nose with my forearm and looked at my feet so no one would notice.

∞

Isabel punched a code into her car door to unlock it, then I slid into the back seat.

"This is Marina." Isabel pointed to the bigger girl sitting behind the driver's seat. "And that's Serena in the middle." I scootched on the bench seat and tried to get a sideways look at my new housemates. Both girls had long faces and dark hair, thick eyebrows. Serena gave me a shy smile when I caught her eye, but Marina glared at the back of her mother's head as Isabel settled behind the steering wheel.

When the doors locked automatically behind me, I felt trapped.

Isabel pulled away from the curb, and soon the girls giggled and spoke to each other in a language that sounded like Spanish, but not really.

"Hey. Stop it," Isabel called over her shoulder. "Speak English. Don't be rude." The family was Portuguese, I learned.

The sisters rolled their eyes. "We were just asking," Marina said, a taunt in her voice, "where's her mom?"

"I told you. She's working. Minka's going to stay with us for a while, so make her feel comfortable. *Like we talked about.*" Isabel's tone told me there'd been words on the way to pick me up.

We drove over the hill from the Valley toward Hollywood, taking one of the winding canyon roads, our bodies sliding and leaning into each other with every twist. I tried to keep myself contained in my corner while Serena and Marina made a game of squishing each other. Marina tried to push Serena into me, but Serena worked to give me a little space.

When Isabel pulled into a driveway leading to an underground parking garage, I craned to see the top of the high-rise above us. This place looked fancy. I carried my duffel from the car; no one spoke in the elevator to the ninth floor.

"Show her where to put her stuff," Isabel said once we were in the apartment.

I followed the girls.

Their bedroom was huge, with a small TV and Nintendo in one corner. I loved video games and couldn't believe these girls had their very own system. I couldn't wait to play, but one look at Marina and I knew she wasn't going to let me get anywhere near that Nintendo.

After Isabel went into her own room, Marina closed the bedroom door.

"You think you're gonna have it easy here?" She kicked over my unzipped duffel and my prized Nikes fell out.

I didn't answer.

Marina loomed over me, her fists gathered into cue balls.

"What, are you a chicken?" She spat her words in my direction while I tried to arrange blankets and pillows into a bed on the floor of her room. She kept kicking the blankets over and tugging away the pillow. Earlier, she'd knocked my backpack from my arms, waiting until we were out of her mother's line of sight before confronting me.

Marina looked like a seething monster, so much bigger and taller than I was, fourteen with braces, acne, and stringy hair that stuck to her face. I was ten. Her little sister, Serena, looked on from the corner of their bedroom, neatly tucked into the closet, careful to steer clear of Marina's fury.

Their bedroom was all Pepto-Bismol pink with white accents and bunk beds, as if staged for a TV show. Was Marina mad that my stuff would mess up their perfect bedroom? It wasn't my fault her mother told me to set up my bed next to their bunk. I didn't want to be here, either.

Marina towered over me, cinnamon breath from the Trident she chomped right in my face.

"Can you fight?" she asked, grabbing the front of my T-shirt and twisting it, drawing my face close, her breath hot on my forehead.

"Marina," Serena called from her corner by the closet. "Leave her alone."

"Shut up, Serena. Don't stick up for her unless you want to fight, too."

Marina pushed me hard and I stumbled. As I tried to regain my balance, she shoved me again, this time with more force. I fell on one knee, the skin of my kneecap burned by the carpet. Another shove and my hip slammed into the bunk bed.

All my frustration bubbled up. Why was Mom gone so long? Why hadn't David come to get me? Why didn't Linette want me anymore? I didn't want to change schools again but I knew that was next, and now I was stuck with this bully determined to mess with me. I was so tired of people telling me what to do, no one asking what I wanted, having to be so careful about everyone else's feelings. What about mine?

I shoved Marina back, just one tiny shove, but more resistance than I'd put up before. The brawl was on, punching, pulling hair, and wrestling, rolling on the carpet like a pair of cats tied together and tossed into a burlap sack. I was out of breath and tried to get her to stop—it was exhausting to keep at it—but she was bigger and determined.

By the time Marina sat on my chest, pinning me to the floor, my breathing was tattered and raw. It was a relief to stop rolling around, but her weight was squeezing all the air out of me. Scratches from her nails stung my forearms and back. My shins throbbed with bruises.

Fine, I thought, *you win*. I wanted whatever this was to be over with.

"Don't make a sound," Marina hissed, spittle on her chapped lips. "Do not cry. Or I will beat you even more."

Isabel's voice floated in through the closed bedroom door. "Girls, dinner's ready. Let's eat."

Marina got off me and walked out of the room. I sat up, wiped my face, and straightened my twisted shirt. Serena came over and tried to fix my hair. We didn't speak but her eyes told me she was sorry.

I didn't blame her for not defending me. I hadn't been able to stop David from hurting his girlfriend Charmaine. I understood how this worked.

Isabel served El Pollo Loco on paper plates, but I couldn't eat. When I asked if she knew when my mom would be back, she just shrugged.

So this was the new normal. I was flexible. I'd learn how to deal.

The rules in this household had been made clear. Like with David in the Hills, I knew better than to draw attention to myself, ask for help, or point out unfairness. No adult was coming to save me and if I let Isabel know that Marina was a bully, nothing but punishment would come my way. Plus, Marina had mocked me for crying. I knew then that the tears had to stop. Never again was I going to cry; it only made the torment worse. I needed to put my head down, stay as invisible as possible, and wait out the days until Mom returned.

◇◇

A new routine was established, with Marina as my jailer. She also kept Serena under her thumb and the two of us forged a bond out of mutual suffering. On the few occasions Marina left us to visit a friend in the building, Serena and I played Nintendo, made cinnamon toast in their beautiful kitchen, and pelted each other with her Koosh balls. We skipped and giggled like those who know their time is limited and need to get in as many laughs as possible before the jailer returns and the door slams shut again.

Day after day, Marina goaded me into a brawl. No matter what I did or said, we ended up rolling on the floor. If I didn't respond to her taunts, she grabbed me and forced me into a skirmish. If I talked back, she assaulted me immediately. There was no winning. I'd find bruises and bloodied marks all over my body in the shower the next day.

The fact that I never knew when she would mete out her next punishment was almost as exhausting as the rolling and scratching, the anticipation always leaving me on edge. Plus we had to keep the brawls as quiet as possible lest we alert Isabel. At that, at least, I succeeded. Isabel never had a clue.

Isabel was the only adult in my life during that endless summer and yet I couldn't describe what she looked like if my life depended on it. She simply faded into the background like the teacher on *Peanuts*; her voice was the "waaa-waaaa-waaaa" in the distance, not a part of the story at all. Marina, though, was a vivid presence, day after day. Thoughts of her interrupted my sleep with nightmares and gave me cold sweats. More than three decades later, I can still smell her, acrid and funky, a girl turning into a teen and staking out her territory, warning me away from her family, protecting her turf.

◇◇

After staying with Isabel for a few months, I was passed off to one unsuspecting woman after another, enrolled in different schools, always the new girl, always needing to prove myself. And Mom stayed away, day after day after day.

Annette, a woman with no kids of her own who took me for a time, offered me chewing gum.

"No, thank you. My mother says it looks cheap and rude."

Annette was impressed. Not only did I have manners, I was abjectly loyal to my mother, whom I hadn't seen in more than a year.

◇◇

A decade later, when I moved back to L.A. as a young adult, I was approached on the streets by middle-aged women I didn't recognize. They always grabbed me in a big hug and seemed thrilled to see me. "Minka, oh my God!"

I had no idea who they were.

"How's your mom? Is she . . . you know . . . doing okay?"

They were asking, in their roundabout way, if she was still alive and were often surprised to hear that she was. My perplexed look, though, let them know I didn't recognize them.

"Don't you remember me? Sarah. You stayed with me on Gardner near Hollywood when you were in fifth grade. We used to make lanyards together."

"I'm Bonnie. We lived off Sunset near Normandie. You loved eating blue Otter Pops until your tongue turned turquoise."

"Stacy. You were best friends with my daughter, Erica."

I had no idea who these people were, absolutely no memory of the scenes they described. My brain was doing what it needed to,

erasing as much of the painful parts as possible, so I could keep
moving forward.

◇◇

Mom eventually returned and to celebrate her homecoming, she
took me to get my ears pierced at Claire's. I was now ten and that,
she decided, was old enough for this milestone. I selected little
cubic zirconia studs.

Oddly, I remember the ear piercing clearly, but nothing of the
day she actually returned. Did I go with someone to the airport to
pick her up, or did she surprise me with chocolates at whoever's
apartment? You'd think I'd remember the smell of her shampoo,
the solid feel of her arms around me, her amazement at how much
I'd grown. I bet I stood taller in the laser beam of her attention,
directed solely at me that day. But there's just a great void, as if her
homecoming never occurred.

I guess, by the time she finally returned, there'd simply been
too many times I'd cried for my mommy, not knowing where she
was or when I'd see her again. I'd forced myself to stop needing
her, waiting for her, expecting her, because it was just too painful.
Whenever we talked by phone, she lied about when she was coming back and was maddeningly vague about where she was and
what she was doing. I deserved to know and yet she steadfastly
refused to tell me. So, I blocked what I could.

I later learned that during that time, she drove a car across the
border for David, transporting drugs. She got caught and went to
jail for a short period of time, but she never told me. Someone else,
years later, filled me in. I learned more about my mother through
strangers than I did from her.

At Claire's, I remember being afraid of the piercing gun, but its
sting was nothing compared to the beauty and dazzle of the earrings that Mom said lit up my face. Every night, I used a cotton ball
and the ear-care solution to tend to my piercings, looking at myself

in the bathroom mirror, feeling grown up. Meanwhile, I wadded up all the pain and sadness over Mom's absence and pretended it didn't exist, focusing instead on the fact that I was becoming a young lady.

◇◇

"Come on, honey, just take a bite." Mom tempted me with Skittles and toffies but I didn't want to eat anything. I was sicker than I'd ever been, lying on the couch for days, watching *Mary Poppins* on an endless loop. The fact that I wouldn't even touch her favorite candies let her know it was serious.

If I tried to stand and walk, I hunched over from the pain. Mom tried to feel my stomach to see where it hurt and I screamed; no one was going to touch me. When I no longer had the strength to make it to the bathroom to throw up, Mom brought a bucket to my side.

I felt horrible in every cell of my being, but if I'm honest, I have to admit that I loved the feel of her attention focused on me. She noticed me and cared for me and was concerned; this was new and life changing.

As I grew sicker, I didn't mind too much because her devotion almost made the suffering worth it. She really saw me.

Meanwhile, Mom agonized about taking me to a doctor. We didn't have health insurance or money to pay the doctor's fee and she kept hoping the illness would pass. Finally, she called the hospital and described my symptoms.

"If she's still like this in the morning," the nurse said, "bring her in."

Mom hung up and sat by my side, concerned.

The illness didn't worry me, though I grew tired of feeling terrible all the time. I was too weary, actually, to care what was wrong with me. Being sick didn't scare me, but the bills that would result if she had to take me to the doctor did.

Still, her attention and closeness in these moments felt like love.

◇◇

"Mink, come on. Wake up."

It was after two in the morning when she roused me.

"This is too much. I can't wait any longer. The cost be damned, you need to be seen." Mom bundled me in a blanket in the front seat. Her maternal instinct had kicked in.

In the ER, the nurses and doctors were immediately alarmed.

"Emergency surgery," Mom explained as they prepared to whisk me away. "Your appendix ruptured. They need to take it out and get the poison out of your body."

Later she told me that, had she listened to the nurse on the phone and waited until the next day to seek care, I would have died. She'd saved my life. And surgery? I didn't really care, as long as they got the pain to stop.

A nurse came in and tried to remove my earrings. I begged her to leave them. "No. My holes are going to close. Please. No!"

She was adamant. I made her promise she'd put the earrings aside in a safe place.

◇◇

Once the surgery was over and most of the pain gone, being in the hospital was almost a delight. I had a tube coming out of my belly, draining the poison out of my body, and I was fascinated by it. I wanted to help the nurse change the dressing and she explained to me how the tube worked. Instead of stitches, a series of staples marched across my right lower abdomen, which I thought was crazy: I was like Frankenstein's monster! When the time came to remove the staples, the doctor let me help take them out. Being in the hospital wasn't traumatic in the least. Unlike my daily life where I often felt overlooked, invisible, or a burden, now I felt cared for. My school sent a bunch of Get Well Soon cards and I didn't feel as alienated from my classmates. I still had my Cabbage Patch doll and I drew a red line across her belly, so it was like she had surgery, too.

Despite the nurse's promises, I never saw those original earrings again. Mom had to take me to get my ears pierced again and I picked out the exact same studs.

∞

We rang her doorbell once again. "I know you've missed us!" Mo cried, crushing Claudia in a bear hug.

Claudia was taken aback. She hadn't seen either of us in ages. She'd just moved into a smaller, one-bedroom apartment, finally ready to live on her own with no more roommates.

"Minka's just out of the hospital," Mom said. "And I told her, 'Claudia will want us. She always opens her door for us.'"

Claudia gave up her bedroom and slept on the sofa. She managed a hair salon now, and when school wasn't in session and Mom couldn't care for me—passed out or too high to function—Claudia took me with her to her work, where I'd sweep up after the stylists and get coffee or soda for the clients.

The owner of the salon pulled Claudia aside when he thought I couldn't hear. "This isn't a day care."

"It's just temporary. She has nowhere else to go."

I tried to make myself useful, tidying up the magazines in the waiting area. All my life, I had been learning how to make myself useful.

∞

One day, Claudia picked me up at the school gate instead of Mom. Her face looked funny, like her features had been taken off, mixed up, and put back on in slightly different places.

"Your mom's in the hospital," she explained. "She'll be there for a few days. Seventy-two hours, actually. It's just a . . . a little infection."

Maybe she'll get some rest, I thought. My time in the hospital hadn't been too bad, so I didn't worry about her being there. And sure enough, when she came home a few days later, she looked no worse than after a night of heavy partying.

There was a distinct change in Claudia, though. She treated Mom as if she were breakable and needed to move slowly. That night, after they put me to bed, they sat on the patio, smoking.

"Really, Mo. This is it. After what happened . . ."

"I just . . ." Mom's voice was rough, like her throat hurt her.

"Look, I love you like a sister, but I don't want to find any more dramatic notes from you. I don't want to have to break down the door of my own apartment to reach you again."

Mom was silent.

"And what about Minka? You may not think your life's worth saving, but what about her?"

"I'm trying, Claudia. Jesus."

Claudia gathered herself. "So we're turning over a new leaf, Mo. You gotta start pulling your weight around here. Clean up the bedroom. Help with the dishes, at the minimum. Don't leave all this shit for me to take care of."

"Oh, I will. I swear to you. I promise." Mom wept quietly. "If not for you, Claudia, I don't know if I'd . . ."

◇◇

A week later Claudia came home from work to find Mom still in bed, dishes everywhere, the TV blaring.

"Mo, we had an agreement!" The kitchen was a mess, food spoiling on the counter. Mom's contrition of a few nights ago was nowhere to be found. I hid in the walk-in closet but watched through the hinges as Mom strode from the bedroom and tossed an empty ice cream container on the pile of dishes in the sink. "Fuck you and your little agreement."

"That's it. I'm done!" Claudia said. "Pack your things and be gone by this time tomorrow." She left and must have spent the night at a friend's house.

∞

Of course, Mom didn't pack. When Claudia arrived home the next night, she found the same mess and so she packed our things for us, lugging boxes and bags out to the hall.

"I can't help you anymore, Mo." Claudia's voice sounded like every syllable was torn from flesh deep inside her. She clearly adored my mom and would have done anything for her, but she couldn't take her shit anymore.

Mom stood in the hallway smoking a cigarette and rolling her eyes as if Claudia was a melodramatic actress. But I knew we were in trouble by the resolve on Claudia's face.

We had nowhere else to go.

"Please, Auntie Claudia," I begged, pulling at her arms. "Please. Whatever I did wrong, I'll fix." She untangled my limbs without looking at me—she adored me and I think she was afraid that if she saw my face pleading with her, she'd buckle. Instead, she shut the door, leaving Mom and me alone in the hallway.

Mom stubbed out her cigarette on the carpet and shrugged.

I went back to the apartment and pounded on the door. "I'm sorry, Auntie Claudia. I'll be good this time. I promise. I'll be good."

When I'd tired myself out, Mom came and got me. "C'mon, Mink. Let's go get a Frosty at Wendy's."

Part II

～

The way we deal with loss shapes our capacity to be present to life more than anything else. The way we protect ourselves from loss may be the way in which we distance ourselves from life.

—RACHEL NAOMI REMEN

CHAPTER SIX

A Fresh Start

Home, they say, is the place where they *have* to take you in.

Still, during my childhood, I yearned for somewhere more open-hearted, a place where I might be integral to the home's makeup. I knew deep in my bones what Maya Angelou once described: "The ache for home lives in all of us, the safe place where we can go as we are and not be questioned."

That ache filled me.

⋈

When I got out of the car to use the bathroom and buy a Coke while Mom pumped the gas, my back hurt and my legs were stiff from hours of sitting.

Exiting the restroom at the back of the service station, I took in my surroundings. Interstate 40, restrained by a shoddy chain-link fence, roared behind me, belching exhaust and fumes. Overhead, the sky was colorless and flat, as if the entire stratosphere had been put under a Tupperware lid. Alongside the convenience store wall, an abandoned planter was a mash-up of jagged rocks, stray tumbleweeds, and spiky cactus. Everything in Albuquerque looked wrong, all the color bleached by the brutal desert sun, all objects coated in dust.

Though we'd only just left L.A., already I craved the greens of my hometown's foliage, the rusty browns and straw-colored expanses of its hillsides, the shady glens I'd discovered in the Hollywood Hills, the translucent blues of the Pacific when we drove to Venice Beach. Albuquerque's woe-begotten air filled my lungs with each breath. Thankfully, we were only here for a visit. Or so I thought.

Mom walked back from paying the cashier for the gas, her hair in a bun on top of her head. I always loved when she put her hair up because it let me see her gorgeous face. She looked cleaner and more mom-like that way, not her usual sexy, unkempt bedhead. Making her way back to the car, her fluorescent green tank top looked corrugated to her ribs from the heat. After driving all night and through most of the day, we were almost there.

We'd come this far in the mustard-brown Saab Mom bought at a used car lot a few months earlier. She'd signed for it before realizing the car had no reverse gear. When she tried to get her money back, the owner just kept repeating the terms of sale. *As is.* Mom and Claudia got good at putting the car into neutral and then pushing it into parking spaces, both developing permanent bruises on their shins. But that was before Mom burned her last bridge with Claudia.

As I buckled myself into my seat, Mom studied the map and wrote down directions to David's family compound. He was waiting for us there. He was the only person we had left.

∞

We exited the main part of the city and wound our way through the outskirts of town. As we drove, the neighborhoods changed. Denny's, the dollar stores, and Walgreens gave way to taquerias, payday lenders, and tiendas. Chain-link fence and wrought iron were popular choices to indicate property lines in this new area, inside of which stood weather-beaten homes and, sometimes, muscle-bound dogs tied in place as early-warning security systems. By the time we pulled up to the two-story house where David was staying, I was pretty sure Albuquerque was going to be a bust.

My impression changed, though, in less than a heartbeat when David's parents, my grandparents, came out to greet me. They bustled out of the house as if royalty had just arrived, squealing with joy, calling to me, hugging me, admiring me, loving on me like I was the long-lost loved one they'd been waiting years for, speaking in a mix of Spanish and English. Grandpa smelled like freshly cut grass, turned earth, and tobacco, while Grandma brought a whiff of roasted chiles and rosewater with her. Grandpa was tall and stood with the moral authority of a giant, and Grandma, who had hair down to her knees, showed up with an intricate hairdo piled into a sculpture on the top of her head. They were like characters from a book and seemed to know my entire backstory; they'd all been present at my birth, though I really didn't know them. They petted me and wanted to touch my pale hair, exclaiming over my beauty and grown-up stature. They delighted in me—there's no other word for it—and I was so taken aback by their affection and praise, I didn't know what to do with myself.

Are you sure it's me you want to lavish all this love and attention on? I thought but didn't ask. *Maybe you have me confused with someone else?*

As much as I was awed by the devotion they heaped on me, I was just as taken by their house—not a cramped and dark apartment like the ones we'd shared in Hollywood, but a proper big ole house with multiple bedrooms that Grandpa had built himself. As they showed me around, I noticed all the walls listed, the doors gapped, and the floors tilted so that anything with wheels tended to roll. Everything was haphazard, and I didn't care in the slightest. All the bedrooms in the jerry-built house were decorated in different colors and the rooms were named by their color. When Grandma assigned me and Mom to the Pink Room, I couldn't have been happier. Albuquerque felt like coming home.

My grandfather was a joyful and smiling man, happiness personified. I've yet to meet a more positive or generous person, truly the most beautiful soul I've ever encountered. Anytime I'd asked him, "How are you doing, Grandpa?" his answer was the same. "I'm fine and dandy, sweet like candy." He had a perpetual twinkle in his eye and I thought of him like a good omen, here to tell me that my luck had just changed.

My grandmother was sterner but no less loving. She immediately took me under her care, teaching me to make tamales, tortillas, and sopapillas. A pot of stew or soup—usually green chile—was always bubbling on the stove and the smell of fresh flour tortillas in the air.

Plus, I had cousins! The units behind the main building, also constructed by Grandpa, housed extended family in need of a place to stay. Little David, who'd long been jealous of me, now lived in one of the back units with his mother, Mercy. Like my mom, Mercy wasn't romantically tied to David any longer, but we were all absorbed as part of this big, boisterous family.

Between cousins arguing about who stole whose clothes, a stepbrother to shoot hoops with, and loads of aunts and uncles, I had everything I needed: playmates, ample adult supervision, warm food at the ready, and a deep sense of belonging.

◇◇

Mom and I had made the trek to Albuquerque to support David because his oldest sister, Roseanne, had come home in the final stages of AIDS. David and his siblings had all at one time or another found a home at this compound; it was where they felt most at ease, and thus, the place Roseanne wanted to be when she breathed her last.

Roseanne was the mother of three daughters: Lisa, Vickie, and Lisanne. David and my mom kept me shielded from the worst of her illness. I didn't know much about AIDS, but I did know that I couldn't catch it from hugging someone or holding their hands, so I didn't shy away from Roseanne. I tried to be a loving niece for the short time we had together.

After Roseanne passed, her daughters were embraced by the family's love and warmth just as I had been. That was how our family worked, absorbing lost souls who needed a place to call home, incorporating all into its welcoming embrace of domesticity, making space for everyone. In no time, I blended into the daily life of the compound, learning ways of being and interacting that were new to me.

∞

Religion, for example. My grandfather was the pastor of his own church and Grandma made me go with her to services. Mom was always asleep and never came and I resented the fact that Grandma didn't make her attend church, too.

Grandpa's church was located off a dirt road and nothing was up to code—the walls, ceiling, and floors were not level, just a square room with a bunch of benches and a podium at the front for Grandpa. Fluorescent lighting lit the pastel-blue-and-white fake floral arrangements, drawing attention away from the dirt-brown low-pile carpet and low ceiling. Grandpa tended a Spanish-speaking congregation and I didn't love going with Grandma because I didn't understand anything, but I enjoyed being tended to, feeling wanted and loved by her. I enjoyed having a grandma. For all my time in Albuquerque, I never did get a good grasp of Spanish and would sometimes fall asleep on her shoulder during services. When that happened she would pinch my leg to wake me up. "But I don't understand what he's saying," I complained.

"This is how you learn! Pay attention to your abuelo!" Her response always confused me; how would I learn if no one was translating what he said? To this day, not knowing Spanish is one of my biggest regrets, but at the time no one in the family thought it was important to teach me, so I never learned. I look at my friends now whose kids are fluent in multiple languages and wish I'd been encouraged more. Still, I respected my grandparents and I did my best to stay engaged and make them proud. Grandpa's sermons were clearly passionate and touched the hearts of those who attended. They found a spiritual home in his words, and sometimes a physical home as well—a few of the church members lived in the little units in the back of the house because Grandpa could never turn anyone away.

I was sometimes startled or taken aback by church. The place was always erupting with wailing and screaming, usually by the women of the congregation. Their hands were always outstretched to God, Jesus, maybe even my grandfather, beseeching, asking for help. I felt their pain as they prayed and knew their suffering was real. Their pain was different from Mom's. Sometimes I felt that if Mom could just get her shit together and do the right thing, get out of her own way, everything would work out for her, for us. She had some choices.

These women were different somehow. Their only hope for survival were the prayers they lifted to God, their suffering tangible and beyond what they themselves could change by the force of their own will. And to them, my grandpa was their savior.

Plus, religion came with mixed messages. Sometimes Grandma told me I was going to hell because I wore pants, cut my hair, and later wore makeup. "You're an embarrassment to your grandfather and the church," she'd say sometimes, but I didn't take it personally. I knew my grandfather adored me and was always happy to see me. Grandma was just very hard-core about her faith. When one of my cousins walked into the house with a cross on her necklace, Grandma ripped it off. "If your husband was killed by a gun, would you wear a gun around your neck?" We all just downplayed Grandma's religious severity and I took solace in how much Grandma loved us. She always called me mija, which felt so good, and she taught me to make tortillas and gave me duties in the kitchen that made me feel at home. I was part of the family.

Because actions speak louder than words, I trusted Grandma's actions and believed they spoke the real truth, despite her dogmatism. And just as the church was a place of hope for many in that working-class immigrant community, Grandma and Grandpa's home was a place of hope for me.

◇◇

That summer, Mom got a job dancing at a local club, leaving each night to work and then sleeping through the day. My grandparents either didn't realize her line of work or were in denial; they never asked too many questions or judged, they just wanted us all to be together. Like in L.A., Mom was often a big fat absence in the daily life of this extended family. Occasionally, David's then-girlfriend Karlotta and I bonded in a mother-daughter-type way that made me feel loved, like joining in on the family's tamale enterprise.

David's family made their living in various ways. David was an incredible cook and the following year, he started his own tamale catering business. But that first summer, the whole family got involved with tamale making. Grandma tended the meat, masa, and chile sauces on a stand-alone range, while David oversaw the assembly line.

Our work surface was basically a board propped on a set of Home Depot buckets. Karlotta and I pulled oja corn husks from where they'd been soaking in water to clean and soften them, then added masa from the large pot Grandma had prepared. Next was the meat: shredded chicken or pulled pork, with more to be pulled once this batch was done. I added red or green chile, depending on the type of tamale, then wrapped my little bundle up in its oja and set it aside. Once they were cooked and we had a tidy stack of dozens of tamales wrapped in foil and ready to go, Karlotta loaded them into coolers, and then put the coolers in her crappy hatchback. Magnetic signs on the doors read, TAMALE EXPRESS.

We showed up at construction sites at dawn, during lunch, and in the afternoons when work crews called it a day, selling our wares from the back of the car. These were the moments when I enjoyed Karlotta's presence as a kind of pseudo-mom and felt enveloped within this bigger family.

◇◇

Summer was coming to a close on the morning I came back from selling tamales with Karlotta to find Mom awake.

"It's not so bad out here, right?" Mom asked, rolling out of bed. "Looks like you're having fun with your cousins."

That was true.

"I think maybe we should stay," she said.

All summer long, I'd wanted to ask Mom if we could remain in this place where I felt so loved, but I'd been afraid she'd say no. I was thrilled.

"I'll start middle school here?"

She nodded.

To this day, I don't know if remaining in Albuquerque had been her plan all along. I liked the idea that maybe she was changing what she'd envisioned solely to accommodate my newfound joy, but the truth is probably coarser. We really had no home to go back to in L.A.

Either way, when she suggested we stay and make a new life in New Mexico, I was all in.

∞

Mom soon enrolled me at Taft Middle School, and if I thought I'd stuck out in Los Angeles, that was nothing to what I faced there. The school was a part of an exurb of Albuquerque made up entirely of Mexicans and Native Americans. I had gotten so used to blending in with my large extended family, I thought I could blend in at school as seamlessly as I'd melded at home. I didn't realize how out of place I appeared, a little blond girl from L.A.

Walking home after the first day at my new school with grown-up lockers and different classes for each period, I was followed by a group of girls. All day at school, I'd been getting dirty looks from them but didn't know why. I dressed like a tomboy in baggy skater-type clothes and tried to keep to myself. What did they have against me?

"Hey, güera," the ringleader called out, using a term for "white girl." I kept my head down and continued walking. I wasn't going to engage.

"What are you doing here?" The girls got closer and when I didn't answer, the tough one yanked my hair. "Hey, Blondie, I'm talking to you."

I pulled my ponytail away from her grasp and kept moving.

"What's your name, Blondie? I haven't seen you before."

Maybe if I gave them what they wanted, I reasoned, they'd leave me alone. "Minka," I answered.

"What kind of weird-ass name is that? Minka what?"

"Gonzalez." I knew instinctively that using my dad's surname would provide some degree of protection.

The girls laughed. "You're one of them white-girl blondie Mexicans?" They were astounded.

I didn't answer. After Marina, I knew it was best to stay quiet when in the sight lines of a bully and to give as little ammunition as possible. They'd get sick of this little game soon.

"You think you're all special, don't you? But you better do something about that unibrow. It looks like a caterpillar took a shit all over your forehead. Didn't anyone tell you that you're supposed to have *two* eyebrows?"

Just then my cousin stepped out from the yard to meet me. Yaz was sixteen, a tad overweight, with big black curly hair, fanned-out bangs, and tons of makeup. She was the chola you didn't want to fuck with. She hung out with the 18th Street Gang and let everyone know she was associated with them. If she wasn't my cousin, I'd have been terrified of her, and yet, her menacing presence was just what I needed now, conveying a clear message to these girls.

See, my family and I are Mexican. And also, don't fuck with me.

Yasmín slung an arm around my shoulder and stared at my tormenters with a look that could kill. "These girls messing with you?" she asked.

The bullies didn't wait for me to answer before scattering.

"We're going to have to do something about your clothes," Yasmín said as we walked into the house. "I can't keep showing up to protect you."

"You don't need to protect me."

"You keep wearing those clothes and I will."

◇◇

Yasmín was Auntie Loretta's daughter and lived in the compound with her parents and her brother Rob. I spent most of my free time with her and our cousin Lisa. Fifteen with long, straight, shiny black hair, Lisa didn't wear makeup like the rest of us and was so pretty just as she was. She was the good girl in the family, the religious one, believing everything Grandpa and Grandma preached.

Her faith offered her comfort when she'd been left bereft by the death of her mother at such a young age.

I moved on as if it hadn't occurred, not discussing it with Lisa, not commiserating with her, not offering her a shoulder to cry on.

On occasions, though, I heard, through the thin walls of that house, Lisa sob and wail, missing her mom, and my heart ached with her. I didn't know how to comfort her.

◇◇

Yasmín decided it was time to address not only my wardrobe faux pas—I needed to stop dressing like a weird skater girl from L.A. and more like a local—but that I also needed to learn to fight.

I thought I'd left all the fighting behind in L.A. the day I saw Marina in the rearview mirror that final time. Fighting was the last thing I wanted to learn and I told Yaz as much.

"You don't have a choice." My cousin was firm. "You can learn here with me, or out there with those pendejas. Either way, you're gonna learn."

We were in the Pink Room I shared with Mom when she started pushing and shoving me around. I was triggered immediately by flashbacks of Marina. *Not again. I don't want to do this again.*

When I tried to get away from her, Yaz pushed me harder until I slammed into the wall. *Dammit. Why couldn't people leave me the fuck alone?* I was ready to scream.

"Come on, little girl," Yasmín taunted. "Fight back."

"I don't want to."

"I don't care what you want." She elbowed me hard in the ribs. "Fight me!"

I pushed her away.

"That's all you got?" She kept shoving me. "You gotta do better than that."

Yasmín slammed me into walls, shoved me into corners, taking a little too much joy from the encounter. I wanted to cry so badly but I'd given that up and held fast to my vow to never cry again. Still, all the rage and frustration of the past years bubbled up in me. *I want this shit to stop now!* I was so frustrated and angry. In a blind rage, I struck out at Yasmín, grasping her around the waist in a hold, then wrestling her to the ground. *Fuck this!*

By the time I regained my senses, I was sitting on top of Yasmín, just as Marina had once perched on me.

"A la verga!" Admiration tinged Yasmín's words. "Now, that's more like it."

◇◇

After dinner that night, Yasmín and I climbed on the roof of the house. She rolled a joint while I watched her every movement, wide-eyed. I'd never smoked weed before.

"Don't worry. You don't need to smoke. Just inhale when I blow it into your mouth, okay?" Yasmín took a big hit and then exhaled into my open mouth. I was late on the pickup.

"Inhale, stupid!"

I laughed so hard, all the smoke dispersed.

"Let's try again," Yasmín said. "When I exhale, you inhale, got it?"

We did it again and this time I got the hang. Back and forth we went, sharing the smoke.

After she finished the joint, we reclined on the roof and looked at the sky, which was beautiful, the upside of living in the middle of nowhere, far from the busy streets of downtown Albuquerque. The stars were just coming out and the night growing chilly. I started to relax and feel a bit high.

Yasmín recited the opening lines of an LL Cool J song. I knew the lyrics and joined in, our two young girl voices intertwining about being alone in a room, staring at a wall, seeing for the first time that "I need love."

Yasmín's home life wasn't much better than mine; both her parents were addicts. Her mom, my auntie Loretta, had been in and out of rehab for years and now had scabs from head to toe. Once, I'd been with Yasmín in her back unit when she found her parents nodded out on the couch, a needle sticking out of her father's arm. After that, David didn't allow me to visit them anymore. If even David wouldn't let me go, I knew it was bad.

But on the evening she taught me to fight and to smoke weed, we found peace and acceptance with each other, drifting in a cloud of forgetfulness. I was thirteen, Yasmín sixteen, both of us lost little girls trying to find our way through life. Our voices lifted the LL Cool J lyrics echoing into the night.

> *The other half needs affection and joy*
> *And the warmth that is created by a girl and a boy*
> *I need love (love, love, love, love . . .)*

I made up my mind that what went on in middle school wasn't going to happen anymore. High school was a fresh new start and it was my mission to assert some confidence and make the right friends this time. I would never be bullied again.

CHAPTER SEVEN

One Person in My Corner

It was my first day at Del Norte High School. I was a sophomore and Mom had just moved us to our own one-bedroom apartment after another round of David's shit.

To be honest, I don't really know whose shit it was she was fed up with, maybe her own and she was projecting it onto him. Either way, she and David were two people stuck in a union of toxicity that spilled over onto my life again and again.

Readying myself for school, I pulled my hair back into a half pony-tail, tying a blue bandana around the gathered hair on top. I didn't have Yasmín around to check my look, but I'd seen others dress like this. I thought it looked cool and was sure I'd simply blend in.

I was worried the neighborhood wasn't safe to walk to school alone—it's just something you feel in your bones—and I noticed all the other kids either found a ride to and from school or traveled in groups, but I had no choice.

"Hey white girl. You all by yourself?" Three girls approached me in the alley.

I kept walking. Here we go again.

"You in a gang or what?" one asked.

"No," I answered.

"Why you got that shit in your hair, then?"

"Because I like it?" I was genuinely confused by the question. They were all wearing blue bandanas in one way or another, hanging out of a back pocket, wound around a wrist, or worn in their hair. Why was my choice so weird?

One of the girls giggled. They must have realized how clueless I was because they just walked away and left me. Then a girl with long, curly dark hair approached. Though she showed a tough demeanor, her eyes were soft.

"Why you have that in your hair?" Coming from her, the question wasn't a challenge, just curiosity.

"Because it matches my outfit." I tried not to let any kind of attitude tinge my words.

"You're lucky they didn't rip that bandana out of your head," she warned in a gentle way, not a threat. She was mostly impressed I'd been so lucky.

∞

At lunchtime in the cafeteria, the girl who'd questioned me in the alley called me over. She was sitting with a group of tough-looking girls as I passed, carrying my lunch tray, looking for a quiet spot to eat.

"Hey lil güera." She patted the bench seat next to her. "Come sit with us."

I looked around to make sure she was talking to me.

"Yeah, you."

I approached her table.

"Sit down. Where you from?" she asked. I thought she was asking about which neighborhood, but she clarified. "Where were you *born*? I can tell you're not from here."

"L.A.," I said.

"Elllayyyyy." She laughed, elongating the letters. The girls around her laughed, too. "So, you in a gang or no?"

I'd already answered her question this morning. Why was she asking again? Besides, it was obvious I wasn't in a gang; I could hardly take the query seriously. I shook my head, nervous.

"You know what these bandanas stand for?"

I shook my head again.

"You're going to get your pretty little ass kicked if you're not careful. People here will think you're in a gang, so after today, leave the bandana at home, okay?"

I nodded.

She looked at my untouched tray of food. "You gonna eat, or what?"

I picked up my fork.

"I'm Rachel," she said.

∞

Rachel and her group of girls became my sanctuary at Del Norte High School. They took me under their wing and called me "lil güera," their term of endearment for me.

I quickly learned what it took to survive. They thought the PE activities were stupid and a waste of our time, so I cut that class regularly to be with them. We'd sit behind the school and smoke weed. Soon, I was cutting other classes and getting into fights. I learned that it was uncool to be a good student, so I let go of my desire to learn. I needed to fit in. Besides, no one ever checked my grades.

Get good grades or survive? I chose to survive.

∞

By this time, my figure was developing, and thanks to Rachel and my new friends, I realized I could look tough and pretty at the same time. That was the perfect mix. Cute, but don't fuck with me. With help from Rachel and a few of the girls whose makeup I studied at school, I adopted this look as my own.

First the eyes: I'd line my eyes with a black liquid eyeliner, stretching out and perfecting the wing to a perfect point at each side. Then I'd heat up an eyelash curler with a cigarette lighter before curling my lashes. After curling and applying mascara, I'd use the blow-dryer nozzle pointed upward to dry my eyelashes and make sure the curl was set, a trick I use to this day. Finally, I'd line my lips with a dark brown wet n wild pencil and lighten the inside of my lips with a dot of foundation to highlight the contrast between the liner and my lip color.

For my hair, I'd apply LA Looks Gel and scrunch my waist-length mane with a towel to make it all curly, spraying Aqua Net or Rave hair spray all over the place, nearly choking myself. I'd dry my hair using a diffuser. The goal: hair as big as possible, the crispier, the better.

Mom hated when I did my hair this way. She wanted me to have a more natural look, but she *did* share her secret of using Sun-In to lighten my hair. By this time, I'd leaned into the "Blondie" name and was proud to be a different kind of Mexican, a unique one, a blond one. After all, I had cousins who were redheaded Mexicans. Why not blond? We come in all colors and sizes.

I'd also started plucking my eyebrows after the unibrow comment in middle school and now attacked them so enthusiastically, they were almost nonexistent, just little anchoring tufts to the left and right of the bridge of my nose. From those anchors, I'd draw in the rest of the brows with my brown lipliner. I was careful to never let anyone see me in the morning or after a shower, though, until I had my brows in place. I looked kind of strange with a mostly blank canvas above my eye sockets. Mom also hated the eyebrows. She said the few remaining hairs looked like "little sperm" on my forehead. She was right, but mostly I ignored her.

I no longer dressed in baggy unisex skater clothes but was getting comfortable showing off my figure in snug-fitting crop tops
and more feminine outfits. Part of my earlier clothing choices, I
see now, were a reaction to how Mom dressed. She chose skintight
outfits designed to draw attention from men, which to me looked
like flirting with danger. By fourteen, I was already getting cat-
called and stared at; why invite more attention? So I'd selected the
polar opposite. If it looked sexy, I didn't want it and would pick
out something else entirely.

Now, though, the pendulum was shifting and I became comfortable showing off my figure. At least, most of the time.

◇◇

One day, I was trying on Mom's old stripper costumes she'd given
me, seeing how I was starting to fill them out, when David spotted
me. We were living with him then and he suggested he take some
photos. I thought, *Why not?*

But then he posed me in provocative ways. I grew uncomfortable when he asked me to bend over in one of her skimpy outfits.
"A little more," he said, urging me to raise my behind for the camera. David had always been my protector, the one who'd looked
after me. This photo shoot felt strange and inappropriate. It confused me. Even Mom was surprised by the erotic charge of the
photos when she saw them.

Still, David was my father and, as scary or uncomfortable as
he could be on occasion, I also loved him. He was fun when he
wanted to be, flamboyant and generous when he had money. He
surprised me in ways that allowed me to keep loving him and to
put all the other shit aside.

This is how crazy he was: That year, for my fifteenth birthday, he
gave me a present in a big box. When I opened it, inside was a saddle.

I looked at him, not understanding. All my life I'd loved horses
and he knew it. He'd been the one to buy me toy horses and barn

accessories when I was a kid; I'd played with them nonstop. I was crazy for everything horse related and would have given anything for one of my own, but I never asked for a horse. I'd learned early: Asking for things is a surefire way to feel rejected.

But for my fifteenth birthday—he got me a fucking horse!

∞

We went together the following weekend to pick her up and bring her home. She was a small paint who had a colt. At David's direction, I kept the two in the yard of an abandoned house across town, encased within a flimsy chain-link fence. I called her Sundance. She was the closest thing I had to a friend at that time and she quickly became my entire world. After school every day, I rode the bus to the abandoned house to care for her, brushing, bathing, and feeding her. I wouldn't put a bit in her mouth or place a saddle on her back because I thought it was too cruel, so I'd unfold a blanket on her and ride her bareback with simply a rope around her neck. I'd ride through the neighborhood and wave to the little kids, convinced I was the luckiest girl alive. Having Sundance to care for kept me out of the kind of trouble my peers were starting to get into: gangs, drugs, and boys.

The place where we housed her, though, was terrible, not a proper stable, just a regular yard, and not really suitable for boarding a horse and her colt. Everything in David's life was always done half-assed and this was no exception. Because it was just an abandoned house with a chain-link fence and no one there regularly to check on things, other people must have noted the horses.

One day, I arrived after school to care for them and found a hole in the fence and the colt gone. Someone had stolen it. I told David and Mom, nearly hysterical, but neither was too concerned. "You still have Sundance," they said.

After that, though, Sundance wasn't the same. We moved her to a proper stable next door to keep her safe, but she became depressed and difficult to manage. I eventually had to use the bit and saddle to ride her because otherwise she'd buck and stand all the way up before slamming down on the ground to throw me. She was heartbroken over the loss of her child.

Not long after, Sundance became lethargic and stopped eating, her health clearly declining. I was told she died of what I assumed was a broken heart. Losing her changed me. Without Sundance to love and tend to, I found myself unmoored.

◇◇

At school I depended on Rachel and her friends to shield me from bullying and fighting. Hanging with the tough girls imparted protection, I quickly learned. I was a sponge, studying how to be threatening, how to look invincible. I wasn't very good at it but I realized that if I was nice to the mean girls, and made myself small for them, they'd protect me, just as David wouldn't hit me when I played meek and quiet.

◇◇

Rachel and I developed a morning routine. I'd "borrow" Mom's white Nissan Sentra and pick Rachel up at her house, careful to park the car in the same spot and to leave the keys where Mom had put them the night before so she'd never know. Then, together, we'd walk the six blocks to school, keeping each other safe.

One morning, when we got back to the apartment to return the car, Mom was awake, standing just inside the front door, her hand outstretched.

Oh, fuck. She wasn't supposed to be up this early. And at this hour, she was likely not very sober. I put the keys in her hand and knew I was busted.

"I'm calling your dad," she said.

"No, please. Don't do that. I can explain. But can I just go to school? Rachel's outside waiting for me."

Mom opened the door to address Rachel. "You're going to have to go to school on your own. She'll be there later."

Rachel looked at me concerned, before Mom closed the door in her face.

"Your dad's on his way over," she said.

She must have seen my fear. "You should have thought of that before you stole my car."

◇◇

I remembered the time when David had assigned Little David some chores before going out. When he got home and found Little David still asleep in bed, the chores untouched, David pulled him from the bed onto the floor and kicked him in the face while he was still half asleep, surely breaking Little David's nose, blood everywhere. "Did I stutter when I told you to clean the kitchen?" David had asked.

I sat on the couch, terrified, and waited. I wanted to explain why I'd taken the car, about how the neighborhood was too dangerous to walk alone and I just needed to get Rachel so she could walk with me, but I couldn't get the words out of my mouth. Fear has a way of doing that. I wasn't very practiced at speaking up for myself.

When David showed up, he looked scary in that far-too-calm way I'd come to know. Unlike Mom, who got hysterical, when David meant business, everything was in a low, menacing voice.

"You stole your mother's car, huh?" he asked, giving me no chance to respond. "I got your report card. You're failing PE. How the fuck do you fail PE?"

"I don't know."

"What did you just say?"

My voice got even smaller. "I don't know."

"I can't hear you, young lady."

After the first smack across my face, Mom sobered up and

realized she'd made a mistake in calling him, but it was too late. "David, stop!"

"Don't interrupt me!" he warned. "Get in the bedroom!"

She did as she was told. He closed the door behind her.

He hit me with an open hand, then a fist, over and over. He found a piece of cable wire on the floor and started thrashing me with it as I curled into a ball to protect what parts of myself I could.

"Answer me, little girl!" he growled.

He yanked my hair, pulling me around the room by my pony-tail. I grabbed my head to keep him from pulling out all my hair but he kept jerking me around. He wailed on me, that damn cable wire coming down on me again and again.

How long the beating continued, I don't know. Welts were rising all over my skin when he finally exhausted his fury. I didn't cry. The promise I'd made to myself years ago to leave tears behind held fast.

He sat on the couch, looking at the effects of his wrath. I finally chanced a glance at him, praying it was over.

"Come here and give me a hug," he said. "This hurts me more than it hurts you."

I couldn't move, I was too confused. But he demanded again, "Come here."

I complied—I had no choice unless I wanted more pain—allowing him to wrap his arms around me even as I flinched at his touch. *You asshole*, I wanted to say. *You fucking monster!* I wanted to cry and scream and tell them both to go fuck themselves, but that would only make it worse. I held it all in.

∞

Mom came out of the bedroom, aware now of what she'd done. "Baby, I'm so sorry! I didn't know he'd do that."

Fury thrummed through me. She knew exactly what he'd do

when she summoned him. That had been her intent. But I didn't argue.

Mom ran a warm bath, trying to tend to me, trying to make amends. I was a complete mess, bruises coming to the surface, swelling everywhere. She tried to brush the mats he'd created in my hair, but that only made me wince in pain. Clumps of hair floated in the water, swirling in eddies.

"My baby," she kept sobbing. "I'm so sorry."

I let her clean me up and fix my hair, sitting naked in the tub, furious and betrayed. *Oh, now you're sorry? What did you think he was coming over to do? You know his answer to any conflict or problem is violence.*

I remained mute.

The minute I was out of the tub, Mom let me go to school. I wanted to be anywhere but there.

◇◇

Is it any surprise, then, that the first girl to give me a funny look in the hallway when I got to school received the brunt of my anger? I flew at her, my fingers like claws, wanting someone else to hurt the way I was hurting, wanting to be on the other side of the violence for once. I punched and kicked and pulled hair and scratched. Venom flowed through my veins. I'd never been so angry in my life. If classmates hadn't pulled us apart, I don't know what I would have done.

Later, in therapy, I learned a phrase that helped me understand this dynamic: Hurt people hurt people. That's exactly what was happening.

The school principal threatened to call my mom and David into his office, but they'd never stepped foot inside any of the schools I'd attended. They weren't going to do so now. A week of the school trying to get their attention was solved when David announced that he'd found a new rental house—a big one with multiple bedrooms!—and invited Mom and me to live with him again. Rather than deal with the mess at Del Norte, I think I just moved schools, but it's also possible I was expelled with a phone call. Either way, Valley High, my third high school (the first was Sandia), was right next to David's new house.

∞

The weird part was that after everything that happened that day, the next day Mom and David pretended that nothing strange or out of the ordinary had occurred. Everyone moved forward as though David hadn't beaten the living daylights out of me and as if my anger as a result of that beating hadn't caused me to be banished from Del Norte. This was the survival mechanism I adopted. It wasn't "forgive and forget" but "avoid and bury." Suppress anything that was hard and make relations with my parents okay so we could get on with living our lives. If I allowed myself to feel my full fury at either of them, what would happen to me? I'd have no one in my corner and might break down completely.

The result of those two beatings—the one David gave me and the one I gave that girl—meant I had to start a new school. So what?

∞

To this point, my life had been about surviving, just making it from one day to the next, trying to figure out how to protect myself and if anyone had my back. Thankfully, that was about to change. Having one person who loved me unconditionally, who accepted me with all my quirks, and who wanted me to be the best version of myself was nothing short of transformational.

I don't remember how Angel and I first met, but I know I saw her at my new school and I studied her for weeks. I had a little more confidence in myself by the time I started at Valley and felt comfortable looking for the place I wanted to belong. There was something intriguing about Angel, an autonomy about her, a sense of self-containment I envied. She kept to herself and was studious, someone so effortlessly tough she had nothing to prove. She moved through the hallways of Valley High without a care or a worry.

Angel seemed to be a planet following an orbit of her own, not needing to belong with the jocks, the stoners, the cool girls, or the troublemakers. At Del Norte, I'd grown tired of hanging with the tough girls and always trying to fit in, working to ensure others didn't see me as meek as I appeared. Still, I never felt like me. I was constantly shrinking myself down to fit. Now at Valley High, I didn't want to be in a group that required me to be someone other than myself. And look at Angel: She'd figured out a way to do that. Maybe I could learn, too.

◇◇

I approached Angel one day and she returned my smile. She was taken aback by how outgoing I was and we became easy, fast friends. This was junior year. Soon, we were eating lunch together and hanging out before and after school. Angel was an athlete and had come from a family of kickboxers. I joined her at the dojo and learned from her. We worked out and sweated until our hair dripped and our breath was ragged, laughing and challenging each other. It felt so good. My body became strong and powerful, and the transformation inside was even greater. I no longer felt like a victim of whatever happened to me. I took out my anger and frustration in the gym, exorcising all the mixed-up, crazy emotions that made life hard until they were out of my system.

I realized that I'd never felt comfortable in my own skin because we'd moved around so much. But now, moving my body and being active and strong in this athletic way with Angel? For the first time ever, I felt like I was home.

She was glad for my company, too. Her mom was going through

a divorce and we were able to distract each other from whatever stress home life had to offer and to share the burdens we each carried. Together, we felt accepted and at peace. We spent hours together and never tired of each other's company. Just knowing that one other person knew me so well and was aware of my struggles made everything easier. I hadn't known that a friend could make such a difference.

Plus, I loved spending time at Angel's house and would sleep over whenever possible. Despite the divorce her mom was going through, she had a real family, a healthy group of people who looked out for and took care of each other. They cooked and ate together. Angel's mom was what I'd always dreamed a mom might be like. She'd peek her head into Angel's bedroom before we fell asleep to let Angel know she'd remembered to get her favorite shampoo and conditioner; we'd see it in the shower when we woke in the morning. I swooned whenever her mother was around. I wanted everything Angel had.

I didn't understand why my mom could never get her shit together. She was the only one of David's ex-girlfriends who couldn't seem to get away from him. I wanted her to make some brave choices, but I was slowly starting to see that was never going to happen.

One day, she and David had been fighting. I remember there was a pool table and she was on one side of it and he was on the other. She was completely hysterical, crying, yelling at him, her makeup smeared, more wasted than normal.

"Pull it together, Mo. You're a fucking mess," David said.

"I took so much." Her words were all garbled. "I hope I overdosed."

"That's great, Mo. Right in front of your kid. Good job."

"I don't care anymore," she cried.

I pretended I hadn't heard what she'd said. Like David's beating, I downplayed it. Whatever awfulness Mom presented went in one ear and out the other. Besides, I knew how dramatic Mom could be. When she was in a rage, anything she did or said couldn't be taken seriously. Sometimes, when she was upset, I'd look at David and he'd give me a little eye roll to say, "It's not as bad as she's making it seem." Whenever I juxtaposed his calmness with her hysterics, she looked that much more irrational.

Say what you will about David, he knew how to keep shit together for the sake of the kid in the room.

◇◇

In the new house, Mom and I each had a bedroom of our own, across the hall from each other. David's room was on the other side of the house where he entertained a procession of girlfriends. By now, I'd gotten fed up with it. I'd fallen in love with some of his previous girlfriends, particularly Charmaine, Karlotta, and Wendy, and had my heart broken repeatedly. I'd become close to these women and their children. Karlotta's daughter Alexandria and I call each other sisters; we're still in touch to this day. And Wendy used to take me to her sign language night class; she was always kind to me. Her daughter Tess and I became the best playmates. These women provided me what little mothering attention I knew. And then they were gone when the inevitable breakup occurred, leaving me aching for the motherly love they'd offered.

One day, we were in the new place with a woman David was seeing who seemed to be getting far too comfortable with her place in the household, talking in the future tense about her life with David.

"You think you'll be here that long?" I asked.

Everyone laughed and thought I'd developed a sharp tongue, but I wasn't trying to be mean. I was becoming hardened.

◇◇

At school, meanwhile, I thought I had moved on from fighting. But one day, the entire student body was abuzz with rumors of a big fight between two of Angel's cousins, Yvonne and Devina, something about one of the girls disrespecting the other. Yvonne was older, long out of school and everyone was pretty sure Devina was going to get the shit beat out of her. Still, she had her reputation to protect and was going to put up a struggle to hold on to it.

A hundred or more students headed to a residential street near the campus after the final bell, ready for the spectacle to unfold. I rode in Yvonne's car with Angel and we slowly crept alongside the parade of the students. Yvonne was ready to teach her cousin a lesson in front of all our friends. The beef between the two girls had been long-standing and now it would finally be put to rest.

As the huge crowd gathered and blocked most of the street in a semicircle, we got out of the car and waited. Soon, Devina pulled up in her blue Chevrolet Camaro, parking perpendicular so she could roll down her window and speak to us before getting out of the car.

"I don't want to fight you, Yvonne," she yelled. "I want to fight Minka." She pointed at me.

Me? Why does she want to fight me? I had nothing to do with their beef.

I turned to Yvonne, expecting her to object, but she just handed me a hair tie. "Put your hair up," she instructed.

Fuck.

Perhaps Devina saw me as an easier target. Clearly, she wanted to avoid the bigger, older Yvonne, against whom Devina didn't stand a chance. Since I had basically been adopted by Angel's family, including Yvonne, I seemed to be a good stand-in target.

I was terrified, certain she was going to beat the living shit out of me, but I threw my hair up anyway.

Thank goodness for the kickboxing. When Devina came flying at me from her car, I instinctively knew how to use the force she was directing at me and counter it with a quick left hook. I didn't know intellectually what I was doing, only acting out of reflex and fear, but it worked. Devina was dazed, which allowed me to grab her by the hair and throw her to the ground, then sit on her and start whaling on her. Soon, though, Angel pulled me off. It couldn't have been easy to watch her best friend beating up her cousin.

I thought it was over, but Devina jumped back up. "I'm going to kick your fucking ass," she screamed, which was kind of funny given the fact I'd just beaten hers.

I looked at Angel. "Please don't," she mouthed.

I was ready to walk away but all the kids around us started yelling. "Let 'em fight! Let 'em fight!" They'd had a taste of violence and wanted more.

So it started again, and the same scenario unfolded again, me pulling her by her hair to the ground, sitting on top of her, pounding her in the face. Again, Angel pulled me off and yet once again Devina rose. "I'm gonna beat your ass, bitch!" she howled.

Three times it happened. There was a moment where everything seemed to slow down while I looked at her face as I was hitting her. I didn't know how I found myself here or what the hell I was doing. Still, I sat on Devina and kept punching. At this point, I couldn't stop myself. I didn't know what I was doing or why I was doing it, only that I couldn't stop; I would have to be stopped.

When Angel pulled me off the third time, Devina couldn't stand on her own. Her eyes were black with smeared makeup and blood covered her mouth. She was staggering. Angel was crying and I was stunned. Thankfully, everyone agreed that Devina showed heart and had had enough. We could all leave.

Half an hour later, when Yvonne and Angel dropped me at my house, I was a sight, my hair a mess and my white overalls spattered in Devina's blood.

The minute I walked in the door, David knew I'd been in a fight. He inspected my face but didn't ask me what happened.

"Who won?" was his only question.

"I did."

"Good," he said.

As a result of that fight, Angel and I became the anti-bullies at school. Girls came to us to defend them from the real bullies. It wasn't what I intended that day when I'd put up my hair to fight, but after that, I was able to let down the tough-girl act. Turns out, I was tough; I didn't need to act it anymore. I could now enjoy myself and have fun. I still felt bad about Devina, though.

I still got terrible grades because Angel and I were having too much fun hanging out and no one asked us about our school-work. By this time, Angel's mom was so caught up in her divorce, she no longer rallied to check how we were doing in school, as she once had.

My mom, of course, was tuned out. On days I didn't want to go to school, I'd write an excuse and ask Mom to sign it. She never even read the notes, because she was half asleep, just added her signature without a question.

∞

Angel and I walked home from school on a warm fall afternoon, late summer, the pavement hot beneath our sneakers.

Usually, when I came home from school, Mom was just getting up for the day, sleep still in her eyes, her hair a mess. Not today.

"Hey, Boo!" Mom's voice came to us from a distance. "Come out and play with us!"

Angel and I looked at each other. What was going on? The house David had rented was big, with a pond in the backyard over-hung by a huge tree.

From the living room, we could see into the backyard where Mom was outside playing with her friends from the club, all of them in G-strings. They had the hose going and were spraying each other.

When we opened the back sliding door, I couldn't believe what I saw. They'd used the hose to make a mud bath out of the pond, splashing each other and shrieking like kindergartners given free rein with fingerpaints. When she saw us, Mom stood in her bikini top and thong, her face that of a seven-year-old, full of innocent joy and childlike bliss.

"Minka! Angel! Hi, my babies! Come out here! Go put on bathing suits. Come on!"

This wasn't the Mom I was used to. Her face was relaxed, no crease of pain or disapproval between her eyebrows, no weight tugging down her shoulders. She was a little drunk, but then again, she was almost always a little drunk, holding her ever-present sports cup with vodka, 7 Up, and sherbet.

I glanced at Angel, ready to roll my eyes, but Angel looked like she'd just been invited to Disneyland and was begging me to let her go. She couldn't believe how much fun my mom was and wanted to get in on the act. I was bored with Mom's shenanigans but couldn't resist the grin on Angel's face.

"You got an extra bikini?" Angel asked.

We ran back into the house, found bathing suits, and joined the fun. We splashed about, slippery and wet and reckless, cool on this hot day, lifting our joyful cries to the flat Albuquerque sky.

Angel and I climbed the tree that overhung the pond and made our way tentatively out on one of the branches, all the women below cheering us on like we were a headlining act. Emboldened by their applause, we stood tentatively, holding on to each other, and then jumped up and down on the branch, tempting fate until the branch gave way and we fell into the pond.

We didn't get badly hurt, though I still have a scar on my wrist from that fall. What I remember most was our laughter, so intense we could barely breathe. And Mom loving on me.

After the fall, she came to where I was and doted on me. She was always so overly affectionate, her nature to be loving, an instinct she amped up when she knew she was lacking in other areas. She knew she wasn't the best mother on the planet and tried to make up for it with an overflow of attention. Usually, I got a bit inured to her gooey emotions, but this day, it felt good. For once, Mom and I were aligned together again.

"My baby, my precious baby," she kept saying, over and over, hugging me close and kissing me all over. I ate it up. If she'd wanted to do a mud bath with me every day after that, I would have been game. Her love gushing all over me was a healing balm.

◇◇

Years later, one of her friends provided the missing clue that fully explained that day. Mom would never have talked so freely with me, but her friend told me they'd all been on Ecstasy. The sense of deep connection we'd shared? It was drug induced.

Even so, the memory remains one of the sweetest moments of my adolescence with her.

And probably the last.

CHAPTER EIGHT

Guys Are the Answer

Miguel Quintana was the most gorgeous human on the planet. He was the school's star quarterback who'd graduated a few years earlier, and everyone knew who he was. So popular, cool, and beautiful. I was smitten and he seemed to like me, too. I couldn't believe it. Me. He liked *me*!

We started hanging together at his house with a group of other kids. Soon we were making out all the time, but I put a halt to things before they got too serious.

"Why do you keep stopping me?" he asked when his frustration built. I avoided him and that question for a few days but eventually called him on a pay phone so I could talk without looking him in the face. I was embarrassed.

"I'm a virgin," I admitted. I was fifteen and didn't know if I should be ashamed or proud of that fact. Mostly, I wondered how he'd receive that news. More than anything, I wanted to make sure he didn't feel rejected.

He paused and I could almost hear the smile curling his lips.

"Well, I would love to take your virginity, if you'll let me," he said, a statement that doubled as a question mark.

I had no particular hang-ups about sex and holding on to my virginity. Everyone around me was doing the deed, and having sex with him would make him my boyfriend, cementing things between us. Plus, I liked him a lot. Why not?

"Okay," I answered. I wasn't in love and there was no real romance, but we shared some good chemistry. Truth was, I'd created in my head a fantasy of who I wanted him to be and was so caught up with the idea that he'd chosen me from all the other girls available to him that I didn't really see him as a person at all.

I didn't know it at the time, but this was the start of my need to use the attention and affection of boys and men to confirm my worth. Miguel Quintana was my gateway drug.

But this was how it worked, right?

I didn't really know. I'd spent a decade and a half seeing how Mom found men to protect and care for her. For years, I'd been trying to do the exact opposite of whatever she chose so I wouldn't fall into the same traps. I knew I didn't want a life like my mother's, so I worked hard to graduate from high school to show I was not like her. In every choice I made, I selected the opposite option from what she would have done.

And that's the weird thing about family patterns: Even though we want to follow a different path than our parents, and in real time we think we are doing just that, we see later that we were, in fact, following in their footsteps the whole time. As Carl Jung says, until you make the unconscious conscious, it will direct your life and you will call it fate. Only, I didn't know that then.

During this time, my sophomore year, I was practically living at Angel's house, which was a great temporary solution for the mess at home, but to have a boyfriend? A strong, older, respected boyfriend? It would be a great way to distract me from the pain at home.

"Do you want to think about it?" Miguel asked before we finished the call. To his credit, he didn't push.

"I want to do it," I said, feeling a little more confident.

◇◇

When we were next together, he was sweet and gentle. It happened, and I remember bleeding and being very nervous. He was considerate and even cleaned up the little mess we made.

"Are you okay?" he asked, and I nodded.

For all the hypersexuality of Mom's work and the life we'd lived, no one had ever explained anything to me. At that point, I still worried that if I masturbated, I'd get pregnant, and I became afraid of my own body for a time. That's how naive and uneducated I was. No one taught me about contraception or STDs or even more important, how to choose a solid partner.

Really, what I was seeking was love and acceptance. And having sex just seemed like the natural order of things, what I was supposed to do in high school. Other girls talked in romantic terms about losing their virginity with one special guy, but I didn't see it that way. *What's this romance of which you speak? I've never heard of it.* My considerations were much more pragmatic.

After our first time, I kept waiting for Miguel to be extra thoughtful and loving, putting his arm around me when we were with his friends, making it clear we were a couple. That didn't happen. Instead, he started bragging about me, as if I were a conquest.

"You'll always remember my name," he crowed, and it's true. I have always remembered his name, but maybe not in the way he wanted.

I waited for the warmth and love to flood me when we had sex, but something felt off. We'd be at a party at his house and go upstairs. The minute it was over, he'd head back down to party without me, leaving me alone in his room.

I argued with myself, going back and forth.

This doesn't feel right.

But he's so nice to me and he likes me.

I don't think this is what it's supposed to be like.

I feel validated by this really cool guy who's giving me attention.

But something's wrong.

Not only had Mom never talked to me about sex, she'd never set an example for me for how a man should treat a woman. Frankly, I never once saw a man treat her with respect or value her and cherish and adore her. I had no idea what that might even look like, nor that there were values I should expect, like kindness and empathy—most important, how to have respect for myself.

Put simply, I felt a little used. And I allowed it.

◇◇

Theresa, the captain of the cheerleading squad and one of the most beautiful girls on campus, approached me and Angel during lunch one day. It was as if a halo lit her up from behind as she came near me, she was so gorgeous. She was the most popular girl in school and I was intimidated. As far as I was concerned, cheerleaders were a different class of animal from the people I hung with, rich bitches who could afford the uniforms and extras required. I had long told myself that Angel and I were cooler than that crowd because we were "real," whatever that means. You tell yourself whatever story you need to in order to accept certain realities.

What on earth did she want from me?

"Hey," she all but barked at me. "You know Miguel Quintana?"

"Yeah."

"That's my boyfriend, so stay the fuck away from him." She turned on her heel, flipping her gorgeous hair as she strutted away.

A few shots of Mom
in her early twenties

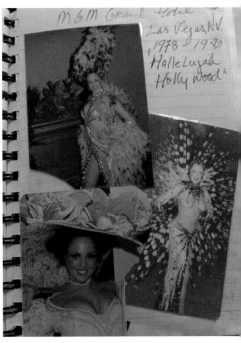

My beautiful momma

Mom modeling lingerie

An entry from Mom's journal

Quintessential Mom and Claudia

Me and Mom

Headshot of three-year-old me
by David

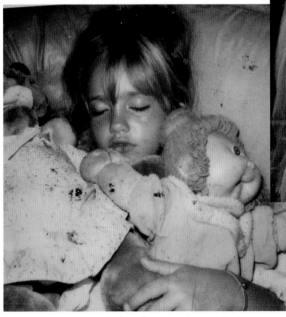

Me and my beloved Cabbage Patch Kid
and Pound Puppy

Rick and Mom in a
moment of lust

Rick getting to know his little girl

Rick doing what he does best

Rick being silly in New York City

My first foray into writing

I'm not even sure if I actually took ballet classes.

Me and Sundance and her colt the day we brought them home

Another entry from Mom's journal

High school yearbook photo

Me and Angel, tough girl kickboxers

Me and Angel on a good day

David and my little sister, Alexandria

Me and Angel, Sears portrait

High school graduation . . .
What I went through to get this diploma!

Me with my auntie and grandma
at graduation

Obligatory road trip "I've arrived in Texas"
photo on my way to shoot season 1
of *Friday Night Lights*

Me and my brother, "Little David"

Me with Zach Gilford, who played
Matt Saracen on *Friday Night Lights*.
My buddy from day one and
still going strong.

Cast dinner preshoot bonding time

From Mom's journal, her as a young girl

Sassy Lyla, *Friday Night Lights*

Mom and her beloved flamingos

Funny thing, I wasn't even mad; I was in awe. I loved nothing more than a beautiful girl who could kick your ass.

Later, Miguel claimed she was a disgruntled ex-girlfriend, but I soon saw the reality. They were a couple, no question. I was just a girl who'd offered him the chance to take her virginity—how could he resist that? He wanted the bragging rights to say that a particular girl would never forget his name (and that's why I've changed his name here).

◇◇

At home, David, Mom, and I shared the house we'd moved into together, but that was about it. She was out each night dancing and slept through most of the days. We hardly talked and avoided each other in the hallway. I was a clean freak, always scrubbing the tub and toilet in the bathroom we shared.

I realize now that my obsession with cleaning was my way of having control of some aspect in my life when I could control so little. My bedroom was always neat and tidy, and I pretty much never went over to David's part of the house, but Mom's room, I could see, was an absolute mess. Candy wrappers on the bedside table, dirty dishes, clothes on the floor, her bag of makeup and costumes left wherever she'd dropped it. I made a point of never going in there if I could help it.

I was so sad about Miguel and couldn't talk to my mom about it, so I tried to make the hurt go away like I'd seen Mom do. I asked one of David's friends to buy me Goldschläger, a cinnamon schnapps with little bits of gold floating in it. Word on the street was that the pieces of gold cut your throat, allowing the alcohol to go directly into your bloodstream, making you incredibly drunk, incredibly fast. Maybe it would help me feel better.

I don't know if the gold did anything to my throat, but I did manage to get blackout drunk alone in my room. I woke the next

morning to my fingertips tapping, splashing even, in a puddle of wetness. When I pried my eyes open, it looked like I'd been throwing up blood all night. I'd been sleeping in a bed full of red puke.

I got out of bed, gathered the sheets, and put them in the washing machine. I felt horrible, so I wrote an excuse note for school.

"Mom, will you sign this?" I tiptoed into her room, trying not to look around, almost certainly still reeking of alcohol and vomit. She signed it and I skipped school to hang with Angel because I was still so hungover and sick. Mom and David never even knew it happened.

◇◇

It was a warm Saturday night and Angel and I were cruising with one of her friends, riding up and down Central Boulevard in his convertible lowrider. We were checking out the other cars and people in them, enjoying the hydraulics and paint jobs of all the cars parked alongside the boulevard, sharing Olde English 40 ounces and blunts. This was how we spent our Saturday nights, and for once we were lucky to have a seat in her friend's car fully equipped with hydraulics. There was no cooler feeling in the world than cruising up and down the boulevard as we bounced while the driver played with the switches. We kept the coolest, most impervious expressions on our faces while everyone watched us drive by. We were too cool to show excitement or fun. Just. Be. Cool.

We stopped at Church's Chicken to examine the other lowriders. Every parking lot up and down the strip, from the car wash to the Sonic drive-in, was filled with vehicles surrounded by teens and young adults hanging around, talking shit, admiring the work, car owners showing off and playing music loud. You knew you had a good sound system if the rearview mirror vibrated with the bass, a detail I always noticed and loved.

A handsome older cholo was eyeing me. He came over and chatted, flirting, giving me his full attention. His name was Rudy

and he was good-looking and a little on the short side. His car was beautiful, too. He had low-profile Dayton Wire Wheels. I liked how strong and quiet he seemed, I guess a little like David in that way. He focused on me as though I was the only woman in the parking lot. I felt my cheeks grow warm from the attention. After Miguel Quintana's indifference, it felt nice. I scribbled my pager number on scrap paper from my purse and shyly gave it to him. The grin on his face was adorable.

◇◇

Back in Angel's bedroom that night, we talked about Rudy, dissecting the evening. I was dizzied by his attentiveness. I asked Angel what she thought about him, but she was evasive.

"He's a bit old for you, don't you think?" He was twenty-two to my sixteen. "Maybe not a good idea." Angel and I stood at her bathroom mirror, taking off our makeup.

Rudy simply hadn't paid her much attention, that was the problem. Sour grapes. I went to sleep thinking I'd found a winner.

I started hanging out with Rudy, and it wasn't long before Angel became more blunt. "There's something about him I don't like," she said.

I paid her no attention. I couldn't see that she was a better judge of character than I was. I was blinded by his cool-looking car, his charm, responsiveness, and maturity. And the fact that he wanted me. Not just on the side but as his main girl.

Rudy and I sent flirty messages to each other with our pagers. By dialing numbers that look vaguely like digital letters, we created words and phrases. For example, 038206237, when read upside down, said *lesgo2bed*. Each person has their own number that identified them as the caller; mine was 27. As we got more serious, we used our pager code to share our deepest feelings. The numbers 143 meant "I love you," so I'd leave 143*27 and he'd know it was from me. This is how we texted before cell phones.

In no time, Rudy became my official boyfriend, the one who put his arm around me publicly, ready to fully claim me. I felt my worth confirmed. He had a quiet confidence, which I found mysterious and intriguing, and he was so beautiful. I loved the way he did his hair, always the perfect fade with a small pompadour up top. It took him as long to blow-dry and hair-spray his hair as it did mine. I loved everything about him and was happy to be his girl.

Rudy lived with his father, Thomás, and his younger brother in a small single-family home behind a chain-link fence with a dirt front yard. That yard was a nightmare because everyone tracked dirt into the house. If I wore sandals, my feet would be grimy from the dust. I coveted the idea of a concrete driveway and a grassy front yard. It didn't take long for me to hate the dust of that place, but I pushed it aside because Rudy was my guy.

Both Rudy and Thomás worked for the city, doing maintenance on garbage trucks; his brother was a few years behind me in school. This little trio was a family unit and I was comfortable there. I thought I could escape the chaos of my own life if I created a household of my own.

And while I loved staying at Angel's, and her mom was always so welcoming, it wasn't the same. Everyone there took care of me and I was considered a guest. Besides, you can't stay with your best friend and her family forever. That's something you do for a weekend or a week or two, max. But a boyfriend? That's a different story, more permanent.

Mom and David of course didn't know I had a boyfriend—technically, I wasn't allowed to have one. I think they enjoyed the performative aspect of being "good parents" but they never levied consequences for breaking their so-called rules. They might preach "no boyfriends" but didn't bother to inquire where I slept every night, preferring to think I was at Angel's.

When I wanted to go to my senior prom, Rudy wasn't having it.

To placate me, we dressed up like we were going and went to the off-site location where the official prom photos were being taken so I could pretend we went. He made me wear flats so I didn't appear taller than him. I could never wear heels with him because he was only maybe an inch or two taller than me. Those photos were the closest I ever got to a prom or homecoming. I didn't care, though. I had a boyfriend who loved me. What more was there to want?

∞

Of course, over time, this new relationship pushed Angel out of the picture. Part of it was that Rudy didn't want me hanging around her; he was very controlling and wanted me available to him at all times. He'd get mad if he knew I'd spent time with her and give me a hard time.

The other part of it was that Angel didn't like Rudy.

Before, whenever Angel and I saw each other in the school hallways, we'd do this thing: We'd limp toward each other, making a big show of the fact that we couldn't walk properly until we were again joined at the hip, reunited with our "other half."

But now, when we saw each other in the hall and she made the motion to start that pantomime, I shook my head and didn't play along. Soon, she stopped trying to connect with me.

I had made my choice. I was going to align myself with the guy, my best friend be damned. It saddened me to see the joy Angel and I once shared dissipate, but that was how the world worked, wasn't it? Mom had always prized her boyfriends over her friends, even over me. And besides, by trading Angel in for Rudy, I got a whole family out of the deal.

Thomás, Rudy's father, was so kind to me, a real father figure. He was short and overweight and had diabetes. He was always giving himself shots and checking his blood sugar. Sometimes, he and I would sit on the couch together all night watching TV. This is what it might have been like, I'd think, if I'd had a more normal dad. He made me feel cared for.

∞

I was walking from English to algebra when Juana, a girl I knew, approached me. She had beautiful eyes and gorgeous light brown, curly hair that fell into perfect little ringlets. I'd always admired her and later learned Angel was a little jealous of how much I revered her.

Juana looked somber and nervous as she bent her head to whisper to me. "I'm not supposed to tell you this, but my dad's a private investigator, and your dad's about to be in a lot of trouble."

I didn't know what to say. I always knew David was usually up to something a little shady. There must be a reason he never had a driver's license, why we never went to the doctor for a checkup, and why the utilities were in my name, but I wasn't sure what was what. Once, when a friend gave me a ride home from school, she was shocked when we arrived at my house.

"Why?" I asked.

"That's where my brother gets his drugs," she told me.

I shrugged it off.

∞

I was nervous to tell Mom because we didn't have a line of communication between us at all. We hardly acknowledged each other's presence these days, but this felt important. Juana had taken a risk warning me. The least I could do was make sure her efforts weren't in vain. Plus, if a raid was about to go down, I wanted to be somewhere else. She and David might be able to handle what was coming, but I couldn't.

When Mom passed me in the hallway to our bedrooms, I just

blurted it out. "My friend says Dad's about to be in trouble. Her dad's a private investigator."

I didn't know how she'd react. Would she hit me? Scream and yell? Throw things?

She didn't do any of that. Instead, she laughed. "What would David be in trouble for, honey? That's silly."

I knew it was an act. I wanted to tell her, *You don't have to admit anything to me, just do what you will with this information. I don't need you to lie to me anymore.*

I held my tongue.

∞

When I came home from school the next day, the house was in complete disarray. Moving boxes were everywhere. When I found my mom, I asked her what the moving boxes were for. She calmly said we were moving to Boston.

"What?"

"You heard me."

"No! Why are we moving? This is crazy."

"Because I said so."

That was the answer she'd given me ever since I could form my first question. By now, I was done with it.

"Where am I going to go to school?"

"We'll figure it out when we get there."

I knew that wouldn't happen. Mom hadn't finished high school. Neither had David. If I left with them, I wouldn't, either. It was a miracle I was still in school in the first place, but I had been determined. Somehow, I had it in my head that I wouldn't be able to get a real job unless I had a proper high school diploma. All I knew was I wasn't going to end up like them.

"This is the longest I've ever been in one school," I pleaded, "and I want to graduate with people I know. I only have one more year left. I can't go to Boston. Please, don't make me!"

"You have no choice, young lady."

I went to my bedroom. She must have thought I was pouting and packing because she left me alone. I called Rudy from the hamburger-shaped phone in my room. "Please come get me."

I threw clothes into a trash bag and when I heard the bass from Rudy's lowrider pull up the street, I ran out of the house.

"Where do you think you're going?" Mom's voice trailed behind me.

I jumped in the car and Rudy took off. I'd escaped for now.

But looking in the rearview mirror, I saw Mom run outside, look around, and jump into her own car.

Shit.

Soon, she was tailing us. Rudy tried to lose her. He was fast but she was even faster.

When he pulled up at his house, I ran inside and hid behind the couch where Thomás was seated. Rudy followed and locked the front door.

The screech of her tires against the curb sounded like it was right next to my ear. I heard her screaming from the porch. "Give me my daughter! Where's my daughter? Minka, get out here right now, goddammit!"

Thomás didn't know much about my home life, but he sized up the situation pretty quickly. He told me to stay hidden. By now, she was banging on the door, screaming at the top of her lungs for me to come outside.

Thomás opened the door. "Ma'am"—he kept his voice low and level—"she's not here. You need to leave my property."

"I know she's here. I saw her!"

Things were going to get violent soon. She was out of her mind with rage. I was terrified.

"I'm going to call the police if you don't leave." Thomás stayed calm throughout.

They argued back and forth and I pressed myself into the carpet behind the couch, praying she'd go away. It was only when Thomás told her the cops were on their way that I finally heard her car peel out.

Thomás turned from the door and I peeked at him from behind the couch.

"Come here," he said.

I inched toward him, afraid he'd banish me forever. Instead, he wrapped me in his arms. "You stay here, mija. We'll keep you safe."

I collapsed with relief.

Rudy, though, looked at his father from across the room as if Thomás was crazy. *We're doing what?*

◇◇

Once I calmed down and fully understood what Thomás was offering, I didn't even pretend to decline his offer, as good manners might require. I called David immediately.

"Hi, Dad," I said. "My mom just came here in a crazy rage, she was out of her mind. I was hiding because I knew she'd pull me out of here by my hair, but I don't want to go to Boston. I want to stay and graduate high school. My boyfriend's dad said that I can stay here with them."

I waited, my breath in my throat, for his response. Until that moment, David didn't even know I had a boyfriend. He'd never met Rudy, much less Thomás. It was a big ask, but David made up his mind in about half a second. "That's a good idea. I'll talk to your mother."

If David was on board, it was a done deal.

The fact that I was jumping from the fire into the frying pan never occurred to me. Rudy, meanwhile, was sulking. He was not at all pleased about this new arrangement. It's one thing to have a teenage girlfriend but another thing altogether to have her move completely into your life, but I didn't see that at the time. I was too awash in relief and the fact that Thomás had offered me safe harbor.

Thomás called David later that day. "I'm going to need some kind of legal custody. I'll have to sign school permission slips, that kind of thing."

I don't know exactly where, when, and how, but Mom met with Thomás in an attorney's office in Albuquerque and signed my custody over to a man she didn't know, no questions asked.

She and David left town two days later.

◇◇

I got what I'd asked for but had no idea what it meant. Driving to school each day after that, I was forced to pass our old house because there was no other way to get to campus. Each time, I'd avert my eyes and try not to think the words that kept haunting me.

They left me.

I asked for it, yes, but really, I just wanted them to stay and care for me here, where I had a home. I had hoped they'd change their minds. They didn't.

I was sixteen.

CHAPTER NINE

Not This Guy

"Hey, baby." Rudy's voice was unusually sweet as he called to me from behind the door to the bedroom we shared. "Come here."

I'd just returned from school and dropped my backpack on the dining room table. His work boots and socks were strewn across the living room carpet from where he'd dropped them the night before. It was his day off.

Ever since I'd moved in with him and his family, I'd become the housekeeper. No one asked me to, it was just my way to earn my keep. I also needed to live in a clean home for my own sanity. I regularly scrubbed the kitchen sink, cleaned the fridge, and cooked for them. A month earlier, when I'd noticed the walls looked dingy, I took the hose attachment with the little bristles from the vacuum cleaner to see if I could make it any better. I was shocked when a bright stripe of clean wall appeared. The whole thing was coated in dirt! The walls alone took days to clean, and then I tackled the horrible toilet we all shared. Three guys had been living there for how long and not one of them had ever thought to clean the toilet?

Before walking down the hall to our bedroom, I picked up his boots and socks, making a note to run the vacuum that night. The place was starting to look shabby again.

When I opened the door, Rudy was sitting on our bed with our friend Nina. A six-pack of cola and a half-empty bottle of Jack made sticky rings on the dresser. Rudy almost never drank alcohol and never in the middle of the day. They were sitting close to each other on the bed.

Nina didn't go to school with me; I think she graduated already or maybe she'd dropped out. Initially, we were friendly only because she was the one person Rudy allowed me to have as a friend. Over time, though, I'd come to adore and trust her.

And now, it was clear, Rudy liked her, too.

"Sit with us, baby." He patted the bed. Nina giggled. They were already a little drunk. I sat next to them, unsure what else to do.

"I want you to look at Nina," Rudy commanded. "Do you see how sweet and beautiful she is?" He was trying to make his voice hypnotic, as if he could convince me of anything if he tried hard enough and used the right timbre.

Nina turned to me, her eyes glazed and a bit unfocused. They'd been partying for some time.

"Nina thinks you're beautiful. Isn't that right? She was just telling me."

She smiled at me and nodded, then looked at Rudy to see if she was playing the role the way he wanted.

"Nina has been wanting to kiss you for so long. She said so just before you came home. Don't you want to make her fantasies come true? Why not give her a kiss? No one here's gonna mind. We're all friends."

◇◇

This was the newest chapter in Rudy's efforts to control me and turn me into the person he wanted. What was most striking was how kind his voice was in that moment. It had been some time since he'd spoken nicely to me.

Usually, he was calling me a slut and shaming me for my clothing choices. Last week, he had taken away one of my favorite skirts and thrown it out when he thought I looked too attractive wearing it. He continually warned me to stay away from Angel—"she's a bitch"—and did all he could to isolate me and make me totally dependent on him. He gave me direct orders: If I wanted to go anywhere, it would be with him, his brother, or his dad only.

I was already completely reliant.

It had been months since Mom and David had moved to Boston. I'd heard from them recently, and unsurprisingly, they were now talking about returning to Albuquerque, but both were broke again. If and when they returned, they'd each be crashing on friends' couches, with no place for me to join them.

Rudy, in the meantime, had been getting into whatever kinky stuff he could come up with. First, he insisted on taking graphic photos of us. He made me bring the film into the one-hour photo at Walgreens for processing. Most of the time, they gave me the pictures without an issue, but the last time, the manager said I couldn't have them. "We don't print pictures like that."

My face grew hot with shame. This man and likely the rest of the employees had seen my naked body in compromising positions; they might also have realized the photos constituted child porn because I was underage. I went home empty-handed.

After that, Rudy bought a video camera—voilà, no need to have anything processed!—and decided we'd do live-action instead. He set up a tripod and monitor so he could watch along as the tape recorded. He played "The Boy Is Mine" from Brandy's newest album, Never Say Never, in the background, art directing the whole shoot. He was really into it.

At the start of the video, I pulled up my top to expose my breasts, thinking that's what he wanted, and then spoke to the camera. It got raunchier after that, but what I remembered most, when he insisted we watch it a few days later, was that I spoke and acted like a small child. I'd long known I'd changed my behavior to placate him—what choice did I have?—but seeing it on video made me squirm. That wasn't me. I hardly even remembered making the tape; I'd become such a master at leaving my body when things were uncomfortable. But watching the video stuck with me. On the screen wasn't a woman filled with desire; this was a small girl doing whatever was necessary to keep herself safe.

After that, he decided I should get his name tattooed on myself. I may have been young and naive, but I knew immediately that was a very bad idea. Still, he was insistent.

"What about if we come up with our own private tattoo, one only you and I know the meaning of?" I suggested as a way to placate him and avoid his name being permanently inked on me. He was game. We decided on an imprint of my lips, which I'd make for the tattoo artist by kissing a piece of paper wearing heavy lipstick. I didn't want the tattoo where someone might see it, and thought I'd come up with the perfect solution: I'd shave my pubic hair (this was before Brazilian waxing was a thing) and have the tattoo placed on the side of my pubic mound. That way, Rudy could feel he'd claimed me—that seemed to be the point—and I could simply grow the hair back afterward to cover it. Easy peasy.

Because the tattoo artist was a friend of Rudy's, we were able to skirt the laws that said I had to be an adult to consent to such art. When the time came to expose myself for his needles, I completely left my body; I was so scared of what we were about to do. Plus, I couldn't believe that Rudy would let another man anywhere near me without underwear, touching me.

The tattoo artist noticed my discomfort. "Don't worry. If I see anything I haven't seen before, I'll smack it."

I had no idea what he meant. Was that supposed to be comforting? Leaving my body in that moment was my way of ignoring what was happening. Since I couldn't object without bringing Rudy's wrath down on me, I tried to pretend I wasn't there.

Little did I know I'd spend the rest of my life explaining to new lovers what that mark was, lying to everyone. "It was just some silly thing a girlfriend and I decided to do together."

I was too ashamed to admit the truth, that at seventeen, I'd been so dependent on a man I'd let him brand me as if I was a member of the NXIVM cult.

∞

I picked at my cuticles while Nina and Rudy started making out. I just sat on the bed, pretending I was anywhere else. Soon, they'd stripped off their clothes and were having sex right next to me. I remained next to them, fully dressed—they'd forgotten all about me. I felt sick and excused myself to sleep on the couch so they could finish. Before the sun came up in the morning, I gathered my clothes and called Angel, hoping she'd forgive me. She picked me and my bag of clothes up immediately.

On the way to her house, I asked her to make a stop at the pharmacy to buy a pregnancy test. I'd been feeling nauseated for some time. I was worried I was in trouble.

I took the test with Angel and sure enough, positive. Shit. I couldn't tell Rudy. He was already so in control of me. This would cement his rights over me and my body forever more. Instead, I called my mom.

"It's okay, honey. We're coming back next week. I'll take you to the clinic. We'll take care of it together."

Mom didn't seem upset about the pregnancy. I'm not sure what I expected, but blasé wasn't it. I made an appointment at Planned Parenthood; Angel's mom had said they'd take care of me there since I didn't have a family doctor, a gynecologist, or insurance.

For once, Mom actually showed up as promised. But when I was on the examining table, I started to bawl. "This isn't what I want," I said. The nurses were so warm and nurturing. The doctor understood and immediately stopped.

"It's okay, baby." Mom stroked my hair. "You can decide whatever you want."

We left the clinic and I was feeling better, trying to figure out if maybe there was a way I could be a teen mother, until Mom spoke on the drive home. "You know, we could do what my mom and I had planned to do. You and me. We could raise this baby together."

Raise this baby together, how? With what money? What home? What insurance? I couldn't imagine bringing a baby into what my mother brought me into. Absolutely not.

That was it. In that moment, I knew the right choice. Raising a child with my mother would only continue this family trauma, another cycle added to so many generations of pain. Hadn't there been enough damage already?

When I got back to Angel's house, I told her the whole story. She held my hand as I called and made yet another appointment. This time, Angel took me and I went through with it. I left with an education about the need for annual Pap smears along with a bag full of condoms, as well as pamphlets of different types of birth control options I could choose from.

Back at her house after, she cared for me and it was like old times; we were close again. I wish I could say I stayed with her and learned my lesson about Rudy. I wish I could say I chose this loyal girlfriend over that asshole boyfriend, but I didn't. As soon as I felt strong enough, and after enough of his begging for another chance and for me to come home, I was convinced things would be different. I took off from Angel's house and returned to Rudy's. I missed him in a Stockholm syndrome–type way.

Plus, I was following the script I'd been given. There'd been an incident a year or so earlier with my mom. She'd been dating a new guy and was excited about things with him. She got mad at me for being rude to him and nearly spit at me a line that had stuck with me ever since: "If I lose him because of you, I'll never forgive you."

This was how it worked. Women sacrificed everything, their children, their friends, to keep their boyfriends. I basically did the same to Angel.

And by that time, she was ready to be done with me. Rightfully so.

◇◇

A package arrived for me from L.A., the return address listing Rick Dufay, my biological father. I held it in my hands, afraid to open it. I hadn't heard from him in years. I believe he still kept up with my mom and asked about me, but we hadn't talked since I was small. For as long as I could remember, I'd wanted nothing to do with him.

Now, after the abortion and the troubles with Rudy, the separation and distance from my mom, I was more open to what he might have to say. I tore into the padded envelope.

The package contained a lengthy letter in which he told me of his life, his marriage to Robin, a gorgeous redheaded British artist, and his music. He also wrote that his mother, my biological grandmother, had recently died. Before passing, she'd told him, "You need to get that little girl. Take care of her. She needs you."

She'd meant me.

"I'd really like to make things better between us," he wrote, "if you'll let me."

Plus, his mother had left me a small inheritance and he'd like to deliver it in person. Was I game?

Along with the letter, he'd included a bunch of photos from his life and a CD. He looked so handsome and happy in the pictures. And his house appeared to have been stolen from the pages of a storybook. His wife was adorable; they looked so normal and sane. Healthy.

I was related to this?

I put the CD from the album he was working on in my Discman. When I pressed Play and his voice came through the headphones, something inside of me broke. I recognized his voice immediately. His voice filled my ears with memories of how loved and accepted I'd always felt with him. His voice sounded like hope. I held the Discman and bawled, playing his songs over and over.

I had a dad. And he wanted me.

When my tears dried, I called him and said, yes, I'd love a visit.

"I'll come right away," he said.

I felt so special.

I called Mom next and told her. She seemed pleased but later reported that David's sister, my auntie Sofía, and the rest of David's family were unhappy about the reunion. "That man's nothing but a sperm donor. We're the ones who raised Minka." They weren't wrong to feel that way. But I didn't care.

∞

Getting ready for Rick's visit, I took up a local hairdresser on an offer. He was a friend of David's and had offered to do my hair for free. He was the most well-known hairstylist in the community, the hair guy everyone wanted to see. I was a little uncomfortable about his generous proposal, but I wanted to look good for Rick. The hairdresser made my appointment for after salon hours. "It's just so you won't be charged," he explained.

When I arrived, he asked me to change into the gown he provided but to wear nothing underneath. "I need to use your back as an easel. Your back will be the canvas on which I'll create a work of art."

I wasn't used to going to fancy salons and thought this seemed a little odd, but I went along with it. He also had me stand as he worked rather than sit in a chair, but what did I know about how artists worked?

As he trimmed the back of my hair, sure enough, he kept pushing the gown aside to see my back, but when he came to the sides, he nudged the gown down in front, so that it dropped and exposed me. I tried to tug it back up, but he held my hand down. "You have no reason to cover up. Your breasts are beautiful."

I froze immediately. I was alone with him and scared. Was he going to attack me? I couldn't move.

Next, he tugged down the other side of the gown and fondled me, telling me how beautiful I was. I stood there, completely rigid, my whole body vibrating with terror. At any moment, it might get worse.

To this day, I don't know why he backed off. Maybe he realized I was still a kid, or he worried I'd tell David, or maybe he saw how completely petrified I was, but at some point he finally allowed me to tug up the gown and cover myself.

"Thank you for the haircut, but I need to go home now."

He let me leave and I didn't tell anyone. This was how I'd been trained. You do whatever it takes to keep men from hurting you and then you shut up and suck up whatever shame is left behind.

◇◇

A few days later, when Rick pulled up out front in his red vintage Jag, I was out the door and in his front seat before he could unbuckle his own seat belt. I looked up at him.

He lowered his Ray-Ban sunglasses. "Wanna get some ice cream?"

I nodded and we were off. He didn't ask intrusive questions and engaged in zero small talk. We simply settled into being with each other like it was natural, like we'd been doing this our whole lives. Rick was effortless to be with.

Driving around Albuquerque, he threw on some Al Green and gave me my first introduction to the blues and soul music. He didn't play the rock and roll my mom listened to, Whitesnake or

Guns N' Roses. And it wasn't the rap I was listening to, Tupac, the Fugees, and Too Short. I'd never heard anything like what he was playing, and I immediately fell in love with him through the music. He was the coolest guy I'd ever met.

We didn't do a lot of talking, just flowed our energy back and forth with each other, surrounded in comfort and this mystical, magical music of which he seemed to have an unending supply: Al Green; Bill Withers; B.B. King; Earth, Wind & Fire—groups I'd never heard of. Being with him and the music blasting felt so fucking good. Everything about the visit was soulful and we connected in a deep way. I kept thinking, *This music, it's in my blood. I can feel it!*

We got ice cream and drove around, talking, but not about anything important, just us vibing and feeling each other out. I felt at ease with him. It had been so long since I'd felt that way.

He stayed for a few days and before he left, he gave me a check from his mother, my inheritance. Before he pulled away for his trek back to L.A., he planted a seed. "When you're ready to get out of here, let me know."

Get out of here? What was he talking about? This was my home. I said goodbye and went back to my life. It had been fun to play around with him for the weekend, to have a different sort of existence for those few days, but Albuquerque was my home.

◇◇

I bought a turquoise Chevrolet Beretta with the four-thousand-dollar check Rick had given me and felt so grown up. That car had muscle and allowed me some freedom. Maybe I wouldn't be stuck like this forever. Maybe there *was* another life for me. I made plans to attend the local community college after high school, but that only angered Rudy.

"I've had to deal with you in high school all this time. No way I'm putting up with college shit, too. If you decide to go back to school, you'll need to find another place to live."

By then, Thomás had seen how things were unfolding between me and Rudy and had taken me aside. "You're too good for my son, mija," he said. "If you save up for first and last month's rent, I'll cosign an apartment for you."

Where was I supposed to get that kind of money?

That's when I got the job at the peep show and started saving in earnest. I hoarded cash in shoeboxes hidden under the bed. I'd make between one hundred and four hundred dollars a night and saved every last dime. I was determined to get away from Rudy.

I never told Thomás about the work I was doing—we had a kind of don't-ask-don't-tell policy—but I was determined to make him proud.

◇◇

Rudy took me along to his attorney's office on a sticky hot summer's day. He was suing the county for something related to his job. He and the attorney were shooting the breeze and somehow got on the subject of men taking advantage of underage women. I'd been quiet the whole time and didn't plan to say anything, but suddenly, out of my mouth popped the story of the hairdresser.

The attorney and Rudy stopped their conversation and looked at me. "What did you just say?"

I repeated the story.

"You have a case here," Rudy said. He was always looking for someone to sue.

"He's right," his attorney agreed. "I'll take you on if you want."

Until that moment, I hadn't realized exactly what had happened and that I could demand recompense for it. Winning such a case might mean I could get my own place even sooner. More important, this information felt empowering. These two men were telling me I could say, *What you did to me was not okay,* and a judge and court would hear me out. Never had I been able to tell someone their treatment of me was wrong. I felt inspired and emboldened. I was going to stand up for myself. Finally.

∞

The first blush of righteous indignation stayed with me for a week or two. And then I got a call from the attorney.

"Minka, is it true you're working in a peep show?" He sounded both annoyed and incredulous.

"Yeah." My voice immediately got small.

"You should have told me that at the beginning. That's it. It's over. Your case is dead in the water."

"What do you mean? My job has nothing to do with what he did to me."

"Actually, it does. No judge or jury is going to believe you weren't asking for it. Case closed."

I was embarrassed and mad. For a moment, I'd allowed myself to trust that a woman should be able to stand up for herself and demand justice when she'd been taken advantage of. How could I have allowed myself to believe that such rights applied to me, too?

∞

Over the years it became abundantly clear how ubiquitous this situation is when it comes to sexual assault.

You dressed alluringly? You were asking for it.

You willingly kissed him? Asking for it.

Make your money by taking off your clothes? Asking for it.

Add in any whiff of sex work, and it's all over.

The answer again and again: The woman is always asking for it. This attitude is so ingrained and deeply offensive, but I didn't know it at the time. I had so much to learn.

CHAPTER TEN

Never Again

Breaking free of a difficult past doesn't always happen in a big dramatic way like we see in the movies—the heroine makes up her mind, and then she's on the path. Sometimes, it's a little back and forth, with some wavering and dithering along the way, and occasional backsliding. As long as the general trajectory is up, though, we know she's heading in the right direction.

For me, that path started when I finally got my very own place.

◇◇

The rental was nothing special, part of a group of densely packed apartments I'd seen on my way to work. I was drawn to it because it was the largest apartment complex around and I thought, if they're that big, maybe they'll have room for me.

After working six months at the peep show, I kept my promise to myself and quit, determined not to follow Mom down that rabbit hole. Sure, the money was good, but I'd saved enough for first and last, tucked away in shoeboxes hidden under the bed I shared with Rudy. To stay any longer was to risk getting lured permanently into that life.

Thomás, as promised, came with me to the apartment complex's leasing office.

"I've been charging her rent for the past two years and she always pays on time," he lied. For his story to be accurate, I would have been paying my way since I was sixteen, but it didn't matter. The leasing agents just wanted to know I was responsible. When they saw all the cash I brought in on top of Thomás's good word, that was enough. I signed a one-year lease on a one-bedroom apartment. I could move in the following week.

∞

That night when I told Rudy I was moving out, he didn't believe me. All along, he was convinced I couldn't manage on my own. He thought working at the peep show was a titillating little side gig I did for kicks—something he got off on. He had no idea I was saving to move out. If he'd known, he wouldn't have let me keep the job. He liked being the one in control.

Honestly, I don't think he was bothered by the fact that I was leaving; he was more upset that I'd found a way to stand on my own. I didn't need him anymore.

Plus, I had an out, one he'd given me. Earlier, when I told him I was considering community college, he told me I needed to find another place to live if I planned to follow that route. Though I'd graduated from high school a month earlier and didn't know how I'd go to college, nor even what I needed to do to get in—no one ever suggested I take an SAT test—for now, it was the perfect excuse. I was going to attend community college.

"That's what you said"—I reminded him of what he said as I packed my few things—"so that's what I'm going to do."

"How? What the fuck?" He played the tough guy and didn't fight me on it, but he never really said goodbye, either.

◇◇

Next stop was Rent-A-Center, one of those rent-to-own furniture places that specialize in people with no credit. I picked out a black velvet couch, a bed of my very own, and a huge wooden entertainment center, complete with a TV and VCR, that felt very adult and legit. Then I jetted to Target for towels and sheets and a few pots and pans. Having my own car, thanks to that inheritance Rick brought me, made everything easier. My life was coming together.

I was excited about my new place, especially because I'd have my very own washer and dryer. All my life there'd been a stash of quarters hanging around for laundry time, coins I'd feed into machines in shared laundry rooms or, most often, at a Laundromat. Now, I'd be able to wash my sheets and towels as often as I wanted; I could have fresh sheets every day if I felt like it. My clothes would smell exactly the way I wanted.

This was the first time in my life I realized I knew how to make a home for myself and that I was not a burden to *anybody*. No one gave this apartment to me. No man helped me get it, other than Thomás telling a little white lie. I'd built this all by myself.

Now that I was going to live on my own, I got to ask myself a few questions: What time do I want to eat? What do I want to watch on TV? When do I want to go to bed? When do I want to wake up? These were questions that had always depended on someone else's answer. Now I would be able to pick what *I* liked.

I bought my very own vacuum cleaner and couldn't wait to make perfectly symmetrical lines in the carpet that no one was going to mess up—no one but me. This was going to be a sacred place that I created for myself.

I had fucking made it.

◇◇

Soon, I found a real job at VoiceStream, now known as T-Mobile, where I did customer service. I bought new clothes that looked professional without being sexy—nice slacks, pretty blouses, no jeans, sometimes a blazer—the antithesis of the stripper costume. I was so proud of myself. At VoiceStream I had my own desk and a cubicle amid a sea of cubicles, but it was mine and I decorated it with a corkboard pinned with pictures of my friends, my mom and me, maybe a couple of inspirational quotes. I surrounded myself with little tchotchkes and all the school supplies I'd always loved: pens, pencils, pencil sharpeners, highlighters. I felt good and wholesome and career focused.

The building where I worked was beautiful and new, everything modern, not all dusty and falling apart like so much of my life had been. At lunch, I sat with the other girls in the breakroom talking about our customers and our lives. Sometimes we'd go out to Dion's for pizza at lunchtime and I'd dip my slice in ranch dressing, enjoying this new reality.

This life was a world away from anything I'd ever known. Talking with my coworkers, I never said a word about my previous line of work, sex tapes and sexual assault cases, how I'd learned ways to keep a man sliding bills into my slot at the peep show and how awful that place smelled, or the fistfights I'd gotten into in high school and the difficulty of getting blood out of my clothes afterward.

It was as if none of that had ever happened. What existed now was all that mattered.

◇◇

"Hi, this is Minka at VoiceStream. Give me a minute and I'll pull up your account." As part of my job, I talked all day with people who had issues with their phone bills.

"Don't put me on hold again," the woman on the phone pleaded. "I've been on hold forever."

"Ma'am, I'm not going to put you on hold. I'm right here. I'm just pulling up your account. Okay. I've got it now. How can I help you?"

"I've been trying to pay my bill but the system won't let me. There's all these late fees that keep getting added on, and I can't be without my phone. If you turn it off, I can't get to work and feed my kids."

My heart always hurt on calls like that. I remembered my own mother talking to creditors, trying to find some kind of escape. When I was a kid, she'd put the utilities in my name since her credit was shot. I felt for them all.

On one of those calls early on, I had to call a supervisor over. I saw him hit a series of keys and then zero out the customer's account. I remembered what he did. After that, whenever it was clear that someone just needed a little help, I took matters into my own hands.

"No problem, ma'am. I've zeroed out your account. Is there anything else I can help you with?"

"What do you mean?" The customer was usually confused.

"The total for your bill this month is zero dollars and you'll start a new billing cycle on the fourth. All the late fees are gone. Is there anything else I can help you with?"

On the other end, I could hear the woman's befuddlement, sometimes tears.

I ended those calls as quickly as I could. "Would you be willing to fill out a survey on the service you received today?"

It's no surprise my surveys were great. I got bonuses all the time, but that's not why I did it. All those young mothers, women in general in financial trouble? Someone needed to give them a break. Even if that break was just taking care of the damn phone bill.

◇◇

I kept my eyes trained on the cars passing by the curb at LAX, looking for Rick's iconic vehicle. His red Jag was my favorite. Its tan leather made the interior feel clean and elegant. The steering wheel was made of solid wood, and he'd changed out the Jaguar engine for a Chevy one that had real umph. That car was his baby, and he showed it the attention it deserved, keeping it in immaculate shape. I could pick it out of a lineup of Jags in a heartbeat.

I stood with my two massive suitcases, my hand to my forehead to shield the light from my eyes, when he pulled up. At his suggestion, I'd come to L.A. for a week's visit.

We had trouble wrestling all my luggage into the trunk, but the minute I hopped in, we picked up where we'd left off with each other, listening to music, totally relaxed in each other's presence. When we arrived at the house in West Hollywood he shared with his wife, Robin, I felt completely at ease.

Rick was a musician and Robin, an artist—she worked for Jim Henson's Creature Shop—and their creativity showed in every aspect of their daily lives. Everything in the house was tranquil, plants everywhere, music playing, all the furniture eclectic and interesting. The house always smelled of some combination of patchouli and incense. Rick kept a guitar stand next to the couch and if he was watching TV or chatting, he'd strum silently away at it; he almost always had a guitar in his hands. Plus, he and Robin seemed to genuinely love each other. He was silly and goofy and playful and funny and she'd put up with it in such a way that I could tell she adored him. I noticed a quality in their dynamic I wasn't used to seeing: mutual respect.

Robin made dinner for us each night, but it wasn't *Leave It to Beaver* in that sterile middle-America kind of way. Everything with Rick and Robin was cozy and bohemian, soothing lighting, and an effortlessness filling the air and allowing me to breathe deeply for

Robin and returned to my job and comfy apartment, but something was off when I stepped into my living room. That black velvet couch and massive entertainment center didn't look as cool anymore. My life seemed small and maybe a little shabby or dark in a way that was new to me.

CHAPTER ELEVEN

Busted

I checked my makeup in the rearview mirror while the cop ran my ID. I couldn't believe I'd gotten pulled over for speeding. Paying that ticket was going to hurt. I wiped the mascara from under my eyes to give me something to do while I waited. I was nervous. Cops always made me nervous.

I'd been driving home with my friend Tricia on a Friday night after we'd gone out with a group of coworkers for a little dancing. I was dressed for a night on the town: a one-piece Frankie B knock-off denim jumpsuit, heels, huge earrings, and lots of makeup. I looked good and hadn't been drinking. I was certain that once the cop issued me the ticket, we'd be on our way.

But when the officer came back to my window, he looked more serious than when he'd first pulled me over. "Step out of the car," he commanded.

"For what?"

"Step out of the car. I have a warrant for your arrest."

"There must be a mistake." I'd been a model citizen since leaving the peep show and graduating from high school, working long days, paying my bills, not getting into fights, being a good and law-abiding person. This made no sense. "Can you try it again?" I asked.

"I've run your ID three times." His voice became no-nonsense. "Please step out of the car."

When I stood, he turned me to face my vehicle and put my hands in cuffs.

"This is a mistake. I'm telling you. I've never been arrested."

I kept arguing with him, under the mistaken idea that a "warrant for my arrest" meant I'd previously been arrested. I had no idea what "arrest warrant" actually meant.

Before pulling me away to his cruiser, he asked Tricia if she could drive my car home and gave me a moment to talk with her.

"The apartment keys are on the same ring. Go there. You'll find cash in shoeboxes at the top of the hall closet. Get the money and meet me at the station to bail me out."

∞

When we got to the station, the booking officer processing me was a friend of my mom's from the strip club. "Mink, what are you doing here?" she asked.

"I don't know!"

She shushed me. "Don't worry, honey. I'm going to get you processed quickly. You won't have to be here long." (Years later, I had to wonder if this booking officer had been an undercover cop, surveilling the strip club [or maybe even my mom], but at the time, I thought it was just an amazing coincidence that I knew her.)

I kept wondering when Tricia would show up.

The arresting officer eventually explained I was being charged with multiple counts of assault and battery from nine months ago, when I was still in high school.

As far as I was concerned, the whole thing was silly. I'd gotten into a lot of fights in high school, had left others covered in blood, and yet no one had ever filed charges against me. But with this one girl, I'd simply pushed her when she got in my face. We hadn't even got into a proper scuffle; I didn't draw a drop of blood. Her father, though, was in law enforcement and he likely helped her file the charges.

According to the arresting officer, I should have received the warrant in the mail, but when I'd moved from Mom and David's place to Rudy's, it never occurred to me to change my mailing address. The papers had been sent to a house we no longer lived in.

The officer put me in the back of his squad car. "I'm taking you to juvenile hall."

I'd just turned eighteen and was offended. I didn't want to be with the kids. I was very proud to be an adult.

"Listen," he said when I objected. "Trust me. I'm doing you a favor." His subtext couldn't have been louder. *Shut the fuck up, little girl* and *you're welcome.*

◇◇

At juvie, I was told to strip off my clothes, shower, and wash my hair with Dial bar soap while a female guard watched. Then I had to put on their uniform, essentially oversized scrubs along with big, baggy, worn-out underwear. Nothing fit. They took away all my clothes, purse, and jewelry. By the time I was shown to my cell, it was the middle of the night. A girl was asleep in one of the beds and I climbed onto the thin mattress on a concrete bench the guard pointed to.

◇◇

I remained in juvenile hall for the weekend because I couldn't see a judge until Monday morning. For that reason, Tricia was unable to bail me out. The other girls, I learned, were incarcerated for innocuous complaints: running away from home, fighting with a parent, small-time shoplifting. When they heard I was up on multiple assault counts, they exclaimed. "Damn, you're fucked."

Over that weekend, I heard the other girls' stories and some of them broke my heart. My roommate, for instance, loved being in juvie. She made it a point to end up there as often as possible; she didn't want to go home. As far as she was concerned, *this* was her home and these were her friends. Juvie was the only place she could count on eating a proper meal three times a day, a place where she felt safe from harm.

I knew I'd had a rough upbringing, but I saw then that it could have been even worse. During the booking process, I'd remembered the phone number of the lawyer who'd been involved with the hairdresser case. When I used my one phone call to reach him, he'd taken pity on me and said he'd meet me in court on Monday. There was nothing to do now but wait.

◇◇

"All rise." The bailiff's voice echoed in the courtroom. I'd been brought in wearing the scrubs they'd given me, my hands and feet shackled, feeling so humiliated, petrified I was in deep trouble. The other girls who'd been transported to court with me, all of us chained together, had done such minor things. Compared to them, I was in serious shit.

When my case was called, a familiar voice exploded from the back of the gallery.

"My baby!" Mom came bursting out from the gallery and pushed through the little swinging doors that separated the courtroom from the spectator seats.

Oh shit, she's here! I didn't even know she was back in town. Her friend, the booking officer, must have told her about the trouble I was in.

Mom ran into the part of the courtroom where usually only the lawyers and defendants are allowed. The judge and bailiff tried to stop her. "Ma'am. Ma'am. You can't be here!"

She grabbed me and wrapped her arms around me, crying. "My baby!"

"Ma'am. You're going to be removed from the courtroom if you don't go back to your seat."

Mom was as dramatic as she'd been all those years ago when I was in the police station as a kid. I was embarrassed by her outburst, but I have to admit, I think it worked on the judge.

When Mom finally went back to her seat, the proceedings unfolded and it was horrible to hear the district attorney speak about me.

"This girl is a threat to society," she said. "She's the reason so many girls are afraid to go to school in Albuquerque. She should be locked up for the sake of all our children."

Thank God I'd called my own attorney. If I'm not mistaken, I was the only girl that day who'd had an attorney. I was also the only one with a parent present.

When my attorney got his chance, he shined.

"Girls fight in high school all the time," he told the judge. "That's just the culture here, and besides, my client was defending herself. Please note that she was only seventeen at the time, and since then, she's graduated high school. She hasn't been in any kind of trouble. She's made a life for herself."

The judge gave me two years' community service and let me leave. I felt guilty because among all the girls I'd met that weekend, I was getting off nearly scot-free, though I'd had harsher accusations leveled against me. Most of the girls I left behind were going to have the book thrown at them. What they really needed was help. They needed to be nurtured and taken care of. They needed new home lives. To be in school. And yet the cards were all stacked against them.

Still, a tiny tendril of hope took root in me that day. Maybe now Mom was ready to be fully in my life. She'd been so animated in court, so convincing. We went to the movies that night and I thought it was the start of something new between us.

It didn't take long for that hope to wither.

◇◇

A few months later, my apartment lease came due; I'd been there a year already. I could sign for another year or I could make a change. By then, I'd seen that Albuquerque didn't hold much for me beyond painful memories. Mom was in and out of town all the time, staying at friends' houses, never at a fixed address; I hadn't seen David in some time. Rudy was in the rearview mirror and Angel had met a guy she was settling down with. And me? The job was still good but I hadn't found a way to go to community college and still pay rent. I considered my options. If I stayed in Albuquerque, this would be my life, stretching off into the distance, forever and ever, amen.

There had to be more out there for me. I needed to get out.

◇◇

I dialed Rick's number. "Okay. I'm ready."

He flew out right away and rented a U-Haul that could also tow my car.

Rick and my best friend at the time, Luciano, helped me pack. I was crying my eyes out, saying goodbye to everything that had been my life, but I knew it was what I had to do.

Farewell, Albuquerque! There was nothing left for me there.

At first, I thought I'd be sad leaving Mom behind, but she called when I was ready to go. "I know you paid rent until the first. Since you're leaving on the twentieth, maybe I could stay there until the lease is up?"

Once again, she had nowhere left to go. I pictured her, staying in my empty apartment, sleeping on the floor. The apartment I'd secured for myself at eighteen was nicer than any place we'd ever had together. I told her yes.

I locked the door for the last time and hauled myself into the U-Haul cab. The minute Rick pulled the truck away from the curb, my tears stopped. All that was left now was relief and deep breaths. I was ready to move forward.

Part III

⌇

Many of us put off dealing with our negative childhood programming until well into our forties and fifties. These issues come politely knocking at our door in our twenties, then rap louder in our thirties. If you delay looking at your programming until your forties, you are likely to have the message delivered with sledge-hammer blows.

—GAY HENDRICKS AND KATHLYN HENDRICKS

CHAPTER TWELVE

City of Angels

Rick and I were driving down Fairfax looking for a place for breakfast. It was a late Saturday morning shortly after I arrived in L.A. and the sun warmed my face through the windshield.

Since arriving to L.A., I'd stored my furniture in a unit no bigger than the space I once shared with Mom, awaiting the day I'd have an apartment of my own. When the memory of that little place came back, a sort of tenderness came over me. Had I really once lived in a storage unit? And a garage? It's amazing how much I'd forgotten or willfully suppressed. I was excited to be in L.A., looking forward to making a new and bigger life for myself.

As Rick turned onto Beverly, I couldn't get over the light filtering into the car. There was a glow here that was different from other places, distinctive. The sun shines just a little differently in Los Angeles—there was a golden quality to the atmosphere that mesmerized me. I stared out the window, taking in my new home, breathing in the scent of eucalyptus mixed with exhaust.

Something was different about this day, though. While L.A.

is known as a driving city, that wasn't categorically true. A lot of people walk in L.A. Just not usually as many as I was seeing now.

Today, whole families were ambling along the streets. The men wore long black coats even though the day was way too warm for that, with large-brimmed, old-fashioned hats. Their faces, every one of them, were obscured by thick, heavy beards with curls at their temples. I craned my neck to watch. The men walked together and the women and children clumped in groups of their own, ladies wearing full, long skirts and long-sleeved tops, many carrying children or pushing strollers.

Rick must have seen the curiosity on my face. "You know about Hasidic Jews?" he asked.

I shook my head.

Rick explained about this subset population that lived in the neighborhood. There was so much about Los Angeles, about the world, I still didn't know.

Back in Albuquerque, in the area where I grew up, everyone I knew was either Latinx or Native American. But here, just about every ethnicity, color, creed, and nationality was represented. It excited me. I was hungry to experience new cultures, to learn all the different ways people lived and loved, made families and found home.

The type of family Mom and I had constructed had been deeply unsatisfying and dysfunctional. How else might it be done? Someone, please show me.

With so many different ways of being in this one city, surely I'd find my path.

◇◇

My living situation was peaceful in the house I shared with Rick and Robin, and she went through a lot of trouble to make me feel welcome. Robin and her British accent always delighted me when, in the afternoons, she'd ask, "Darling, have you put the kettle on?"

I've carried that comfy little detail with me to this day. My kettle is the first and most important piece in any space I occupy.

Robin prepared a bedroom for me, appointed with linens far nicer than any I'd ever touched before. I always bought the cheapest sheets and didn't know that something as simple as good bedding could make a difference in my level of comfort. She added a delicate little lamp on my bedside table that she turned on whenever I was out late so that when I came home, a light was waiting for me. Little details like that meant so much.

But that wasn't the best part. Each night, Robin put a hot water bottle under the sheets at the foot of my bed so that when I climbed in, my feet would be snug and warm. You know those old-fashioned, flat red rubber hot water bottles? I'd never used one and had only seen them in the movies; I would have told you such a thing was silly before I'd tried it.

Coming home to that little hot water bottle on a chilly night was the most astounding indulgence I'd ever experienced.

Without letting on, I studied Robin when she wasn't looking and tried to learn from her. Robin applied minimal makeup and wore Issey Miyake perfume. She was an artistic, confident woman with an interesting career designing "creatures" in the film industry. Later, she was part of a team that created some of the monsters used in the movie *Where The Wild Things Are* and just about every other furry creature you've seen in movies. In those early days, when we were free in the afternoon, we painted together in their living room. My artwork looked like stick figures next to hers. I could point to anything in the room and ask her to paint it for me and the most amazing designs would flow from her fingers. I fell in love with Robin on so many levels and learned from her how to be a woman in this world without having to defer to a man. She was fun and had a dirty sense of humor that snuck up on you. Robin swore like a sailor and loved beer, which, juxtaposed with how classy she was, removed any possibility of her being stuffy or boring. In her relationship with Rick, Robin held her own. She was the breadwinner and I loved that.

The deal was that I'd stay with Rick and Robin for a month and then find my own place. I felt good about the work I'd done at Voice-Stream and knew I could land a similar job quickly. Then I'd be ready to stand on my own.

Looking back, I can see that I hadn't considered that the cost of living in L.A. was more than fifty percent higher than in Albu-querque. Still, I was pretty confident I'd figure it out and was ready to get to work.

∞

The Monday after I arrived, first thing, I planned to go to the AT&T call center on the corner of Hollywood and Vine. I printed out directions from MapQuest and had my résumé and references ready to go. VoiceStream was a small, regional company; AT&T would certainly be a step up, and, I hoped, better pay.

I took at least an hour to get ready, frustrating my dad with all the time I spent in the bathroom. My outfit looked great, my hair was big and teased, my makeup heavy, just like I'd done back home. I was about to start my California future.

When I arrived, though, the offices were nothing like the fancy ones at VoiceStream. The whole department was housed in the basement level of an ugly building in a gritty part of Hollywood. I wondered at first if I had the address wrong, but when I double-checked, I came to a different conclusion. Maybe working for a cell phone company here wasn't as sexy as it was back home in Albuquerque.

The first thing I noticed, besides the subterranean ugly space, was that the people who worked there were not at all friendly; most seemed annoyed at having to show up for work at all. I was interviewed and when the woman read my experience, she offered me a job on the spot. But there were catches. She could only give me a few shifts at a time, each of them only a few hours long. Full-time was out of the question.

And the pay? It was miserly. Less than half of what I'd earned back home. How was this going to work?

I took the job, of course. I had to work. But now, I was also going to have to find an additional job. Plus, I didn't have a ton of free time because I had to spend my afternoons doing community service at the AIDS Healthcare Foundation to make reparations to the legal system from when I was arrested. It was a ridiculous number of hours that were required over the course of two years, and I worried I'd never pay off that debt.

I went to the dreary AT&T offices at five each morning, but instead of taking calls from customers and getting to be the fairy godmother who wiped away their debt, I was instructed to make outgoing solicitation calls. I hated every minute and wasn't good at it.

At this rate, I knew I'd never be able to afford my own place. My deal with Rick and Robin had been for a month, but now I realized that expectation was insane. Very few nineteen-year-olds can get on their feet in one month in L.A.

It was a tough day on all fronts when I went to the Beverly Center to fill out applications for an additional job. I hadn't made a single sale at AT&T since I'd started the job and I worried they were going to fire me. After that morning shift, I spent hours at the AIDS Healthcare Foundation filing paperwork, feeling completely out of place. By the time the evening rolled around, I hadn't eaten in hours and was desperate. I was willing to take any job that paid.

At the Guess store, after I filled out the application, the assistant manager took me into the back room for an interview. Marie was gorgeous, green eyes, caramel skin. A few years older than I was, she seemed in charge and yet so friendly.

"Have you ever worked in retail?" she asked.

I tried to answer the question in a straightforward way, but somehow the whole messed-up story of my life and this terrible day came tumbling out. I'd reached a breaking point. I was hungry and tired and without meaning to, I spilled my guts to Marie.

"I have to find a job. I just moved here from New Mexico and I have to move out soon and I'm not making enough money and I'm a really hard worker, I swear, but . . ."

Marie hired me right then and there. That job soon became a highlight of my life, and my experiences with Marie shifted everything about living in L.A. In no time, she became my best friend, teaching me how to navigate life in Hollywood, correcting me when I did something stupid. To this day, I still hear her voice when I'm about to do something reckless: "Minka! You can't *do* that! That's not okay!" She would laugh at the absurdity of whatever I was saying or doing while yelling at me, so her corrections never felt aggressive or like a scolding parent.

She was the first person in my life who cared enough to call me on my shit. She didn't give up on me when I was slow on the pickup and had the grace to see that I would grow, if given the space and opportunity. She told me what was right and what was wrong in how I dealt with people, filing away my rough edges. I'd spent my whole life literally fighting others to survive. I was super scrappy and it took very little to set me off. Marie taught me to take a breath, to realize that not everyone was out to get me, and to respond from a place of calm and centeredness. Basically, she showed me how to be an adult who wasn't raised by wolves. She never judged me but saw me and loved me. And I felt it.

∞

"Minka, we need to talk." Rick pulled me aside one weekend morning when I didn't have to be at AT&T at the crack of dawn.

By this point, I'd been getting sick a lot: colds, bronchitis, whatever was going around. I was working from 5 a.m. to 1 p.m. daily doing phone solicitation, then my community service job from two until five, before heading to the store to work from six until closing, and staying there until one in the morning, resetting the displays, cleaning the store, making sure everything was perfect for the next day's crew. I wasn't getting enough sleep, wasn't able to eat well or regularly with all these demands on my time, and was a little stressed out.

Whenever I mentioned to Rick that I thought my schedule was making me sick, he simply said, "It builds character."

This morning, though, he looked serious. "My wife and I need our house back. We agreed to one month. It's been four," he said.

In that moment, something inside of me cracked. I spent my entire life fearing I was a burden to someone, terrified of that ever happening. Nothing on this green earth seemed more disgraceful to me than to be a liability to someone else. From the moment I could walk, I'd done all I could to take care of myself so as to never, not in a million years, find myself in that position. And yet here he was, telling me I was a burden.

I was embarrassed. "I'm so sorry," I said, wanting the ground to swallow me up. I pulled myself together. "Okay, I will be gone soon."

"You'll thank me for this later," Rick replied.

I cried in the car the entire way to my shift at the Guess store.

◇◇

I was still crying in the break room when Marie came in.

"Come home with me tonight," Marie said. "I live in this building that's all studio apartments. You can stay overnight and then I'll introduce you to the landlord. I think there's one unit still available, and they're all $475 a month."

I sniffled and nodded.

"If you want, you can quit your other job, too, and I'll hire you here full-time, okay?" she continued. "You'll make enough. You'll be okay."

Marie saved me, time and again. She was so good to me.

∞

I moved into the unit directly below hers and restarted my life, once again on my own. I was still pissed at Rick.

When I told Mom, she blew up. "He didn't have anything to do with you for eighteen years, and now, it's too much for him after four months?!"

As it turned out, though, Rick was right. I *did* thank him later. By laying down the law, he got me to move on, and I needed that. Living near Marie opened up one of the best seasons of my life; we had so much fun together, going to the movies, dancing, boys, cooking—she taught me so much. Rick, in asking me to move, had also taught me, though his way was less compassionate, a more tough-love approach. Marie's care for me was always gentle.

∞

Mom was still living in Albuquerque but came out to California a lot to visit her friend Kim who lived in San Diego; then the two of them would make the trek north to see me in Hollywood.

Kim was one of Mom's best friends from the stripping world, but their lives had grown in different ways. Mom was now working at a gas station as a cashier, while Kim was rich because her husband founded a company that made dolls, initially just torsos, modeled after Kim and the other strippers she worked with. Over time, his company did very well and started making life-size dolls. These would become RealDolls, which is to say lifelike sex dolls, and their success raised Kim's standard of living in a big way. Still, she always made time for Mom and welcomed her like a sister.

They came to visit me in my little studio apartment.

"Why aren't you modeling?" Kim asked, almost the minute she arrived.

Mom jumped in. "I've been asking her the same thing."

"I'm really not model material," I told Kim, waiting for her to drop the subject. "I'm five foot five, not nearly tall enough, and I have a big butt. It wouldn't work. And besides, I work all day just to cover my rent. There's no way I could go on castings during the day, too."

"Yes, Mink, you *are* model material." Kim was adamant. "How much is your rent?"

"Four seventy-five."

"If I pay your rent for a year, would that free up your time to pursue modeling?" Kim asked.

I demurred. "Thank you, really. It's a very generous offer, but I'm managing now on my own and I don't think I could do that."

After that day, Mom kept calling and asking about Kim's offer. "Why not take her up on it?"

I didn't have a solid answer, except that I didn't want to burden or owe anyone to pursue a dream that wasn't mine.

A few days later, I told Marie about Kim's proposal.

"She's right, you know," Marie said. "You'd do a lot better as a model than selling Guess jeans at the mall."

Marie did a little modeling herself so she knew a photographer who'd do free sessions with actors and models in exchange for their time and suggested I get some headshots done. It wouldn't cost me anything and I could decide once I saw them if I wanted to take Kim up on her offer. Soon, I had a photo shoot scheduled. I still wasn't sure this was the right path, but at least I'd check it out.

I brought my own clothes to the photo session as requested and thought I'd be doing my own hair and makeup, but the photographer's wife, Tina, was there to fill that role. She toned down my heavy makeup and styled my hair in a softer, more natural way.

As she worked on me, Tina chatted. A lot. She used to be a

Playboy Playmate, she told me, and now she managed the careers of other models in that world. She offered to represent me.

"But I'm not really a model," I explained. "I'm just trying this out, seeing what's possible."

"How are you paying your bills now?"

When I told her I was working a ridiculous number of hours a week, including the community service, she almost spit out her coffee.

She convinced me to leave my job at Guess—Marie had just accepted another job and it seemed as good a time as any to leave. Thanks to Tina, I would now answer phones in the offices of a plastic surgeon. In addition to managing the careers of up-and-coming models, Tina also managed the surgeon's office. "The hours are flexible and that way, you can go out on calls when I line them up for you," she explained.

∞

The hours were similar to what I'd done at AT&T, super early in the morning, which I didn't mind because it freed up the rest of the day. Soon, I met the surgeon, nurses, and scrub nurses who worked there and settled in. It wasn't bad.

The office included a surgical suite, and on days when the doctor was performing surgery and the phones were quiet, I would stand in the window to watch. Eventually, I was invited into the operating room to observe up close.

"You don't get queasy or faint at the sight of blood, do you?" the scrub nurse asked.

"I don't think so." I thought of the fights I'd been in or witnessed. Blood had never bothered me.

They waved me into the operating room, where they were in the middle of a breast augmentation. The patient was knocked out and draped, so all I could see was the surgical site. This woman's nipples were completely gone and forceps had been inserted through the circular incision where her nipples had once been. The forceps now held up her empty breast tissue and her chest had become a construction zone.

I was too stunned to know what I thought about it all. The surgery didn't turn my stomach, though, and I didn't think it was gross. In fact, as my shock wore off and I grew more comfortable watching, I realized how I felt: This was awesome!

I loved everything about the surgery: the caps and gowns, the masks and gloves. I loved the order and organization of the surgical instruments on the scrub nurse's OR table, how sterile and organized everything had to be. I watched the scrub nurse with intense concentration. She had to keep track of all the instruments and sponges to make sure everything was accounted for and in perfect order. In my eyes, she was the most crucial member of the team, working diligently to make sure everything went as planned, anticipating the surgeon's needs, and offering instruments and assistance to him before he asked, a silent ballet between the two.

After that, as long as the office was empty on surgery days, I talked my way into the surgical suite, watching or assisting in some way whenever possible.

◇◇

"Guess what?" About a month after I started working there, Tina came to my desk carrying a calendar. "We've got you scheduled!"

Since I'd started the job, Tina had been giving me advice, grooming me to be in her portfolio of models and suggesting different plastic surgery options to improve my chances. The fact that I worked for the doctor, she explained, meant he'd do the procedures at no cost. According to Tina, I needed a lot of work, but first we'd focus on teeth veneers, breast augmentation, and liposuction.

I stared at the calendar she showed me. My name was penciled in for both the breast augmentation and the liposuction, each procedure just a few weeks apart.

"I don't want to send you on calls until we get this work done," she explained, "but soon you'll be good to go."

I wanted to object. Having seen surgeries firsthand, I wasn't sure I wanted to go through all that, and I didn't really want my body messed with. But Tina had been so good to me. Maybe she knew what was best.

◇◇

Marie and I often made dinner together and caught up on our days. She was always very impressed at my ability to turn Top Ramen into a more gourmet meal (thanks, Mom) and loved when I cooked for her. What we put together wasn't the delicious pho we eat now, but it was our cheap-ass, living-in-studio-apartments-in-your-twenties version of that pho, and we had so much fun in each other's company.

This night, I asked her if she'd be available to help me with the upcoming procedures. I wouldn't be able to drive or lift anything for a while after the first one.

"What procedures?"

I explained about Tina and the doctor's offer. It was very generous that he was going to help me out this way and so helpful of Tina to have arranged it for me. "I'm just a little nervous," I told her.

Marie stood and slammed her hand on the table, making our bowls of ramen jump. "Are you fucking kidding me?! You have the most gorgeous figure in the world. Why would you even consider letting that man take a knife to you?"

"She says I need a boob job."

"Minka, your boobs are one hundred percent perfect! People would kill for those boobs. You are perfect as you are. You are not getting your boobs done! I'm sorry. I will not be part of wrecking your body. No way."

∞

Reinforced by Marie's words, I told Tina I needed to cancel the surgeries the next day at work. Marie was the one person who always had my best interests at heart. I trusted her and knew she was right.

"You'll never be Playmate of the Year without a boob job," Tina scolded, clearly unhappy with my choice.

"That's okay. I don't think that's what I want to do," I said. I didn't really *want* to be Playmate of the Year. That was *her* dream. I just wanted to make a decent life for myself, pay my rent without getting sick, and be happy. Working as the receptionist at this surgical center was a pretty decent gig. Maybe I'd just stay here for a bit and chill out until I knew what I was going to do next.

The next day, though, when my shift ended, I was summoned into the surgeon's office. Tina was there, too, standing behind him. He seemed to be reading cue cards she'd written for him.

"I'm sorry, Minka, but we're downsizing and we just don't have enough hours to keep you on staff. It's been great working with you and I know you'll find something else soon." He stood, indicating that our chat was over. "Please use me as a reference. You're free to take your things and go."

I was stunned. I looked up at Tina. Her straight face offered no condolences, making it clear this was her doing.

I was sad to lose this job but I wasn't about to be bullied into altering everything about my body. I didn't know it yet, but once again, this moment that felt like a rejection was just another opportunity for growth in disguise.

CHAPTER THIRTEEN

Boundaries Are a Bitch

The fact that I stood up to Tina was a remarkable step for me. Yes, I was punished pretty quickly, but I was also undaunted. There was something about taking that leap that meant I was coming into my own.

I spent so much of my life conforming to what others wanted me to be, ready to contort myself into whatever shape was requested. But now, that dynamic was starting to change. I began to have the first, earliest inklings of what kind of life I wanted to build for myself. I knew a few things for certain: I wanted to be self-supporting and not dependent on someone else. I wanted to create a calm and peaceful home and to do work that mattered. I wasn't dreaming of becoming an actor or being famous—not in the slightest. My objectives were to create a simple yet deeply satisfying life, and I started moving toward that goal.

It was hard, though. There's something about getting clear with yourself about what you want that can cause turmoil in your other relationships. When you set boundaries, sometimes other people aren't so happy.

Dear Kim,

Thank you so much for your very kind offer to pay my rent for a year to allow me to try my hand at modeling. I so appreciate your generosity and, until now, have not been able to accept it. But some things in my life have changed, and I'm wondering if you'd be interested in supporting me in a slightly different way.

Recently, I was working as a receptionist at a plastic surgeon's office. One of the young women who works there is a scrub nurse who assists the doctor in surgery and I've become fascinated by her job. I called her to ask about her training. I've since reached out to the Concorde Career College, where she studied, to learn more. It's a one-year vocational program in North Hollywood, six months of schoolwork followed by six months of hands-on training. I've already been approved for financial assistance. Being broke means I qualify for just about everything! Between grants and student loans, I could do this. I've always wanted to go to college.

The only problem, of course, is covering my living expenses. If your offer still stands, and if you'd allow me to use it to train to be a nurse rather than a model, I'd be so grateful. I'll never have this opportunity to go to school full-time again and I'd like to have a career that will sustain me, one that's not solely dependent on my looks.

Would you consider this? I promise to make you proud of what I do with your investment in me.

Love,

Mink

I waited and worried while the letter made its way to Kim, hoping she'd see things the way I did. When she called, I held my breath, afraid she might say no or that maybe she'd changed her mind. No one had ever offered to help me out like this with no strings attached. I wasn't sure I could trust it.

"Oh, Mink." Her voice was soft, though not as enthusiastic as usual. "I'm sad you don't want to be a model. I *do* think you could be super successful in that work and I don't think you fully understand your own beauty or appreciate it. But of course I'll support your dream of being a nurse. Go for it, honey. I've got your back."

My heart fluttered with excitement and my shoulders relaxed for the first time in weeks. I had a path forward.

∞

I started school and loved every second of it. On the weekends, I sat in the Beverly Hills Public Library six hours at a time to study. I can't even describe how good it felt. I carried around anatomy and physiology textbooks in a backpack just like the other students and applied myself like crazy, realizing for the first time that I was smart. In so many ways, this was a do-over, allowing me to make up for my high school experience, when I cut classes all the time, focused simply on surviving. Now I was finally able to indulge my hunger to learn, a craving I'd tucked away after elementary school when being curious about the world around me was no longer considered cool. Thanks to Kim and the fact that my rent was paid, my full attention was available for my brain to grasp what I'd just absorbed, amazing myself with my ability to retain information and to comprehend difficult subjects. Once I let myself feel that desire to learn again, I blossomed.

I memorized the names of all the bones, muscles, and ligaments in the body, learned how all the organs worked, and completely geeked out on every aspect of biology and anatomy. Next, I learned how all the surgical instruments worked and learned the names of them all by heart. Every day, I woke up with a clear idea of what I was doing. I had purpose. I worked my ass off and got all As— even an award for perfect attendance. Me, the student who used to cut classes all the time! My name was on plaques on the walls for good students. I was so proud of myself.

Going back to school as an adult taught me something about myself that was utterly and completely life changing: I could set my mind to a task and accomplish it. Not only accomplish it, but excel at it. Until that experience, I never knew.

◇◇

"I'll be like twenty minutes late for dinner on Saturday. I hope that's okay."

I was at Rick and Robin's house, visiting. We'd patched things up and now spent time together whenever we could. Rick had just pushed the button on his answering machine while I was walking around the living room. I was confused by the sound I heard, the sentence from his machine filling the air. The voice sounded so strange and yet familiar. I hadn't heard that inflection since I'd left Albuquerque a year earlier. There's a very specific accent to that region and now, it seemed, I was hearing it for the first time as it unspooled from his recorder. Had one of my old friends tracked me down at Rick's?

"Who *is* that?" I asked.

Rick looked at me, his brows raised. "Honey, that's you." He rolled his eyes a bit, as if to say, *Look at what I have had to deal with all this time.*

My face immediately grew hot. I sounded like that?

"Play it again," I commanded.

He hit the button and when I heard those rough-edged consonants, I blanched. That was me! I had no idea. All along, I thought I'd succeeded in turning myself into a California girl, dressing the part, no longer wearing the full face of makeup, not as coarse as I'd once been. I was blending in.

Or so I thought.

All along, though, my thick Albuquerque accent was a dead giveaway. From that moment on, I worked hard to hear myself, to become aware of how I presented. Still, the accent remained a sore spot. To this day, whenever someone asks me, "Where are you from? You have some kind of accent," I bristle because it reminds me of the pain of my childhood.

Initially, I tried to deflect or erase my history. "I don't know what you mean. It's an American accent!" was my earlier response. But now, I explain where I grew up and that my accent might be a remnant from my previous life in Albuquerque. When I was younger, I spent so many years trying to hide who I was, ashamed of my experiences, trying to sugarcoat my backstory. But I'm proud of the culture in which I was raised. It's a relief to be free of the shame I carried for so long.

I remember that time as an important part of this unending quest of learning who I am as an adult and how I became this person. It amazes me that even today as I write this book, I'm still discovering the imprints of this time pressed indelibly into my psyche.

Now, I see the good from this epoch, firmly rooted in Mexican culture and this family who raised me as their own. I identify deeply with and celebrate the family-centric ethos, the way I was raised to have manners, loyalty, and respect for my elders, and the food. There's no flavor quite like those found in Albuquerque, the only place you'll get that Hatch chile taste. Even at McDonald's, the number one question is always "red or green chile?" No race or ethnicity is a monolith. This is not to essentialize Mexican culture but only to share what became an important part of my character.

◇◇

I cannot overstate how much going back to school helped me flourish. To this day, having finished that vocational program is one of my proudest accomplishments. My career as an actress can vanish tomorrow, but no one will ever be able to take away from me what I can do with my mind and my hands.

After I completed six months of anatomy and physiology, the

next six months was training in a real OR. After enough hours in the school's mock OR, I was assigned to California Hospital, an inner-city facility in the heart of downtown Los Angeles, located between the Staples Center and Santee Alley, where knockoff luxury goods and clothes were sold. I shadowed another scrub nurse until my instructors decided I could handle surgeries on my own.

At first, I was assigned to the central sterilization and processing department where all the instruments utilized in surgery were cleaned and prepped to be sterilized for surgery, scrubbing away the blood and tissue, then prepping and organizing the instruments back in their containers. When I told anyone what my day had been like, they were very grossed out. But me? I couldn't wait to see how the tissue got there, where the blood came from, to finally be let into the OR with a job to do.

Instead of wearing street clothes to school every day, now I wore scrubs and felt professional, like my work mattered. Everything about the job fascinated me. Washing the instruments was a lot like doing dishes and I'd always been good at that. I took my time and was meticulous, finding gratification in being useful in this way. When the surgical drapes and linens came back from the laundry center, I folded the towels perfectly, creating little bundles exactly as I'd been shown.

I graduated from washing instruments to finally attending in the OR, where my job was to anticipate the surgeon's needs and to provide what the doctor required without ever having to be asked. The doctors didn't want to have to talk about the surgery at hand, I learned, but they liked to tell us about their dinner with their spouse the night before or their golf game. If they needed to talk about the surgery at all, that would be a sign I wasn't doing my job. I was determined to do this work as perfectly as possible.

And I did. I'm really organized—likely the result of having grown up with such mayhem and needing to create a little space of calm in my own life—and I'm good at keeping calm under pressure. Plus, I learn quickly. Those skills, with the training I received, helped prepare me.

But the biggest preparation of all, it turns out, came long before nursing school. All my life, I'd been anticipating the needs of others in order to keep myself safe. From the time I could walk, I studied my mom for signs of drug use or irritability, guessing at what I needed to do to disarm the moment before she blew up. Same with David, Rudy, and Rick. It's no surprise I excelled at this work.

Plus, I was fascinated by surgery. There's something about getting to see behind the scenes and understanding the inner workings of the human body that is humbling and awe-inspiring. I was amazed by surgery from that very first breast augmentation I witnessed, but the experience of assisting for the first time on a C-section is the moment that changed me forever.

∞

People don't really appreciate that C-sections are one of the most intense and invasive operations a woman can have. It's an underappreciated trauma, I came to see in my time in the OR, and one that left me reeling with amazement at the miracle that is the female human body.

On this particular day, I was there to assist. The patient was awake and her husband was in the room, but a surgical drape protected her from seeing what we were doing. The doctor first opened the skin on her distended, taut belly with a scalpel, while we blotted, suctioned, and cauterized to mitigate any bleeding. I kept the site clean of any blood and handed him instruments as he needed them. Next, the layer of subcutaneous tissues had to be cut, which he did painstakingly. Finally, once we got past the oblique muscles (I'll spare you the details of how we get past those muscles in case anyone reading this might have a C-section in their future), we made it to the uterus.

Up to this point, I'd been following along, noting what the surgeon was doing, sponging away blood so he could see, behaving as a silent and consummate professional. All that changed when he sliced open the uterus. There, cradled in this woman's pelvis, was the amniotic sac, the last layer between us and the fetus, wholly intact (her water hadn't broken), and inside it, visible to my eyes, was a fully developed, perfectly matured, beautiful little child. A person! A whole, ready-to-join-the-world person—and I was honored to be present in this moment between being in utero and being born.

The baby was curled in upon itself with a full head of black hair. Everything froze in that moment and the only thing in the room still in motion was the fluid in the sac swaying the baby's hair, as if he or she were a little mermaid in there. I was motionless, stunned by this miracle of life. *This* was a whole new person, right here, about to make its entrance into the world, and I was privileged to be a witness. I became so overwhelmed, tears started to fall down my cheeks under my surgical mask.

The scrub nurse I was shadowing elbowed me. "Not now," he said under his breath, sharp.

I snapped to. I had a job to do and I got busy doing it, handing the doctor instruments, returning to my professionalism. But the wonder at what I'd witnessed did not go away. I kept thinking, *Whoa, what am I doing here? How did I get so lucky? This is a miracle!*

The scrub nurse had jolted me out of that moment of awe because there was no time for astonishment in this kind of operation. A C-section is a fast-moving, no-time-to-mess-around surgery. Once the amniotic sac was cut, the delivery moved into hyperspeed. At that point, the doctor wasn't talking about dinner with a spouse or a golf game; we had to get the baby out as fast as possible. We removed this fully formed beautiful human with its flowy black hair and handed him off to a pediatric nurse so we could tend to the mother and close her up. The doctor removed her entire uterus and put it on her stomach and chest. We used gauze and wet sponges to clean out every inch of the uterus before the doctor replaced it back into the patient and then sewed up the layers after layers we'd cut to facilitate the birth. This was no minor surgery, and any time I hear anyone downplaying what a woman goes through with a C-section, I make sure to let them know every feature I remember. I spare no detail as to how we get past the abdominal muscles to get to the uterus. This lecture usually puts people (often men) back in their place.

When it was all over and my assistance was no longer needed, I took a quick break and let myself feel all the feelings before heading back to another OR for another procedure. I'd never been part of something so extraordinary.

In my time at California Hospital, I attended every kind of operation you might think of other than open heart and learned that surgery is basically carpentry. I loved every moment of it. Once, we had to amputate the gangrened foot of a houseless man, and I held one end of the saw as the surgeon and I dutifully severed the part of him that would have eventually killed him if left intact. I felt so fortunate. *This* was what it meant to do honorable work.

I finished school and graduated with the highest honors, then started working at an outpatient orthopedics center. While I preferred working with the many kinds of surgeries we saw at California Hospital, the pay wasn't great. If I was determined to be self-supporting, and to have a schedule that didn't require me to be on call 24/7, I'd have an easier time of it at the outpatient center, so that's where I went.

CHAPTER FOURTEEN

Old Patterns, New Resolve

He was so handsome that when he first walked into the suite at the Staples Center where I was invited with friends to watch a basketball game, I could hardly take my eyes off him. His name was Sean and I was immediately smitten. I tried not to let on, but I think he knew. In our first interaction, though, he was kind of a jerk and that helped put me on solid footing. I would see him as just another human being, a friend of my friends, and take it from there.

Sean and my friends and I started hanging out regularly as a group. Eventually, he and I spent more time one-on-one and started to see each other as more than friends. I do think the fact that we were just buddies first was a huge gift.

We had so much fun together, playing like kids, both of us ready to make a game out of anything. We needed groceries? We'd turn a trip to Ralph's into the silliest outing possible. Doing laundry? Let's recite Jay-Z lyrics and have a blast at the Laundromat! We were both very childlike, with no shortage of joy in our hearts, always acting as goofy and giddy as possible, delighting in each other's company. We were in our twenties and free, living every moment to its fullest, surrounded by friends as often as possible.

By then, I was working full-time as a nurse and feeling fulfilled in all parts of my life. The relationship with Sean was good. When he asked me to move into a house we'd pick out together, I felt ready. I let go of my apartment and moved the same furniture I'd brought with me from Albuquerque into the home we shared. Together, we were building a life.

∞

"Do you model?" A woman approached me while I was sitting with Mom at a street-side café in Beverly Hills, this question coming up alongside Mom and Kim's efforts to nudge me into that profession. From what I'd experienced with Tina and the plastic surgery debacle, though, I wanted nothing to do with that world. Besides, I was happy with the nursing. I felt proud of myself.

The woman questioning me that day, though, wasn't just any woman. She was Jackie Salem of Elite Models. She knew what she was talking about.

"Here's my card," she said. "Come see me at my office sometime. I'm certain I could get you work that would fit around your nursing schedule. Please. Give it some thought."

"What have I been telling you?" Mom elbowed me. She couldn't wait to call Kim and fill her in.

I waved them both off but later decided to check it out.

∞

When I arrived at Jackie's office, I was nervous but kept reminding myself I didn't care if she liked me and wanted to sign me. I was just taking this step so Mom and Kim would finally stop badgering me. Jackie and her coworkers all studied me and then conferred for a moment.

"Minka, you have a great look and we'd like to sign you. But first, you'll need to lose fifteen pounds."

After the rigamarole with Tina and the plastic surgery, I was sick to death of being told I needed to change to their standards. Besides, *I* wasn't the one who'd requested this opportunity. *They'd* asked *me* to come in. This was ridiculous. I was furious but kept my tone civil.

"Okay, thank you," I said, packing my things to leave. I hadn't come to their offices just to be told to lose weight.

Before I reached the door to the street, though, another agent stopped me.

"Wait! Wait!" she said. "I'll take you. Just as you are."

"No losing fifteen pounds?" I asked.

"No, just like you are today. My name's Kati and I want to work with you."

Kati brought me into a room where she showed me how to pose and taught me to "find my angles" while she took Polaroids. Before I knew it, she was sending me on castings for jobs that needed models from the shoulders up, where it was okay to be five foot five—makeup ads, accessories at Macy's, as well as a few music videos.

The work was far from high flying but was a nice supplement to the nursing income, and Kati is still one of my best friends to this day. Before long, Kati introduced me to a commercial agent and I started going on auditions for commercials. I was able to add this work around my nursing job because my hours at the orthopedics center were early in the day, leaving my afternoons free. Modeling and the music videos were just a side hustle to earn extra cash. I took none of it seriously.

∞

Hurricane Katrina hit that year, and on the nightly news, Sean and I watched stories of people taking displaced Louisianans into their homes, people they'd never met before but who needed help. There was this sense that we all needed to care for each other, even if we were helpless to do anything in the immediate aftermath.

My mom, meanwhile, had been saying how much she missed me and wanted to be near me. We wrote letters to each other all the time and though we could have used the phone and email to stay in touch, there was something lovely about receiving one of her missives, her handwriting on the envelope so familiar and beautiful. I could almost feel her mood by the way she shaped her letters. Now, she wanted to come to L.A. to be close by.

Katrina had left so many people houseless, I felt even more sensitive to my mother's needs. She wrote that she had some money saved up and would just need a couple months to get a new job and find a place. She seemed to have a thought-out plan.

I called her on the phone, too excited to wait for her to get a return letter from me. "Get out here!"

We had the extra bedrooms. Why not? I'd discussed it with Sean and he was supportive of anyone needing help. I don't think he would have objected, even if he hated the idea.

Then, before we knew it, Marie moved in, too. She'd broken up with a boyfriend and hadn't yet found a place of her own.

While Mom, Marie, and I all lived under the same roof with Sean, our household was like a TV show about kooky roommates up to outlandish hijinks together. Mom got a job as a messenger and drove all over town, dropping off scripts and bringing packages hither and yon, coming home each night to tell us of the crazy things she'd encountered. Every night after work, we all came together and had a blast. Everyone adored my mom because she was just so loving, calling everyone "my baby" and "my love," telling Sean and Marie how much she adored them. They loved her, too. She wasn't hard to love. She was nothing but unbridled excitement and joy and love—when she was healthy. We had fun together and it was nice having her in the house.

On our days off, Marie and I (and sometimes Mom) would get up early to walk the stairs in Santa Monica, then have a breakfast of cinnamon sugar pancakes at The Griddle Cafe on Sunset near Fairfax. We were regulars, so the staff gave us clues about off-menu items like the Supercalifragilistic, which was sugar-and-cinnamon French toast with icing on the side. We hung out, maybe window-shopped for a while, listened to Jay-Z's *Reasonable Doubt* or Kanye's *The College Dropout* in the car, or went to a movie at the ArcLight on Sunset. Other days, we headed to the beach, Venice or Zuma, to lay out. Or we ate at El Compadre and then went dancing until two, three, or four in the morning. Mom joined in with me and Marie whenever she could and was like a big kid with us.

That Christmas we had a feast and Mom did the lion's share of the cooking—Stove Top stuffing, everything from boxes, our favorite. She made yams with marshmallows and brown sugar, as well as mashed potatoes and turkey. She even did all the decorating, a Christmas tree in the living room and stockings for all of us. Though she was never good at day-to-day cooking and life maintenance, she loved holidays and went out of her way to make it special. She would have preferred that we not invite Rick over on Christmas but made an exception when she learned that he and Robin were getting divorced.

I, frankly, was furious when I heard about it.

◇◇

A week earlier, Rick had taken me aside to tell me the full story. Robin had been having an affair, he said.

I was so angry with her. How could she? Theirs had been the one healthy-looking relationship I'd ever witnessed, and here, she'd blown it all to smithereens. I was livid.

"Don't be mad at her," Rick said. "Believe me, she's already hating herself more than she can stand. And, honey, listen to me. It wasn't all her fault."

"What do you mean? She cheated!"

"Yes, she did. But it was my fault. This is how I see it," Rick said. "A woman needs to feel sexy and wanted and desired. That was my job as her husband, to make sure she felt that way. And I stopped doing my job. Somewhere along the line, I let our relationship settle into a roommate-type situation. We became like brother and sister. And so she did what she needed to, to rediscover her worth. She found someone else who would desire her. There's no getting away from the fact that I share a big piece of the blame."

It was an indelible moment for me. After hearing my mom fault everyone else for each shortcoming in her life, this was a whole new perspective. By taking responsibility for his part, my dad was refusing to be a victim.

"If you know all that," I said to him, "then maybe you two can work it out?" I still yearned for a happy ending.

"No, we're getting a divorce, but it's okay. We'll always be in each other's lives and always remain friends."

Which they did. They're still friends to this day, and Robin remains in my life as well.

Still, that experience was eye-opening. Not only had Rick seen the part he'd played in the relationship's demise, he also knew what he wanted.

Meanwhile, I was taking notes.

◇◇

After some time living together, Mom fell back into old patterns. She kept telling me she was saving up to get a place of her own, but she didn't seem to be going to work very often anymore. She was spending more time in her room, eating those painkillers like gummy bears.

Her OxyContin use was getting worse, and when I tried to talk to her about it, I couldn't get through to her.

"Mom, that much OxyContin? That's really intense."

"Honey, I need it for my back. I just have a bad back."

Soon, Marie found a wonderful new place for herself.

"You and I could be roommates!" Mom suggested, overjoyed at this thought.

Marie tactfully deflected. She was ready to live on her own, even if my mom was not.

◇◇

It was a couple of weeks into the second month of us living together, and Mom had been sleeping or watching TV in bed all day long for days on end. Often, I came home from a long day at work and she was still in her pajamas. Sean mentioned something about it—she didn't seem to be making plans to leave—and that jolted me into action. I became very protective of him and our relationship. I needed to have a very difficult conversation with her.

It would be one thing if this were my house, but I didn't live alone. It was Sean's house, too. We'd been together two years, were not married, and I didn't think it was appropriate or healthy for my mother to be living with us permanently.

The next time I had a day off, I went to her room.

"Mom, can we talk?"

She was wrapped in her comforter, snuggled in the bed. I stood there. "Two months are almost up, Momma. Do you have a plan?"

That's all it took. She lost it and in no time was standing on the other side of the bed and screaming at me.

"I can't believe you! You're throwing me out into the streets. How could you do this to me? I can't believe you would kick me out!"

"Well, no. You said if you didn't find a way to make L.A. work after a couple of months, you'd go back to Albuquerque. Right? That was our deal," I said, and then tried to explain that this wasn't just my house. She just kept yelling.

I didn't fight back but kept my voice calm. "All right. Today is the seventeenth. You have until the end of the month, but you need to move."

I now understood how Rick had been able to say the same thing to me. There comes a time when we all need to stand on our own. He'd seen that I was ready, even though I didn't yet know it. And now Mom, one way or another, was going to have to make herself ready, too. Also, she wasn't nineteen years old. I was trying to make a life for myself and tired of being the parent in this relationship.

But, was she pissed! She grabbed her purse and threw on clothes in a huff, then stomped downstairs, slamming doors. Soon, I heard her car squeal away. I felt sick, and knew the worst of her anger wasn't over.

A few hours later, she called. "Let's meet. You, me, and Sean for dinner tonight, okay? Like old times. We'll talk it all out."

She picked my favorite restaurant, a Korean barbecue place on La Cienega near Wilshire, miles from our house. The plan was that we'd drive there together.

"I'll be home by seven," she said.

∞

First thing I did was call Rick. "What do I do?"

"She's going to ask you for money. When she does, just say that you guys will have to think about it and that you'll let her know tomorrow. Then call me and we'll figure out what to do next."

We had a plan.

I filled Sean in on the details before Mom came home and we all headed to the restaurant together. He and I were on the same page, agreed with how to handle this.

Surprisingly, Mom didn't look too upset that night and I started to think that maybe we'd get out of this confrontation without too many hurt feelings. At the restaurant, though, the air scented with the delicious bulgogi beef I adored, before we even had a chance to order, she started in.

"Thank you both for agreeing to have dinner with me. And thank you for housing me for these two months. I just need a little help getting on my feet. I've been looking at my finances and I think it'll take about five thousand dollars for me to get my own place. I have nothing in savings, but if you'll front me that money, I'll be happy to get out of your hair. And I'll pay you back, I promise."

Sean jumped in, ready to follow the script Rick had given us. "Okay, Maureen. Let us think about it for a night."

I knew I was supposed to follow his lead, but I couldn't do it.

"No!" I slammed my hand on the table. "Absolutely not!"

"But *he* said to let him think about it," Mom said, tilting her head toward Sean.

"I don't care! You're not borrowing five thousand dollars from my boyfriend."

There was no question that I didn't have that kind of money and that if anyone was going to come up with that sum, it was going to be Sean.

"Mink." Sean gave me the eye. "Let's just think about it for the night."

"No! I cannot let that happen. I'm so sorry," I said. I was embarrassed and determined.

She knew it, too. I can be stubborn and she knew she wasn't going to get what she'd come for.

Mom stormed out of the restaurant and Sean got up to follow her.

"Let her go," I said.

Sean and I ate and hung out for a bit, thinking she'd return once she'd exhausted her fury. She didn't.

"How is she going to get home?" Sean asked. "Where could she have gone?"

"I don't care," I said. I'd hit the point of no return.

"She doesn't have her car," he reminded me.

"That's okay. She'll probably be back at the house when we get there," I told him. But she wasn't.

∞

It was after one in the morning when she finally came home. Had it taken her that long to walk home or did she get a ride somehow? I heard her in her bedroom, packing her stuff, then struggling to get it all to her car. When I went out to help, rubbing sleep from my eyes, she refused my assistance. I'll never forget that night. She stood next to her car, the vaporous mercury lights adding deep shadows to the scene, fog creeping its way along the street.

"Stay away from me," she hissed. And then she hit me with what I'm sure she thought was the most lethal weapon in her arsenal. "You were never my daughter! I want nothing more to do with you."

I waved as she drove away. "Real nice, Mom. Goodbye."

And that was it. I was done. I drew my line in the sand and I was ready to stand by it. I had put up with so much from her just because she was my mother, and I couldn't do it anymore. I was now fully willing to take her anger and her abandonment in order to be true to myself.

I was one hundred percent determined, and though I'd hardened my heart as much as I could toward her, I'd be lying if I didn't tell you that I cried myself to sleep that night.

CHAPTER FIFTEEN

Acting Class

I sat in the darkened theater/acting classroom, not at all sure what I was doing there. A friend had suggested I sign up for the class given that I was now regularly doing commercials and music videos. Why not? I was able to fit the afternoon class in after my hours at the surgery center.

I was just starting to get a handle on the class.

This day our teacher, Janet Alhanti, gave out acting exercises to pairs of actors who took the stage, while the rest of us sat in the darkened space and watched, noting nuances in the actors' behavior. She taught the Meisner technique and we were doing a "repetition exercise" in which two actors sit across from each other and one actor makes an observation of the other, like "You're smiling." The scene partner then repeats what's been said, agreeing with the first. "I'm smiling." In time, the exercise becomes more complex, introducing mood and behavior.

The point of the exercise was to get each actor focused on the other rather than themselves, and to draw their attention away from the words they were speaking and toward the emotion underlying the exchange. It was fascinating to watch how the actors became less stilted as the exercise went on and how deep feelings began to emerge. All the actor had to work with was the vulnerability of the present moment, absorbing exactly what the scene partner provided, subtly and emotionally. Sometimes, the actors smiled or giggled; at other times, tensions rose. Though the exercise might sound straightforward, it can actually be kind of intense. Sometimes the actors got angry or cried, all due to the subtle changes in vocal inflection, meaning, and interpretation of the words spoken, coupled with mood and the energy shifts in the room. Sometimes just sustained eye contact and being seen by someone without being able to hide or deflect could bring a person to tears.

The whole thing captivated me. That is, until my name was called and I found myself on the stage for the first time, all eyes on me and a young man sitting across from me, knees touching, eyes in contact with each other's. I was so terrified, I could hardly move. I'm sure my body was quivering. I felt exposed and raw and wanted to hide. I was not ready for this level of connection with a perfect stranger, and with additional strangers watching, no less.

We started out with instructions from Janet.

"You're nodding your head," I said to my partner, a handsome young man about my age, and he repeated it back to me. "I'm nodding my head." Soon, we moved into deeper territory.

I was simply trying to copy what I'd seen the others do in my few days in the class and I attempted to fake my way through. I didn't yet know how to be vulnerable or present with someone so I just kind of parodied what I'd seen. I shrugged my shoulders and giggled a little, making it clear I felt awkward and hoped the watching students would look past that. I might have been a little flirtatious in my body language because that's what you do when you're talking with a guy.

I thought the exercise was going okay until Janet's voice ripped through the darkened space. "Stop, stop, stop!" she yelled.

Had we done something wrong?

"What the fuck are you doing?" Janet called from the darkness.

I pointed at myself. "Me?"

Her voice rang back. "Yes, you! What are you doing? Why are you manipulating him?"

What? Manipulating! How does one even manipulate? What are you talking about? I'd always tried to blend in and I had been good at it, the consummate chameleon. Why was she calling me out? I was doing exactly what I'd seen the others do.

"What? I don't—"

"Why are you talking like a little girl?" Janet asked. "You're using that small voice and being all coy. What's going on?"

I sat there and started to shake. Jesus. What was I doing here? Everyone was looking at me and I didn't know what to say to get them to look away. I was horrified this was happening.

"There's a woman in there," Janet insisted.

I didn't know what to make of her words, how to put into practice what she was saying.

"I'd like to hear that woman speak," she commanded. "Let her out."

I just sat there, befuddled.

Janet didn't back down. Her no-bullshit Bronx accent became even more adamant. She suffered no fools and was not going to let me off the hook. Either we were going to have some kind of breakthrough in that moment or I'd never be back to the class again. She didn't waste time on people who were playing around.

"Don't give me bread crumbs and call it a meal," she said. "There's more to you than you're showing. Why don't you let the full *you* out?"

"I don't know," I all but squeaked.

She was pushing me to a limit I didn't know I had. This wasn't what I'd signed up for and I didn't know how to cope. I couldn't hide or run. I started to cry, the entire class staring at me, tears running down my face.

Janet's voice softened a bit, probing. "Were you abused as a child?"

Did she really want me to answer that? Here? Now? People were staring. I couldn't see them over the lights, but I could feel their eyes. I'd always been a magician with my ability to make myself invisible. How come I couldn't do it now?

Flashbacks played in my mind's eye as I sat on the stage.

Mom telling David she hoped she'd overdosed. "Great, Mo. And in front of the kid."

David holding Charmaine by the throat against the wall, slamming her head until her eyes lost focus.

David wailing on me with the cable TV cord until I was bruised and broken.

Rudy forcing me to make a sex tape.

I'd always been able to control my tears, to withhold them in order to deny another person satisfaction, but now they streamed along my cheeks unimpeded. With my hand shading my eyes from the lights, I shrugged, not wanting to answer that question in front of an entire class watching me. But mostly because I'd never really even considered, before this moment, the fact that maybe I *had* been abused as a child.

"You can come down now," Janet said.

Back in my seat, I shrank. Someone patted my shoulder and I gave a polite smile. Were Janet's words true? Had I really been abused? Was there a woman in me who wanted to get out?

When class ended, I headed straight to my car, not wanting to talk with the other students. I dialed Rick's number and when he answered, I blubbered as I hadn't since I was a small child.

"Mink?! What's wrong?"

I tried to tell him what had just happened but my words were all garbled.

"Are you okay? Were you in an accident? Where *are* you?"

"No, that's not it," I was able to get out. "This woman, Janet. My acting teacher." I sniffled and blew my nose. "She saw me. She paid attention to me in a way I never experienced before." I was talking and crying all at once. I could barely get the words out. I don't think he fully understood what I was saying. He was just relieved I hadn't been in an accident.

Despite my tears, I was happy. Ecstatic, even. I had been *seen*, maybe for the first time ever. Janet had seen through all my defenses and located the real me hiding inside. Her attention felt good and nurturing, like she really cared about me. Who I was and who I had the potential to be. In the heat of her attention, I'd felt stripped bare and far too exposed. But I also felt that maybe I could finally relax.

Maybe I could just be me. Whoever that was.

All I knew in that moment was that I would follow this woman until I learned *all* she had to teach me.

◇◇

That was the first time I confronted the pain of my childhood with another person, and though it was hard and exhausting, I kept at it and soon felt myself starting to blossom. I became so completely engaged with the acting classes and what they were doing inside of me, I decided to pursue the craft with everything I had.

Plus, for the first time in my life, I felt like I'd found where I belonged. I finally had a safe place to express all these feelings, to feel all the pain that I'd long denied and suppressed. I started peeling back all the layers, learning who I was. While I don't believe in using acting as therapy, I can see how discovering who I was and learning to stop hiding behind the masks I'd acquired to survive was most definitely an introduction into self-awareness, though I didn't realize that at the time. Either way, I was hooked.

I felt swallowed up, but in a good way. Delving into my psyche in the acting classes hurt like hell, but at that time, I thought that if something didn't hurt, it wasn't worthwhile. The places that were tender? That's where I needed to dive even deeper. That's where there was more to uncover. And I did.

I became a fiercely loyal student, following Janet around, taking every class she offered, opening myself up to the process, taking private lessons from her, learning to be honest with my emotions and experiences. Janet always sat in a little corner in the dark against the wall, and I positioned myself as close to her as possible. I wanted to hear every note she gave. I wanted to learn everything she knew. I wanted to discover the woman she said was hiding inside me. One of my favorite sayings of hers was that "sensitive people change the world, and the rest don't give a damn." And so, of course, I wanted her to like me.

I learned that I'd developed a survival technique I used whenever I felt threatened. I turned into a little girl who spoke with a tiny voice. That was to ensure someone wouldn't hurt me and might even take care of me. That was how I'd made it through life thus far. If you're small and appear innocent or helpless, maybe they won't wound you. This was completely unconscious. It embarrasses me to admit that this voice thing still haunts me to this day. When I'm nervous or intimidated, I have to remind myself I'm safe and to release the tension in my throat so I can speak from my diaphragm.

∞

I told Sean about my breakthrough in acting class, and in the weeks and months that followed he saw how I was growing and changing. It made him happy.

"I have an idea," he said one night after I'd told him I couldn't go on a particular audition because of my full-time nursing schedule.

"Why don't you let me cover the bills and let go of the nursing for right now to focus on the acting?"

It was the sweetest offer, and though I was annoyed that I wasn't going to remain as completely self-supporting as I wanted to be, I took him up on his suggestion. Or at least part of it. I never wanted to be dependent on a man, and needed to be able to cover my own occasional meals out, trips to the movies, makeup and clothes, that kind of thing. Still, I let him cover my part of the mortgage and utilities, and that allowed me to reduce my nursing hours dramatically. I started going on auditions and to classes all day, every day.

Soon, I was hired to guest star on Amanda Bynes's show *What I Like About You*. I did a couple of episodes and was petrified on set, insecure and scared. I literally trembled delivering my lines.

After taping the shows, I'd watch them alone when they were broadcast, not wanting anyone else to see, and I'd think, *Hmmm, I need to loosen up*.

I did a Clean & Clear commercial, and one for Old Navy that also featured Kristin Chenoweth, which totally intimidated me. I'd just seen her in *Wicked* on Broadway and could recite every lyric to every song in the play. She was Glenda the Good Witch and, as far as I was concerned, was a goddess. I was completely starstruck.

Fortunately for me, the girl I was playing in the commercial had to speak really fast and so I had the perfect place to express all that nervous energy. It worked out perfectly and that commercial still delights me.

While none of these jobs was particularly noteworthy, I was making steady progress.

∞

My agent called a month or so later with another opportunity. A TV series was going to be created out of the feature movie *Friday Night Lights*. Did I know the film?

Of course I knew the film! Sean had made me watch it with him at least half a dozen times. It was his favorite movie and he was obsessed with the football players in that rural Texas town and the obstacles they faced. He loved an underdog and adored everything about those characters. I, however, didn't care about football in the slightest and couldn't really see myself as a cheerleader. I went for it because, if it actually worked out, what a fun surprise for Sean. I'd not only be able to contribute to the bills, but I'd be on a show based on his favorite movie.

I kept the audition a secret from him. If I didn't get the part, he wouldn't be disappointed. And if I *did* get it? Then I'd pop a bottle of champagne and tell him all about it, giving him full credit for having helped me come so far. He'd be so pleased.

After the first audition, I was pleasantly surprised when my agent called to let me know they wanted to see me again. Really? I wanted to let myself believe I could get the part, but I wasn't sure it was possible. I was still so new to this world and because of all the nos I was now accustomed to, I didn't get my hopes up.

Over a period of weeks, though, I started to believe, as the repeated callbacks exceeded my expectations, offering me chances to try to impress the producers and, eventually, Peter Berg, the creator and director—the man, the myth, the legend. Still, every callback, I thought, might be my last, that they'd see through my not-polished acting skills and find someone better. But they kept calling me back.

By the time I was in the room with Pete, everything was different. Up until this point, the callbacks had all been the same, acting out the same scenes, the same way every time. But Pete wanted nothing to do with that.

After my first read, he said, "Yeah, that's great. Now do the same scene like you want to fight him."

I did this, enjoying the novelty of his approach.

"Great. Now do it like you want to seduce him."

"Now do it like you want to kill him."

"Now do it like you're on heroin."

He didn't care that we weren't polished actors; what he was looking for was the ability to play. To take direction and improvise, to take notes in the moment. I had a blast and he seemed convinced I could do it.

The next step was a "chemistry test" with Scott Porter, who was up for the part of the Dillon Panthers star quarterback, Jason Street. They wanted to see if we worked well together on camera. Scott was really sweet and so easy to improvise with. I instantly felt our chemistry. I left the room that day with a really good feeling.

∞

Things at home, though, weren't so great. Sean seemed so withdrawn. This had been going on for some time and I didn't know how to bridge the gap. How do you invite someone to be closer to you when they've clearly made a decision to pull away? We'd been together two years by this point and I was hoping we'd be closer than ever. But everything felt off. I could see he was doing what he could to bring us back to a good place—leaving me sweet notes and cards, telling me how much he loved me—but the distance kept growing.

∞

It was an early Sunday when I woke and tiptoed down the stairs to feed the dogs without waking Sean. He had a dog of his own and, for my twenty-fifth birthday, had given me Chewy, my beloved cockapoo whom I adored more than anything in the world. Once I scooped out their food, I noticed his BlackBerry on the counter, flashing. I looked to see who was trying to reach him—maybe it was a work text he needed to handle. If I'm honest, I have to admit that my intuition told me I needed to see that message. I'm not a snooper—this would be the first time—but because of our distance lately, something in me told me I needed to check.

The words flashing across the screen confused me. "*Next time you come over, I don't want to just suck your dick. I want you to fuck me.*"

Whose phone was this? Did someone leave their phone here?

My vision narrowed to a pinpoint, everything focused on those appalling words next to her name.

I couldn't believe it. He was cheating on me.

In my heart, I knew what I needed to do, and in some ways, I was relieved. All this time, I knew something was amiss, and no matter what I did, I couldn't fix it. But with this information, everything fell into place. The distance I'd been feeling wasn't just in my head.

I went to the bedroom where Sean was still asleep and tapped him on the shoulder. "Hey. Wake up. You have a message." I put the phone on his chest, then went to the closet and closed the door.

From there, I called Marie. "Can I come stay with you?"

"What happened?" she asked.

"He's fucking someone."

"What? Minka!! Get over here right now!"

I packed some clothes and wondered why Sean wasn't barging into the closet, making his case, trying to stop me. When I finally returned to the bedroom, he was in exactly the same position, staring at the wall.

"Do you have anything to say?" I asked.

He shook his head.

"I'm going to Marie's. I'll make arrangements for movers to come get my things." Most of the furniture was stuff I'd moved from Albuquerque years ago, including that black velvet couch. I wasn't going to let it go.

Marie's place was only like five hundred square feet and I wouldn't be able to stay there long, but I knew I had to place my own emotional well-being above all. It had taken me a long time to learn to care for myself, to stick up for myself, and to finally know that I deserved to be treated well. And that would only happen, I realized, if I insisted on it.

I left Sean's place and spent days crying to Marie.

◇◇

"How long has this been going on?" I asked Sean over the phone a few days later. I needed more information. If it was a onetime thing, maybe I could forgive and forget. If I had to leave him for good, everything about my life was about to get a lot more complicated. Now I'd have to come up with rent money. There was no question I'd have to quit acting to focus on making a real living. Plus, I adored Sean. I really wanted to believe it was a one-off mistake.

It wasn't.

"On and off for a year," he said.

I felt sick. A whole year? How could that be? I was gutted.

I couldn't give it another shot. I'd learned from Rick. When someone betrays your trust that deeply, there's no going back. I now had self-respect.

◇◇

The movers were coming to get my things from Sean's house and put them in the U-Haul I'd arranged and I needed to be there to direct them. I was hoping he'd be gone, but when I arrived, he sat in the living room, waiting for me. When he saw me, he reached out to hug me, then started crying in my arms. The movers lifted coffee tables and end tables around us as he sobbed.

"Please don't go. I'm so sorry. Please don't go."

"It's okay," I said. "We're going to be friends. Everything's going to be okay. But I can't stay."

I don't know what changed, but I felt strong. I thought of all the times my mom had gone running back to David when she really needed to get out on her own, all the times I'd excused bad behavior in my own relationships and thought that's just how it works. Women were supposed to put up with this shit. But no more. I was done. I was telling the universe I deserved better. And for once, I believed it.

◇◇

Back at Marie's apartment, I could see my filled-to-the-brim U-Haul parked at the curb from the living room window where I sat on the couch. The inner strength I'd felt at Sean's had evaporated, and now I saw truly the depths of my predicament. I had no idea where I was going to live, how long I'd need to hold on to the U-Haul, if I should get a storage unit for the furniture. How was I going to support myself? I could go back to nursing full-time, if that's what it took, but I was heartbroken at the thought of leaving acting.

Still, I did know one thing. Over the past few months I was crystal clear about what I deserved in life. I said goodbye to Mom and all her bullshit. And now, I was refusing to put up with betrayal from Sean. That was growth, I tried to convince myself.

This was a good thing. Wasn't it?

CHAPTER SIXTEEN

Friday Night Lights

I was miserable company, picking at my lunch, not up to making conversation. My friend Rose took me to Hamburger Hamlet on Sunset to try to cheer me up, but it wasn't working. After, we were supposed to go get our nails done or something of the sort one does to make themselves feel better, but I just didn't have the heart.

"Do you mind if we call it a day?" I asked.

"Of course not." She reached across the table to take my hand.

I was upset over Sean and needed to figure out what I was going to do with my life. Where was I going to live? How was all this going to work out? I kept asking Rose these questions, the same ones I asked the universe. I couldn't find a satisfying answer.

"You'll figure this out," Rose said.

I shook my head, my hair sticking to the tears along my cheeks.

"This, too, will pass," she added.

I couldn't be convinced.

"Want to order dessert?" she suggested.

 ⋅ I should have been more grateful for her compassion, but I felt like such a mess. How was I going to fix all of this? My heart hurt, like I could almost feel the organ behind my rib cage leaking its insides into my chest cavity. Every part of me felt raw.

In her car on the way home, I was hiding from the beautiful day behind big sunglasses when my cell phone rang. I almost let the call go to voice mail but knew I needed to deal with life, so I wiped my face on my sleeve and answered.

"Minka, this is Mark." It was my manager. "I have news for you."

I was ready for him to tell me that the part I'd been called back on so many times had fallen through. Of course it had! Nothing was going my way.

He must have heard the despair in my voice. "It's *good* news," he clarified.

"Yeah?" A little crack in my chest opened to make room for what he was about to tell me. For a split second, I allowed myself to believe that good things could still happen.

"You're moving to Austin!" Mark's voice thrummed with an enthusiasm that seemed out of place for this day.

"I am?" I couldn't fully understand what he was telling me.

"Minka. You got the part!"

"I did?" Helium began to fill my chest, buoying me, lifting me. Maybe I wouldn't be in this morass of pain forever. Maybe life was going to get good again at some point. Maybe there was hope.

"You booked it. They want you there in a month. It's time to start packing."

I blew my nose and lifted the sunglasses. "You don't need to worry about that." I thought of the U-Haul with my stuff still parked at Marie's curb. "I'm ready to go."

After I hung up, Rose and I celebrated in the car. I had a sense of direction! There was a way forward! I had absolutely no grandiose thoughts about the show itself. To me, it was just a stepping stone. After all, had a movie ever been successfully turned into a television series? I didn't think so. And, besides, the series was about football. I could not have cared less about football. All that mattered was that I knew what was next and I was ready for it. The ache in my heart was still there, but I felt like I'd just turned the corner after a bad case of the flu.

∞

Rose dropped me back at Marie's tiny apartment and when I walked in and told her the news, we danced together in the living room, shrieking and crying. Under my breath, I kept saying, "Thank you, thank you." I thanked Marie for having given me safe harbor during this painful time and for being such a great friend. I thanked the universe for giving me a break when I desperately needed one. I thanked my agent and my acting teachers and all the people who'd helped me this far.

I even called the surgery center to thank the doctors and nurses I'd worked with for supporting me on this journey. They'd always made sure I worked enough hours to get by, but that I was out in time to make my auditions. I promised them that I would always be a scrub nurse and that as soon as I was back from Austin, I'd be right back in my scrubs with them again.

I called a few people to tell them the news, including one very close friend, Cat, who reminded me of my mom. She was a little bit older and a free spirit, completely open-minded, and the least judgmental person I knew. That's why I adored her. Plus, she loved everyone the way my mom did, with open arms and utter enthusiasm. Her protective energy made me feel safe and nurtured. It wasn't like Cat was a replacement for my mom, whom I hadn't spoken to in some time. Cat was more like an encouraging big sister. When I told her my news, she squealed and celebrated with me.

"When are you moving?" Cat asked.

"I might go tomorrow. I mean . . . there's no reason to stay in L.A. I'm just going to fill up my car and go. It's a twenty-hour drive and I cannot wait to get there. I want to start my new life. I'm ready to leave all this drama behind."

"Listen, if you give me three days to organize some stuff for work, I'll go with you. I can do a lot of my work remotely, as long as I have my phone. We'll make it a road trip, a little Thelma-and-Louise action but with a happy ending. What do you say?"

"You'd do that drive with me? It's really long," I warned.

"Oh my God, Minka. We're going to have so much fun!"

◇◇

I crammed all my clothes into the SUV and made a little space for Chewy in the back seat with a blanket. The production company agreed to transport my furniture to Austin, so I didn't have to worry about that. I picked Cat up early in the morning on a summer's day, and together we hit the road.

Cat and I took turns driving, listening to music on CDs we'd burned, dancing in the car. When we got tired of music, we listened to *Memoirs of a Geisha* as a book on tape, though there was no "tape" involved, just a seemingly never-ending series of CDs.

We stopped in tiny little towns to have a look around, ate all the junk food one does on a road trip, ordered meals at hole-in-the-wall diners, took pictures of each other, and never stopped laughing. Whichever one of us was in the passenger seat invariably had her bare feet up on the console, tapping out a rhythm with the music, Chewy nestled in her lap. We peed on the side of the road when needed and no restrooms were to be found—garden-variety road trip stuff.

After ten solid hours of driving, we made it to the Texas border. I couldn't believe we had to drive the same distance tomorrow and would stay within the same state the whole time. I'd never before appreciated just how big Texas is.

We were getting weary when a neon vacancy light caught our attention. Night was falling and we needed to stop and get some rest. Cat checked us in and when she reported that the motel wouldn't take pets, I swaddled Chewy in a blanket like she was a pillow I had stuffed under my arm, and snuck her in, beaming a smile at the desk clerk.

The next day was more of the same—miles and miles of brown landscape—and having Cat's company made all the difference. By this time, I was putting the Sean debacle behind me and looking forward to this new chapter. I had already made peace with the fact that I was estranged from my mother. And though I had no idea what was to come, I was excited.

◇◇

The minute we arrived in Austin, that little city had my heart. It was nothing like I was expecting. All I'd seen and heard about Texas before had created a vision in my mind of a place that's dry and desolate. But Austin was nothing like that. The city is surrounded by lakes and trees, nature exploding wherever you look, everything so green and lush. I'd never pictured so much water!

Cat and I drove around taking in all the sights. Joggers and cyclists sprinted past wherever we looked. Everyone was so healthy and fit. Plus, a ton of people were out walking their dogs, or eating outside at restaurants with their dogs. Signs everywhere said, KEEP AUSTIN WEIRD. It was my kind of place.

In no time, I recognized Austin as a music-centric city. L.A. was full of actors, and there are upsides and downsides to that, but Austin was bursting with musicians—such a different vibe and nothing but upsides. Of course, that's easy for me to say since music wasn't my business. I was able to innocently enjoy all that the city offered.

To my eyes, all the musicians seemed to play their music for the sheer love of it, not worrying about becoming rich and famous. You could hear it in their songs: the freedom of their choices, the delight they took in adding beauty to the world, playing in just about every little dive bar, every day of the week, for tip money.

◇◇

The production company had given me a few thousand dollars to facilitate my move. When you book a regular role on a new TV show that shoots at a location away from home, production gives you a onetime relocation fee to help get you moved out and settled in the new place. At that point, you're then considered a "local" hire so you're now responsible for your own housing and getting yourself to and from work. On the other hand, if you're on location with a shoot, they put you up in a hotel and transport you to and from work every day. Being a local hire, which I was, is a lot less expensive and less stressful for the production company. The relocation fee is a bit comical because rarely does it cover even first and last month's rent for a new apartment in a new city—or sometimes a new country. But I was young and the fact that they'd given me money at all felt miraculous.

They also provided a list of recommendations for the new city, including great housing options with everything I might need in easy walking distance. Thanks to that help, Cat and I found an apartment for me right on Congress, the main street in Austin. It was clean, had a kitchen, a bathroom, a bedroom, and looked safe—that was enough for me. Jo's Coffee, this great people-watching spot serving the best coffee in town, where dogs were not only welcome but treated with a jar of dog treats at the pickup window, was right across the street.

Cat and I scoped out the food scene and quickly realized we'd hit a gold mine. We got very into the Tex-Mex cuisine of the region, especially Austin queso, also known as chile con queso, the food that reportedly allows Austinites to thrive. An addictive combo of melted cheeses and chopped peppers, it sometimes features added ingredients like chorizo, guacamole, or beans—all served with a heaping side of tortilla chips. I could eat that stuff all day, and pretty much, Cat and I did.

Like Jo's Coffee, many of the dining places in Austin had little patios where I could bring Chewy. We felt immediately at home.

∞

Once we leased the apartment, Cat and I headed to Target. The moving company wouldn't arrive with my furniture for a week or more, and we needed blow-up mattresses, sheets, and kitchen items.

After years of scraping by financially, for the first time ever I could relax a little about the cost of what I bought. Under my new contract for *Friday Night Lights*, I wasn't paid a lot by Hollywood standards—I was still a newcomer to the realm, after all, and no one had any inkling of how well the show would do. But still, I had an ongoing contract and was being paid more than I'd ever made as a scrub nurse. This one day, I decided, I could afford to let loose.

Cat and I went up and down all the houseware aisles in Target, tossing in stuff without comparing prices, without wondering if I could have gotten a better deal elsewhere. It was a far cry from the times I'd gone shopping as a kid with my mom, always afraid we'd have to put items back when we overshot the mark. This day, I didn't have to double-check my bank balance to make sure I could afford the dishes I wanted. If I wanted them, they went into the cart. I don't think I spent more than three hundred dollars that day, but it was an epic haul for me. It felt like I might actually be on my way to freedom from the financial insecurity that had long plagued me.

∞

Cat stayed a couple of weeks as I got settled, then flew back to L.A., leaving me on my own.

At first, I spent my days exploring the city on foot, eating at as many different restaurants as I could, learning my way around. Because I came out right away when I heard I'd been hired, I was the first cast member in town. But soon, others began to trickle in, making their own living arrangements, setting themselves up.

The first one I met was Zach Gilford, who plays Matt Saracen in the show. He and I became fast friends, buddies pretty much instantly. We still are to this day. He was easy to talk to and very much like the character he played on the show, a real sweetheart. I loved that he had a side job taking kids on backpacking trips through Iceland. I thought he was just so cool. We'd get together to hang out and eat all the time because for those first few days, it was just the two of us.

The next cast member to show up was Adrianne Palicki, who plays Tyra Collette, and I was excited when I heard she was in town. "Yes, another girl!" I was looking forward to making friends. She was fun and we became friends right away. She was a five-foot-eleven, gorgeous bombshell from Ohio with the kindest smile and the most joyful spirit—a very down-to-earth girl's girl.

She was also more experienced in the acting world than I was, not nearly as green. At one of our first dinners together, I mentioned how much fun it was going to be to have our hair and makeup done every day.

She looked at me with a flat expression. "It gets old. Trust me."

She was right, of course. Having people touch and poke at you all day, every day, can be tedious. I'd learn that soon enough and was just happy I had a new friend.

Part of me thought that this was my chance for a do-over with high school. I missed out on so much, never going to the formal dances or football games, cutting classes, too busy caring for Rudy or trying to keep my mom from pulling me out of school to run off to Boston. I was an outsider in school, never anywhere near the popular girls. So now that I'd get to play the popular cheerleader and girlfriend to the star quarterback, I'd have the chance to know what that kind of touched-by-grace life might feel like. I was certain all the cast members were now going to be my best friends.

When Scott Porter, who plays Jason Street, showed up, I was instantly at home. I knew him from the chemistry test and he felt like a friend already. The whole burgeoning group of us would go out to bars, drinking, hanging out, getting to know each other. Everything was easy and everyone got along. Soon, Connie Britton (Tami Taylor) and Kyle Chandler (Coach Eric Taylor) arrived. Eventually, the cast gatherings grew to include Jesse Plemons (Landry Clarke), Taylor Kitsch (Tim Riggins), and Gaius Charles (Smash Williams). Aimee Teegarden (Julie Taylor) had also arrived in Austin, but she couldn't really go out with us at night because she was under eighteen. Everyone was excited to be there, and I felt honored to be part of this crew.

◇◇

We started filming the pilot and I was literally trembling with nerves. During one of the first scenes, in the diner, I only had one tiny line to deliver, and yet every time we got to that part, I'd say my line shuddering with terror. The pressure was intense.

Okay, girl. Yeah, this is your show now. You can do it.

I was in way over my head, but eventually I loosened up. Peter Berg, the director, was able to see that I had the ability to play and could improvise and take direction well, which was definitely a plus. But I wasn't trained and had such little experience knowing my way around a set. I had zero confidence and was learning as we went.

Later, when I watched that first season, I could hear the level of fear and intimidation in the high-pitch tone of my voice.

I was filming a scene with Scott Porter, who plays my boyfriend, Jason Street, when Pete was playing around with getting different options for the scene. He kept throwing out suggestions for us to be more playful with each other. *Try this. Try that.* At one point, I was kind of nuzzling up with Scott/Jason when Peter called out from behind the camera, "Bite his cheek!"

Bite his cheek?! I was confused and unsure of how that would help, but I did as instructed and that scene, to this day, makes me smile. I bit his cheek and we laughed with each other, revealing the kind of intimacy Peter Berg was looking for. He was an amazing director to work with.

Our little cast group was gelling when Taylor Kitsch, who plays Tim Riggins, took my breath away. All I could think was *Oh, man, this looks like fun.*

I had just gone through the betrayal with Sean and here was this guy who was so beautiful to look at with this quirky Canadian accent. The chemistry between us was intense. I had a crush on him immediately. He was funny and adventurous and didn't take himself too seriously. It was as if he had no idea how gorgeous he was. He was so humble and down to earth, it sort of disarmed whatever pretense you might have about someone so pretty. He made me and everyone else laugh constantly.

Flirting and laughing with him on set and off became the sweetest salve to my recently injured heart. We fell in lust fast and hard. I would have told you back then that we were madly in love. Mad, yes. But love it was not. We were infatuated with each other. I had no idea how to give or receive love back then.

One day, Peter Berg asked Taylor and me to meet him for breakfast. Taylor and I had woken up together that morning, but for the sake of appearances, we decided to arrive at the restaurant at different times, very pointedly *not together*.

Pete had summoned us to give us a warning. He could see the chemistry between us. Looking back now, I'm pretty sure everyone could, though we thought we were slick.

At breakfast, he basically said, "Don't fucking do it. It's not a good idea and it always ends badly."

We kept our faces straight and nodded. "Yes. Okay. Whatever you say."

He didn't know he was too late. Or he at least pretended he didn't.

Later, Pete said he knew exactly what was going on. He also knew we wouldn't heed his warnings, but he had to try.

∞

During this time, I hadn't spoken with my mom since she'd stormed out of the house, saying I'd never been her daughter. She called and wrote to me, but I didn't listen to her messages and tried to ignore her pleas for contact. I wanted to carve out space for myself, to get to know myself as a person not connected to her. Her letters all said that she missed me and she was sorry for the way she'd behaved and that she loved me. That may have all been true, but I was tired of going through the wringer with her. It was time to focus on me.

But then she sent a letter unlike the others. "I really need to talk to you, Boo. It's important. Please call."

Something about her calm tone got my attention. She was never calm about things. I dialed the number.

She made small talk and asked how I was doing. After months of no conversation, it felt weird. Something was up. I could feel the tension rising. And since there's never a good time to say something like this to someone you love, the truth just fell out of her mouth.

"I have cancer, baby," she said.

I can still hear her uttering those words to me. *I have cancer, baby.* When I heard that, everything happened at once in just a fraction of a second. My head spun around on its axis, possibly falling on the floor while I simultaneously left my body looking for another one that didn't just hear this news. Every possible outcome and scenario flashed before me, and then in that split second, I returned to the present moment and all my body's survival mechanisms came back into play. I needed to minimize this heart-shattering news. Deny. And get angry. And while I was at it, blame her for all of it.

My first instinct was to think, *Of course you do! Everything is about you.* Maybe she had some minor form of the disease and now she was going to milk it for all it was worth, turn my life upside down again to help her, make herself a victim once again looking to me to be her savior. I wasn't going to fall for it.

I was mad at her. And clearly in shock. Every time I'd started to get on my feet, there she'd come, ready to mess it all up for me. I struggled to find compassion for her and failed. I resented her so much for not taking care of me and, now, for not taking care of herself.

Still, I asked her how the diagnosis had come about.

She'd been constipated for a long time and taking ex-lax, she said. When she went to the doctor—I still don't think she had insurance—the doctor just gave her more laxatives. That had gone on for a time until the strongest laxatives didn't work anymore and she went to a different doctor. The newer doctor found a tumor the size of a grapefruit in her colon.

Inoperable, they said.

Two years, they said.

I was in denial. "They'll fix it, right?" I asked. She didn't dissuade me.

◇◇

As soon as I got off the phone with her, I called my dad.

"Rick, Mom says she has colon cancer." I told him the whole story. "I'm not sure what to believe. She has a way of stretching the truth to suit herself."

I expected Rick to reassure me that she'd be fine, to agree with my take that she often put herself into the victim role to get sympathy and was likely doing the same thing now. I waited for him to tell me that the doctors would be able to fix this. He didn't.

"You need to start seeing a therapist immediately."

What? What did my seeing a therapist have to do with Mom having cancer?

"Why?"

His voice became somber. "There's a ticking clock now for you to sort things out. There's a lot you two went through together and you're going to need to work out your resentment with her before she dies. Otherwise, you will regret it for the rest of your life."

My world began to spin. As mad as I was at my mother, I still needed her. I still wanted her in my life. I couldn't allow what Rick and she were saying to be real. My mom wasn't going to die. That wasn't possible.

CHAPTER SEVENTEEN

Cancer

My character, Lyla Garrity, cried a lot in the early episodes of *Friday Night Lights*. Her boyfriend had just been paralyzed and she was doing all she could to help him. Crying became far too easy for me. Between my mom's cancer, about which I kept mostly silent on set, and the now-brewing tensions between cast members, I was pretty miserable after the first blush of being on the show.

All the good feelings that had been present at the outset began to deteriorate. I guess that's just what happens when you work together on a show; it's a lot of pressure, and filming scenes again and again with the same people can sometimes bring out aspects of personalities that are less than stellar. There was often stress between the people I'd thought of as my friends, and I was left feeling lonely and confused.

I was so new to this world, and so young. So naive. I had just assumed everyone on the show would want to be the best of friends on this new journey together, and when that wasn't always the case, or didn't magically happen on its own, I felt lost. Plus, having come straight out of the betrayal with Sean and shacking up with Taylor so quickly, I can see now how that created a diffi-cult dynamic. Taylor became my medicine to help ease the pain. I was living by the ol' adage, "The fastest way to get over someone is underneath another."

I can be a little messy when my heart has been broken. All the effort I might have invested in connecting consistently with the girls on the show went to Taylor. So when my relationship with Taylor became toxic, I had no one to turn to.

In relationships, I'm usually the one to end things. My super-power is to run away at any sign of either stability or trouble, so hooking up with me at this time was a lose-lose. No matter the guy, it was only a matter of time before I found something to pick apart that would convince me I shouldn't be with him. That is a *me* problem. Never theirs. Either I didn't have the self-esteem to know I deserved the love in front of me, or I didn't have the self-esteem to know I'd be okay if I walked away from an emo-tionally unavailable or toxic relationship. I repeatedly fell into that dynamic because it was familiar to me, so it's where I felt safe, even though I was in constant pain and confusion. That's a whole other chapter for therapy.

Anyway, after breaking things off with Taylor, I'd show up to work with a smile on my face thinking I was being professional, while everyone else felt sorry for the guy whose heart had just been broken. My castmates weren't taking me out for drinks after work to mend my broken heart; they were taking *him* out. And to be fair, I didn't let anyone see that my heart was broken. Taylor was much better at being vulnerable and sharing his feelings. He was very much in touch with his feelings and all I knew was to put on a brave face and not burden anyone with my shit. But vulnerability begets connection, as evidenced by the outcome of both of our coping mechanisms. My tough-guy approach only left me alone. If you behave as if you need no one, if no one around you knows any better, most certainly no one, in fact, will be there.

Life became very difficult both on and off set whenever we broke up. We were young and had very few tools to handle our emotions and personal grievances. Plus, it was difficult for him to separate me from the person he had to work with every day. I, on the other hand, was too good at compartmentalizing. I didn't see what all the fuss was about. My heart was so guarded that I couldn't even acknowledge that this was a real relationship with real feelings. I minimized what we'd shared, the way I did everything else in my life.

On the days we had to work together and were broken up, he didn't want to be in the hair and makeup trailer at the same time I was. We couldn't ride in the van together from base camp to set for the same reason. On those days, the tension on set was high and everyone at work felt the awkwardness.

Since I didn't know anyone in town besides my castmates, I was very lonely and would get back together with him to avoid being so isolated. Of course, that wasn't the only reason we got back together, but to say that loneliness wasn't a part of the equation would be a lie. I loved being with him. It's just that the good only lasted so long before our incompatibility reared its ugly head. We ended up getting back together and breaking up more times than I can count.

There are only so many times you can refuse to look at or acknowledge someone's presence until on set and the director yells, "Action." At that time in our lives it was almost impossible for us not to be consumed by the chemistry we shared. In your twenties, sexual chemistry can be very confusing. You're convinced that if you have this kind of chemistry, surely you're meant to be together.

When it was good, it was good. But we were very young and very sensitive people with our own personal unhealed traumas, so when it was bad, it was really bad. I have to admit I wasn't very receptive to the times he'd tell me what he needed from me. From my hardscrabble past, I'm afraid I'd lost some of my sensitivity for men, particularly given the fact that I'd just come through the Sean betrayal.

Add in the pain with my mom's illness—which, to be honest, I still didn't fully believe or comprehend, though I knew it was bad—and I had all the tear-making equipment I needed whenever Lyla had to break down on camera. All I had to do was put on my headphones and play "Fix You" by Coldplay right before they yelled, "Action," while thinking of my mom, sick and possibly dying, as well as the tensions at work, and I cried on the spot, over and over.

◇◇

I want to clarify that this isn't the way I work today. I used to make myself miserable for the entire day when I had an emotional scene to shoot. I'd wake up in a depressed state, listen to depressing music all day, barely saying hello to any of the crew as I arrived to work so as not to allow even an ounce of joy. I kept my headphones on the entire day up until the very moment I heard "Action." The assistant director knew what I was doing and gave me a look and a thumbs-up to let me know we were rolling. I'd remove my headphones at that moment and pass them off to a production assistant, ready to bawl my eyes out.

Thankfully I don't do this to myself or anyone on set anymore. I've learned to trust myself and the material. I've learned to allow my heart to be open to the situation my character is in. Now, I can have a wonderful morning and say hello to everyone with a smile on my face and know that I can trust my instincts to be there when the time comes.

On *Friday Night Lights*, the way I was working was making my work messy and maybe even sometimes a little unnecessarily melodramatic. Like I said, though, I was learning on the job. You can take all the acting lessons you want, but nothing teaches you how you'll work or what works for you until you're actually on set.

Now, when I think back to that breakfast with Peter Berg, I wish I'd listened to him.

◇◇

"This is so exciting, Boo!" Mom said when she first walked on the set, assisted with a cane because the cancer treatment and chemo had weakened her so much. She was living in San Diego with Kim, who made sure she got to all her doctor's appointments. Kim went above and beyond to care for her; she was her best friend and an absolute angel. Now that Mom had a break in her treatment regimen, I invited her to Austin to see me at work.

I set her up in "video village," the area behind all the monitors, so she could watch what we were filming, and gave her headphones. After every scene, I'd look over to where she sat and she'd just beam at me, silently clapping with excitement no matter how good or bad the take might've been, love flooding at me from across the space, and I could feel every ounce of it even across an entire football field. For all our tensions over the years, I knew she loved me and was so very proud. When she was younger, she did a lot of modeling and she wanted to act and had been in a few minor roles. She was so thrilled to see me in the place she'd dreamed of for herself. And of course, people on set loved her and loved having her around.

For this period of time, it was like I had my old best buddy back. There was something about the cancer that had humbled her, that really made her want to be my mom in a way that was new. Even though she was ill, the healing in our relationship during that time was deep.

Still, though, I was very much in denial about how sick she actually was.

I dragged her all over that city, refusing to see that she was unwell. We went shopping because I wanted to spoil her. When I was little, going to Payless for new shoes or Target for a new outfit was always our favorite thing. And now I had some money and I wanted to do something nice for her. She was so frail and I just could not accept the reality in front of me.

We walked from the car to the entrance of Target one afternoon, and I was nudging her to speed it up. "Come on, Mom. Put some pep in it."

"I'm coming, baby," she said. She didn't complain.

She never talked about how tired she was or how much pain she felt. And I was too happy to be in harmony with her again to acknowledge what was really going on. She was sick and tired and breaking down, her life ebbing away, and I was blind to it all, determined to see her the way I needed her to be.

∞

When we had a break in filming, I went to visit Mom in San Diego. No one loved animals or found more joy in them than she did, no matter how big or small, so I got us tickets for a safari ride at the Wild Animal Park. She wouldn't have to walk much—we'd be shuttled around in a van—and she'd get to see her favorite animals. It was the perfect outing. My plan worked like a charm.

She lit up like a child on our safari and my heart filled to see the delight on her face. When the giraffes came close, she got to feed one and her excitement was contagious. These magnificent animals were taking leaves from her hand! Her barefaced pleasure made me so happy.

This period of time was such a respite—from all the pain Mom and I had shared in our past. The cancer gave me permission to let go of all the resentments I'd been holding on to. For the first time, I really leaned into the affection she'd long offered me and that I had sometimes taught myself to resist. No matter what I did, I felt myself swaddled in her love.

∞

"Tell me about your mom," the therapist said when I first sat down. At Rick's insistence, I'd made the appointment when I knew Mom was sick and was trying to clean up my relationship with her. Just in case. I still refused to entertain the idea she might die, but we could unpack the nuances of our relationship for the overall health of both of us.

So I told this woman my story, the whole story, over a number of days. This was the story almost no one knew because it was such a dark part of my past. I seldom told friends and kept a low profile about my history. Whenever I was interviewed on talk shows, I'd demur when I was asked about my background. How do you reduce your experience down to a sound bite when you haven't processed or even had the time to understand and accept or make peace with all that's happened?

The rest of the world seemed to think my life looked like Lyla Garrity's, that I'd been born into wealth and found myself adored, judged, and maybe even envied by so many. But I knew the truth and was finally starting to let it out bit by bit as I got more comfortable sharing my story with this new person.

The therapist, when she heard about all the ins and outs of my life with my mom, was enraged on my behalf. "Your mom didn't love you." She let her words hang in the air for a moment, giving me time to take them in.

"Your mom didn't love you," she repeated.

This was a concept that had never crossed my mind. Not even in our worst of times did I think she didn't love me. Though she could be fun, for the most part she'd been a shitty mom who also loved the shit out of me in her own unique and childish way. Was she irresponsible and selfish a lot of the time? Yes. But her love was not something I ever thought I lacked.

I realize now I had a very skewed idea of what love was. Her example was all I knew. She was a dreamer and struggled with addiction, which means she will lie, steal and, cheat—whatever it takes to get her fix, children and loved ones be damned. It's not personal, just survival. At least, that's how I saw things.

Children whose emotional needs are not met by their parents end up blaming themselves. It's the root of shame, a sense of wrongness that can be so hard to shake. Childhood trauma is so tricky because the kid doesn't know any better or different. This is the only story they have and they have to draw their own conclusions. That's why I think it is so important to do the work as an adult, to see one's past with adult eyes and not through the frightened eyes of the child, while also honoring and loving and tending to the frightened child that's still alive within us—and often making decisions for us!

So at the time, in this office, my first introduction to this thing called therapy, I was confused. Of course my mother loved me! I was here, alive, because she loved me. I attributed my surviving all the shit I'd been through because she loved me. I was the sun, the moon, and the stars to her, the very air she breathed. She couldn't stand to ever be away from me for any length of time. I felt it and knew it was true.

I explained to the therapist that she had it wrong and yet she disagreed. "That's not a mother's love. A mother doesn't choose a man or drugs or partying or anything else before her child. That is not love."

I didn't know what to say. I refused to agree. This would shake my entire reality if I accepted this perspective.

"You need to tell her all the ways she hurt you before she dies," the therapist said.

She had me write out a script of what I needed to say to her. I was hesitant to follow what the therapist suggested—Mom and I were finally on really good terms and enjoying each other's company intimately. Still, I wanted to do things right and I figured this therapist knew what she was doing. She thought an air-clearing conversation with Mom would set something free in me, would allow me to get off my chest all the ways I'd been hurt.

This woman was a professional, I reminded myself. I needed to trust her.

◇◇

On my next trip to San Diego, I approached Mom when she was in bed, which she often was by then. She sat up to face me, sick and very weak.

I sat on the edge of her bed and followed my script. "I've been seeing a therapist and there are some things I need to say."

Mom listened.

"You were a really bad mom," I said, reading her the litany of the hurts she'd inflicted on me. "Here's where you put me in danger." And, "I almost died several times because of your negligence."

I was about halfway done with my list when her entire being quite literally crumpled right in front of me. Her shoulders dropped forward, her head as low as her neck would allow, using up whatever precious reserves she still had left within her. I don't even know if she heard the rest of what I said after "You were a really bad mom." I hoped she hadn't, because that was enough.

It was like she was a structure composed entirely of toothpicks, delicate and brittle, barely holding herself together. And my words were sledgehammers, dismantling every shred of dignity she had left. She was already carrying so much guilt. She already knew the very specific ways she'd wronged me and every mistake she'd made. And there I was, calling them all out for her in big red letters.

It was such a bad idea. Just remembering this conversation still brings me so much pain.

Everything inside her, so much of which was already broken, shattered to bits before my eyes. She closed in on herself, like a building that's imploded, collapsing deeper with my every word. She was destroyed.

Seeing her break like that, I snapped out of my trance and saw this poor woman for who she really was. She tried. She was a woman who'd been held in place by the societal norms she grew up with, who had learned to use her looks as her only source of currency. She hadn't had any good role models. No guidance. She'd never gotten a break. She'd had a hard job to do as a single mother with no real skills to speak of, and she did the best she could with what she had. She had no family to support her, no home to run to. They'd all abandoned her for her free-spirited lifestyle and called it "tough love." More than anything, she'd loved me, in perhaps her own very flawed way, but loved me with every fiber of her being nonetheless.

In that instant, I knew that this conversation was utterly misguided. *How in the world do I reverse this?* Wasn't it enough that I'd seen her in pain? Did I have to pour salt on her wounds and break her heart, too?

"But it's all okay, Mom!" I said. "Look at me: I turned out pretty great. You must have done something right. Look how well I turned out. I'm strong and healthy. I don't do drugs. I have a great job and am making a good life for myself. Everything's gonna be okay. You don't have to worry. I love you so much."

"I know I wasn't a good mom," she said in a quiet voice from somewhere deep in her chest, as if her voice was a shelf of ice inside her rib cage that was cracking apart. "I'm sorry. I'm just so sorry for everything." She didn't defend herself or justify. She simply apologized and cried.

◇◇

I can see the truth more clearly now, years later. Once she developed cancer, she stopped pretending that everything in her life was fine and started taking responsibility for her choices. And with that shift, together we found the space we'd needed for healing.

We'd already been well along on that journey before my therapist made her suggestion, organically moving toward a full reconciliation. My therapist may have meant well, but her advice was corrosive. I never went back to see that therapist again, and that day with my mom is one of the most painful memories of my entire life.

At that time, Mom and I were doing so well for the first time in forever. I begged the universe for more time with her. It felt so good to be realigned. She and I were getting along so beautifully. *Please, give me more time.*

CHAPTER EIGHTEEN

How Is This Happening?

"I can't do this anymore," Mom said at the start of that summer. It was 2008.

She'd grown tired of the chemo and its effects on her body, the chemicals making her so sick. "The doctor says if I stay on the chemo, I'll live another year. But if I stop, I'll die in six months. I'm not sure it's worth this."

I listened and helped her weigh the pros and cons of this decision. She wanted quality of life over quantity, and I supported that choice. I got it. She felt terrible all the time. On one of my recent visits, I'd spent the whole time outside her bathroom, listening to her throw up. It was brutal and exhausting for her. She didn't have a strong enough immune system to pay the price the chemo was extracting.

If she stopped the chemo, we convinced ourselves, she'd feel, if not good again, at least better. And we'd have six wonderful months together.

We were both deluded.

Even after stopping the chemo, she was still tortured daily by the cancer. This was so maddening because I finally had my mom back in my life in a new way. She wanted to know what I was doing, was interested in my dreams, was one hundred percent behind me and focused on me. I'd been hungering for that kind of maternal attention my entire life, and now her every thought seemed to be concentrated on me.

We'd found this different footing with each other since I'd confronted her—on some level, perhaps that therapist had been right. Mom had apologized to me and I had accepted her apology. That was enough for both of us.

But the cancer? We didn't talk about it besides that one time when she said she was sick of the chemo. I was still scared, of course, but I steadfastly didn't consider that she might truly die. We just enjoyed each other's company when we were together, and I was thrilled to be able to put all my resentments and the bullshit I'd long carried toward her aside. My only thought was *We've lost so much time.*

For the first time, I started to see her as a fellow human and woman, not just my mother. My heart broke for her because, this poor baby, she'd never gotten a break. She'd taken blow after blow after blow from life, nothing but hard times. Sure, she'd made a lot of bad choices, but she also had a lot of really miserable luck come her way. I was so happy to have my mom back. She was lucid and genuine and pure, and I could see her humble heart again.

∞

That fall, Mom decided she wanted to move back to Albuquerque. Kim in San Diego was great and so full of love, but she had four kids and her house was always hectic. Mom just didn't have the stamina for that kind of chaos now, and since she was in bed a lot, she often felt lonely. A lot of people she really loved were back in Albuquerque, and so when her best friend Holly suggested she come and live with her, it was settled. Mom used a wheelchair to navigate the airports and made the journey back to Albuquerque without too much hassle. Then, Holly took her home.

Holly had an infant daughter she'd named Minka after me, and Mom was happy to be with Holly and have this little Minka nearby to cuddle and coo to as she grew frailer and more ill.

⬦⬦

All along, I kept picturing her the way I'd last seen her, slowed down quite a bit and tired out but basically the same person. I was in for a shock when I flew out early in November for a visit. Her hair was brittle and thinning, her face sunken in, her eyes lined in shadows—and she was so skinny.

Oh, God. She really might be dying.

On one level, I knew what was happening. But when crises happen, a shift takes place inside of me. I become very calm and pragmatic, doing whatever needs to be done in the moment with as much love and tenderness as I can. It wasn't the time to process or think of my feelings, so I didn't. I didn't admit what was happening, just cared for her and did what I could to make her feel safe and comfortable.

Still, for as awful as she felt, she didn't complain, just mustered up all her energy to be excited to see me.

"Look, honey," she said when we were alone in her bedroom, lifting her shirt. "Look what my body is doing." Her stomach was closing in on itself. But she wasn't looking for sympathy; she was genuinely awed by what was happening. Like, *Isn't it wild?*

I was bewildered by what I saw. All her life, her body had been her greatest asset. She'd always had the most knockout figure around. Always slender, but with flesh on her bones. But now, I could see her rib cage; her stomach was completely concave. She was being eaten away by the cancer from the inside out.

⬦⬦

On that visit, we hung out together and watched a lot of TV. She had little energy and needed help, sometimes, to go outside to smoke. Yes, I know, it's crazy. She had cancer and was still smoking. But you know what? I wasn't going to give her a hard time about it.

Smoke all the fucking cigarettes you want!

Eat all the junk food you can get your hands on.

Candy for breakfast? Great!

That visit was surreal, seeing how the illness had robbed her of so much of who she was. She was so vulnerable and delicate. She'd always been a force of nature, with an ironclad will, so filled with vibrancy, strong, a fighter.

But that was all gone now.

∞

Given how happy I was to be reconciled with her, I still have trouble understanding why I didn't go see her that Thanksgiving as she requested. But I think just seeing her like that was too hard. I clearly didn't have the strength.

After that early November visit, I went back to Austin and threw myself into my work, avoiding her a bit because it was simply too hard to see her deteriorate right before my eyes.

She'd call and text and either I wouldn't return the calls or I'd text a short answer. She kept asking me to come back and I put her off. She wanted me to come for Thanksgiving and I just couldn't. I lied and told her I had to work and couldn't travel. None of it was true.

By now, the *Friday Night Lights* cast had all met her and had seen her when she was doing well, though walking with a cane. They'd ask every so often how she was doing but I didn't really open up to anyone about it. Because if you talk about it, you make it real.

I was avoiding the topic. And avoiding her. My auntie Sofía, Holly, and everyone around my mom was furious with me for not coming. I was numb. Thanksgiving had always been her favorite holiday and yet, instead of being by her side on that special day, I spent the day alone in Austin. It was such an unloving decision and I regret it to this very day.

I didn't have the tools then to handle it better.

◇◇

"You need to come. She's not doing well."

We were just wrapping *Friday Night Lights* for the season, right after Thanksgiving, when I got the call from Holly.

My first thought was *fuck*, and then I called my dad.

By this point, Mom hated Rick. She was jealous of the attention I gave him, felt left out whenever we were all together. Maybe she even regretted having encouraged me to have a relationship with my father. No matter how I looked at it, she wanted nothing to do with him.

"I'm coming with you," he said.

"But she won't want to see you."

"That's okay."

"Other people will show up, like David. You're not going to want to be around then," I warned.

"I don't care. I'll hang back in the hotel room. I will be there for you when you need me."

We both hopped on flights and met up in Albuquerque. Holly offered me a bed in her house and Dad got a hotel room nearby.

When I saw Mom for the first time, it nearly killed me. It had only been a handful of weeks since my last visit, but she'd fallen even more ill. Mentally, she was mostly absent and when I first entered her room, she didn't recognize me.

Me. I was always her everything, the reason she got up in the morning, the reason to keep going. Now, though, she had no idea who I was. It was stunning, but by then, I'd become a master at minimizing difficult things. I kept playing down the severity of the situation and just went through the motions of what I had to do.

And right now, my job was to take care of her. Whether she recognized me or not, I was there and not budging until the very end. My denial had crumbled and I had to accept that this was it.

∞

When you're dying, so many parts of you go, one by one. Though her mind was mostly gone, she'd have little moments of lucidity and I'd want those moments to last forever. And then she'd descend into bursts of genuine confusion. She was still able to talk but she kept calling things by the wrong names. She said the clock was a door, her cane was a steamer, and her phone was her car. Watching TV, she picked up her glasses, thinking they were the remote.

∞

One day, she wanted to take a shower.

"Do you want help?" I asked.

"No, I can do it." She was still very proud. "I can shower by myself."

But she couldn't really walk anymore. I wanted her to let me help hold her up, but she refused.

"Okay, I'll put a little seat in the tub so you can sit. And here's the showerhead. You can shower all by yourself. I know you don't need my help, but I'll be sitting right outside the shower curtain if you need me. I'm here." I peeked in every minute or so to make sure she was okay.

"Honey?" her weak voice called out.

"Momma, I'm right here."

She opened the curtain and handed me a razor. "It's not working."

I looked at it; it seemed fine, so I gave it back to her. She closed the curtain again.

"Baby?"

"Yeah, Momma?"

"It's not working."

I took the razor from her and shaved my arm. "See," I said. "It's fine." I didn't think to question why she wanted to shave herself, given the state of her health. *Who are we shaving our legs for right now?* I still trusted her to know what she was doing, the last bits of my denial still in action.

"Boo?" She handed me the razor again.

"Show me how you're using it, Mom."

She took the razor from me and stuck it in her mouth as if it were a toothbrush.

"What are you doing?" I jumped to pull it away from her, afraid she'd lacerate her tongue or cheek.

She looked at me with the eyes of a four-year-old, a confused baby girl worried she was in trouble.

"How am I supposed to brush my teeth?"

"Do you want a toothbrush?" I asked.

"I don't think so."

"Okay, let's get you out of here." I got her out of the shower and dried her off, then put lotion all over her body. I put her in her pajamas, all the while so startled and berating myself. *Why did you let her use a razor? What the hell was that? This woman does not need to have sharp objects in her hand.*

◇◇

I spent every day and all night caring for Mom. After initially leaving Rick back at his hotel, I let him come with me to Holly's house because Mom never left her bedroom. She'd never see him. Besides, judging by how infrequently she recognized me, her beloved daughter, I didn't think she'd remember him even if she did see him.

I had to give her morphine every hour. Liquid morphine, with a syringe that I'd squirt into the back of her throat or under her tongue. She came to hate that syringe and if she saw it in my hand, she'd freak out and hit me, trying to fight me away.

"You're trying to kill me!"

"I'm trying to help make you more comfortable, Momma," I said. "This is medicine. It's going to help."

She hit me and pushed me. "Get out of here. I don't know you."

"It's me, Mommy. It's Minka."

She stared at me and appeared confused. She was so tired.

She'd drop off and once she was asleep, I'd stick the syringe in her mouth and shoot the morphine in. That would get her attention and she'd open her eyes again, terror filling her face.

"You're okay," I'd tell her. "You're okay." Eventually, she'd close her eyes and drift off.

But this day, she was really restless. All day, she'd wanted to get up and go to the window in the bedroom. I helped her over to it and she leaned on the dresser, just looking out the window. To me, it looked like she wanted to run and couldn't figure out how.

In a rare and brief moment of lucidity, she said, "I'm dying."

I was shocked. She knew what was happening. What could I say? What do you say to that? All I could do was be honest with her.

"I know, Momma, but it's okay. Why don't you come sit down and rest with me?"

She didn't. She just stood there longer.

"I want to go outside."

There was no way I could let her go outside like this. She was wearing only a T-shirt and a diaper, and besides, to get outside, we'd have to walk through the living room and past Rick.

"Why don't you come lie down?" I tried to show her to the bed and she pushed me away. She's five foot eleven and all my life has been stronger than me and now, with a burst of adrenaline, she easily overpowered me. I struggled with her. She kept pushing me out of the way and hitting me. Of course, she had no idea who I was. If she was wailing on me like this, I couldn't let her see Rick. She'd murder him.

She started screaming at me. "Get the fuck out of my way, whoever you are! I want out of here!" She burst out of her bedroom and into the living room where Rick was sitting on the couch. The sight of him stopped her in her tracks.

He looked at me, silently asking, *What do I do?*

I raised my eyebrows. I had no answer.

For a moment, we all stood there in silence.

"Hi, Mo," Rick said.

"Rick?" she said.

Whoa, I thought, *she's lucid again. She knows who he is.*

"Yeah, baby," Rick said.

And with that, she climbed onto the couch and curled up on his lap like a baby, at peace and fully content at last.

He just looked at me. All this time, all this fighting, that's all she'd needed. I'd been hiding Rick from her and she was just happy to be in his arms again. For all her anger and protestations that she hated him, the truth was clear. She loved him and always had.

◇◇

Over the next couple of days, caring for her got harder and harder. I was trying to make it so that she could die in her own bed but she became so erratic and combative, I couldn't keep her comfortable anymore. Moments of lucidity grew rarer. She couldn't sleep because every time she lay down, her lungs filled with liquid and the sound of that liquid rattling around woke her up and scared her. "What is that?" It startled and confused both of us and neither knew what to do. I didn't know what a death rattle was at that time.

"It doesn't happen when you sit up, so let's try sleeping sitting up." I propped her against the wall since the bed didn't have a headboard, but then she'd fall to one side. I sat up next to her, holding her, wrapping my legs around her to keep her upright. She kept getting frustrated and restless and just wanted to fucking run. Who could blame her?

Eventually, I had to call hospice. I needed help. The medicine wasn't working. She was in pain and I didn't know how to help her anymore.

When they came, though, she didn't want to go with them and they had to force her. I hid in the other side of the house because I couldn't bear to watch.

∞

"You need to eat something," Rick said after the medical transport vehicle left with her. "You and me, before we go to the hospice facility, we need to take care of you. They'll tend to your mom until we get there."

I'd been up for the last three days straight fighting with her, trying to keep her comfortable. I wanted to go straight to hospice with her, but I let him take over.

We stopped at a diner and I tried to eat. "I want to see my mom," I said. I couldn't swallow and needed to be by her side.

∞

When we got into the facility, I found her in the hall, strapped on a gurney.

"What's going on?" I demanded at the nurses' station.

"We need to keep our eyes on her. We've had a hard time making her comfortable and didn't want to leave her alone in a room. We just finally got her to calm down."

Apparently, she'd needed enough tranquilizers to fell an elephant. That's how high her tolerance had become.

Once she was calm, she was moved into a room and the parade of visitors coming to say goodbye started. Her best friends, Holly and Rachel, came. Auntie Sofía came. And eventually David, my dad, which was tense because Rick was also there.

I hadn't seen David in years.

"Hi," he said, a somber hello. He was walking with a cane by then from his own injury. He'd picked a fight in a liquor store some time ago and hadn't been the same since. I'd heard about him from Mom and I was mad at him. As she was dying, he'd wanted to know what she was going to do with the money she had left. She told me he'd asked her for a thousand dollars for a new TV and to go skydiving.

I didn't want to be around him.

Everyone was cordial, though, and put aside their grievances. David didn't stay long. He kissed her on her forehead, told her he loved her, and then left.

∞

The next day, I crawled in bed with her and wrapped my arms and legs around her. I told her how much I loved her. Her friends were all sitting on the couch in the room, and the hospice nurse came in to check on her. He was so soft and tender, with the most compassionate bedside manner. Hospice nurses are a special breed of people. Angels, really. They and doulas, guiding people so tenderly in and out of this life.

This one nurse started to give me a countdown.

"All right, honey, you got about six hours."

I couldn't believe it. *That's all? Six hours?*

I wrapped myself around my unconscious mother even tighter and kept whispering in her ear how thankful I was for everything she'd tried to do right and that I forgave her for everything she thought she'd done wrong. I knew she could still hear me. I rubbed her head and kept telling her how much I loved her, that she didn't have to fight anymore, it was okay to rest now. I tried to dim the lighting in the room and played music for her.

When Bill Withers's "Ain't No Sunshine" came on, my dad made a little noise.

"A little on the nose, Mink," he said. "Let's skip this one."

Now, every time I hear that song, I think of that moment. It was a little melodramatic, I guess, putting that song on my list. But that's how I felt.

∞

For hours, I lay in bed with her, listening for her every breath, wondering which one was going to be the last. There was a lot of time between her breaths now, and I never knew.

The nurse came back in. "Two hours."

Shit. I need more time.

When it finally happened, when she finally took her last breath, everyone in the room seemed to understand what was happening.

A moment later, the doctor came in. How had he known?

Still curled up with my arms and legs tightly wrapped around her, my face buried in her neck, I looked up at him. "I don't think she's breathing anymore," I said.

With deep compassion in his eyes, he nodded his head yes, quietly calling the time of death. He offered his condolences and then left me to be with her.

All the others were standing around when Rick said, "Let's give her a minute with her mom."

In that moment, everything came pouring out of me. I just fucking wept twenty-eight years of tears. I'd never cried so hard in my life. I buried my face into her, not wiping the tears and snot, holding on for dear life.

"I love you so much. I love you so much. And I'm so sorry. I'm so sorry life was so hard for you. But you're free now, my mommy."

I soaked the sheets with my tears, grabbing her as if my love could call her back. But it didn't.

When I finally stopped crying and everyone came back in, I still wouldn't let go of her.

An hour later, a nurse came into the room. She rubbed my hand. "Honey, I don't want to rush you." Her voice was so gentle. "But she's going to start turning soon. And I don't want you to see that."

I lifted my head for the first time. "What?" I looked up at her, then down at my mother's hands. Her fingertips were turning blue.

I finally got up, kissed her all over her face and her beautiful hands, then said my last goodbye.

◇◇

The next day, Rick took me to a funeral parlor to see about having her cremated. That was what she wanted. That's when it became real. For days after, I tunneled myself away into sleep and prayed that it was all a bad dream, but I kept waking up again. She'd always promised me that everything was going to be okay, but nothing was okay.

When she was dying, she told me she'd leave a treasure chest of mementos for me in her room and that the journal she'd been keeping the last few years would be mine to read when she was gone. I wasn't ready to deal with any of that.

My disbelief over her passing lasted years. I kept feeling the urge to call her and would have to remind myself that I couldn't. I'd kept a voice mail of her that I listened to over and over again. What was extra heartbreaking was that that voice mail was from when she'd wanted me to come and visit her at Thanksgiving when I didn't.

"*Hi, Boo. I miss you so much, honey. I hope you come soon.*"

I loved hearing her voice and the way she'd say, "Hi, Boo." Over and over again I'd listen to that voice mail, but mostly just the "Hi, Boo" part. I couldn't bear hearing her ask me to visit, knowing I hadn't. I hated myself for being so selfish. I'd give anything for just one more moment of her in my life again. Just to see her smiling face and hear her loving voice say just one more time, "Hi, my Boo."

CHAPTER NINETEEN

Having You Was the Best Thing I Ever Did

The doorbell rang at Holly's low-slung stucco house in Albuquerque where Mom had lived until near the end, and when I opened the door, David stood on the stoop. His face was vacant and downcast. He looked old and tired, walking with a cane, a bit hunched. There was little left of the man I'd once adored and who'd long terrified me. I welcomed him to our little gathering, a kind of wake Holly and I had planned to honor Mom, knowing there wouldn't be a formal funeral. I'd set up the room with a table featuring beautiful photos of Mom; she was always so photogenic. I thought everyone might want to gather, tell stories of her, and find solace with each other in our pain.

As I greeted him, everything I thought and felt about David seemed to recalibrate. I was aware for the first time that I'd never sought his approval; I'd respected him simply out of fear. He'd long taught me to show deference to him and how to behave, but I'd looked to others for guidance: other people's parents or older friends—never David.

I think that's why I fell in love with Rick so hard—because I respected and admired him. He felt so normal and stable and, most of all, sober. Rick was the first family figure I wanted to impress and make proud, feverishly trying to change myself to get his validation. I'd begun to grow and evolve as a human because of Rick's influence, and thanks to the conversations we had about having compassion for the people who hurt you. That might be a tall order, but the practice of asking, "What happened to you?" rather than, "What's wrong with you?" has proved a much easier toll on my spirit and allows me to not take hurtful experiences personally (though I fail at this regularly).

Seeing David on the stoop, I realized how little I needed his approval because I could finally contrast my relationship with him to my relationship with Rick.

Still, I had compassion. He was just as devastated at my mother's death as I was—she was probably the longest relationship of his life. Though their bond had swung from romantic to platonic, they'd been in each other's lives for the last twenty-eight years. And now he stood there, shattered, a shell of himself.

As I welcomed him, I kept waiting for a spark of connection, for him to pull me into a big bear hug and say, "Minka, I'm so sorry. Your mother. Your life! I'm so heartbroken for you. And *with* you."

I realized that connection was never going to come.

David entered the house, giving me a distracted side hug. Until the visit in the hospital, I hadn't really seen or spoken to him since they left for Boston when I was sixteen. Maybe there was just so much to talk about that we didn't talk at all. At the time, though, I was perplexed.

"Hello, hi." He offered a polite and compassionate smile, then immediately made his way through the room to the bar where I'd set up the drinks and food, pouring himself a cocktail. It was surreal.

When Rick, organizing snacks in the kitchen, saw David, he

headed to another part of the house. Clearly, he didn't know what to say to David, either.

As I prepared a tray of cheeses, I thought about how much Mom's illness had eviscerated me and how, until the very end, I couldn't handle watching her be diminished day by day by the cancer. And so to protect myself, I stayed away. It was so strange because I was a nurse, after all. Surgical nurse, yes, but I was used to seeing all levels of people unwell. If Mom had been a stranger or friend, I would have been able to care for her with so much love and tenderness.

I'd never before been repulsed by illness and nothing can make my stomach turn. In fact, when I was a kid, about thirteen, Mom had taken me to see her father, my grandfather, when he was dying. Throughout my lifetime, her entire family had distanced themselves from both of us, as if by withholding their love and support she'd straighten up and fly right, according to their dictates. A lot of pain and not much forgiveness—that was the standard in her family. Still, Mom wanted to be a good daughter and see her father before he passed. My grandfather had never been very nice. He was downright abusive to her, and the few times I'd visited him as a child, he'd been mean to me. From my perspective, he was an old and scary alcoholic, and I felt nothing particularly warm toward him, but I accompanied Mom because it was important to her.

The day we visited, he was in a hospital bed in the dingy living room, passed out as Mom said her goodbyes. While she was talking to him, holding his hand, telling him that she forgave him, he started to vomit. He was lying flat and still unconscious, a recipe for trouble, but Mom didn't know what to do. Immediately, I went to his side and began shoveling the throw-up out of his mouth so he didn't choke and die. Mom took a step back, awed at how I kept my head and knew what to do. Here was this man, who'd been mean to me when I was just a little girl, and I instinctively scooped puke out of his mouth with my bare hands, no problem.

But when Mom got sick and began to fail, it was different. I was so afraid of her illness. If she had been any other person on this planet, I could have faced it, but she wasn't. She was my mom, my one person, the only one who'd been by my side in one form or another my entire life. I couldn't bear to see her hurting and deteriorating, getting smaller and frailer by the moment, as if she were drawn in disappearing ink and evaporating before my eyes. Even at the end, when I finally came to be with her before she died, I had trouble doing the simplest things for her, like using the wet sponge on a little stick to moisten her mouth, something so basic. I just couldn't do it. It was hard to see her so weak.

My aversion, combined with my many resentments, including her not having taken better care of herself, had kept me away.

But now the truth crashed into me. I needed her. How was I going to journey through my life without her?

◇◇

We all congregated in Holly's living room, with drinks, sitting on the couch. The room felt dark and heavy. I shredded the napkin cradling my club soda, waiting for someone to speak. I thought people might want to tell stories of Mom's crazy escapades—I could use a laugh and the chance to see things through a prism of lightness—but no one volunteered. Why had I thought this wake would be a good idea? I couldn't wait for it to be over.

David remained quiet throughout. If I thought there'd be a final reckoning with him, I was wrong. He paid his respects and didn't stay long. For him, discomfort was to be avoided at all costs. I never saw him again. He died a few years later from injuries he'd sustained in the liquor-store brawl.

The wake didn't last long, and as Rick and I cleaned the kitchen, I was grateful everyone had left. I packed up the photos of Mom and thanked Holly.

I had just one more day left in Albuquerque. Tomorrow, I'd

finally open the treasure chest Mom had prepared and take the journal she'd written to me. After that, there'd be nothing left to hold me here. Or to hold me anywhere.

◇◇

After coffee the next morning with Rick and Holly, I knew it was time. "I'm going to open the treasure chest now," I said.

"You okay doing this on your own?" Rick asked.

They both wanted to give me privacy. Holly handed me a box of tissues.

I took a deep breath. "I'm ready."

I made my way to what had been her room and the steamer trunk Mom had used as a kind of coffee table. For months, she'd gesture at it whenever I was around. "I'm packing this for you. I'll put in special things to remember me by. But you can't open it until I'm gone, just like I don't want you reading my journal until then."

I was already picturing what might be inside. Little love notes and pictures of the two of us. She loved charm bracelets so I was sure she'd have kept at least one special one for me, though I'm not a fan of them myself. I was ready to hold on to and cherish whatever she'd left for me. She loved tchotchkes of every kind, and I was sure there'd be a bunch of them, ones she'd collected over the years, particularly ones of flamingos. I don't know when she'd come to see flamingos as her special animal but all my life, they'd been her favorites. She had the same long, skinny legs, and when she cooked, she'd often pull up one of her legs and rest her foot against her knee, flamingo-like. We had flamingo fridge magnets, lawn statues, little porcelain figurines everywhere, even pink birds tattooed on her: one on her arm of two flamingos making the shape of a heart with my name tattooed on the inside, and another that covered the entire outside of her hip and thigh. I knew I'd find flamingos in and among whatever she'd left for me.

Rick and Holly stayed in the kitchen and I can only imagine their thoughts as they heard me laughing hysterically. They both came running to the bedroom. My arms were deep in the treasure chest, tossing socks—plain, white athletic socks—all around the room.

"Where's the treasure?" I mumbled, my face buried in the chest in disbelief. When they walked in, I looked back up at them, smiling and giggling.

"What is it?" Holly asked.

"Socks," I said.

"What?" Rick said.

"It's just full of all these socks. Either there's another treasure chest somewhere in this room or she never got around to filling it." I dug through, looking for the flamingo that had to be hiding in there somewhere. Was this a joke? I didn't understand.

Socks. That was my entire inheritance. Not even perfectly matched, rolled-into-tidy-little-balls socks. Just cozy socks, the kind you'd use to stay warm when you didn't care about how you looked.

"She must have lost track of what she'd planned to do," Holly said in her defense.

But she didn't need to be defended. She'd left me comfort and warmth. She may have meant to do otherwise, but she left me with about forty pairs of simple cotton socks to remember her by.

Plus her journal. Her writing definitely meant more to me than anything she could've put in that treasure chest. Not to mention, she'd made me laugh. I'd take it. I needed that laugh.

◇◇

Once all the arrangements in Albuquerque had been made, I got back to Austin and focused on my work. I'd made friends of my own in Austin and was no longer dependent on the other cast members for my social life. And to be frank, my mom's death put all the on-set drama into perspective. I could no longer rally enthusiasm to worry about what others thought of me. I'd also learned to stop taking everything so personally. I realized that we all had a job to do and we were just here, doing those jobs. I was going to do mine to the best of my ability and not look to the cast and crew as the pseudo family I'd wanted them to be. Finally, I'd found balance at work and it suited me.

When I left Albuquerque that day, I took Mom's journal with me. She started it when we were estranged, and all the entries were made out to me, letter-like, as if this were her opportunity to tell me her side of the story. The journal was like a kid's diary, with colorful flamingos on the cover (of course!), and she'd added stickers and stars on every surface, reminding me yet again that she was truly a child at heart. When I first picked up the journal at Holly's house, I had to be careful how I handled it unless I wanted all kinds of stuff to fall out. The journal was bursting at the seams from where she'd taped in photos, news clippings, and souvenirs. Some of the pictures, which I treasure to this day, were partially ruined by the tape. She must have thought she was laminating them in place, not knowing the tape would degrade over time and all but ruin the photos.

I first glanced at her writing the day I found the socks, but after reading just a line or two at random, I had to stop. *Not today! It's just too much.* Since then, I'd taken the journal back with me to Austin and had read an occasional entry. *My Boo, where are you? I miss you.* I felt so sad and sorry about how I handled her illness. *We haven't spoken in two weeks. I'm so mad at you. Don't you understand what I'm going through?*

Every time, I'd have to put it down.

◇◇

I'd wanted to tell my story since I was in high school, not yet aware it might hopefully mean something to someone somewhere, struggling to find her place in this world, struggling to understand the cards they'd been dealt and how best to play them. The way we make sense of life is through our stories so, to tell mine with depth and honesty, I came to see, I needed to know hers better. I was ready.

When I first started writing, friends asked me, "Is it really cathartic?"

It wasn't. I was just making notes of my memories. But then I read her journal and it all changed. I was crying all the time and working hard to balance her perspective with mine, to be fair to both of us, to get it right.

Oh, so this is the cathartic part everyone was talking about.

It was hard.

She'd started the journal while we were separated, and in it, told me about her struggles. In reading it, I came to see her as a full, beautiful, deeply flawed, and deeply pained human who never really got a damn break. I saw how our society convinced her that her currency was to be found in her looks and, as those looks faded with the years, she had nothing left of herself to hold on to. She only had me.

◇◇

During that time, I wanted to get a tattoo to memorialize her. I didn't want a whole flamingo—they're really not my thing—but I thought maybe I'd do a flamingo feather or the outline of the bird. I was trying to decide when I was reading the journal, and in an instant I knew: Aha! There it is.

In one of the journal entries, she'd written my name in such a way that I could almost see and hear her again. I felt her love in the affection of the big exaggerated loop that preceded the capital letter *M*. I'd always loved her handwriting; she had a very distinct and specific style of penmanship. You'd recognize her handwriting a mile away and it never changed. I always thought it was so beautiful and it taught me to care and want to write beautifully, too. All my life, we'd written to each other as our way to stay connected whenever we were apart, even when I was a small child. In this journal entry, she'd written *my sweet Mink*, and for some reason that *M* in *Mink* was shaped with so much love. It captured her.

I asked the tattoo artist to copy it and inscribe that *M* on my right arm below my elbow. This made sense. It was the perfect way I could carry her with me always.

∞

"Have you been seeing a lot of birds?" the medium asked just before we hung up at the end of our hour-long conversation, as if a last-second thought just occurred to her. I was looking for answers or clues, trying to understand more about my mother and about loss, and to ease the way I missed her.

"Now that you mention it . . ." I realized I'd very recently been seeing flamingos in all kinds of places I didn't expect but hadn't thought too much about it.

"Okay, great! She wants you to know that's her."

I wasn't sure I believed her when I hung up the phone, but the next four hours changed my mind. I went to a store that afternoon, and staring at me were flamingos on a huge display of socks. I took my dog for a walk at the park and behind an energy-drink stand stood a massive bouquet of flamingo balloons. Back home, I turned on the TV show *Sex Education* and the main character was discussing with his paramour what their safe word would be, only to pick "flamingo." When one of my best friends sent me an Instagram post that evening of a flock of flamingos taking off and flying together, all I could do was smile and think, *Okay, Mom, now you're just showing off.*

A few years later, I went to Paris for my birthday. I asked silently if or how my mom might show up for my birthday, doubting I'd ever see flamingos in Paris. But sure enough, as soon as I walked off the plane, while still in the airport, I saw a huge mural of flamingos. And at dinner that night, the first person in the restaurant we saw as we walked in had flamingos all over his button-down shirt. In case that wasn't enough to convince me of her presence, my glass of rosé was etched with a flamingo. No one else in the restaurant seemed to have the same glass. It should be noted, there was absolutely nothing to do with flamingos in this restaurant whatsoever. A completely random coincidence, one might suggest. But I know it was her.

This still happens all the time and in so many different ways. I was on a beach in Mexico with my girlfriends and we looked up to see one big bird flying across the sky. I looked a little closer and asked, "Is that bird . . . pink?" It was, in fact, one lone flamingo flying by. I didn't know flamingos flew alone and I didn't know they were in Costa Careyes, Mexico. I asked people who lived there and they'd never seen one before. I've decided and embraced that it's her way of letting me know she's with me. It's what I choose to believe.

◇◇

One of her journal entries, though, hit me between the eyes and stuck with me for years; I still haven't made peace with it.

The best thing I ever did was have you, she wrote.

I had to sit with this a long time because I'm not sure it's true. Abortion was legal when she conceived me. She'd already had three abortions because she knew she wasn't ready or able to be a mother at those times and she didn't want to do that ever again. She just knew this time was different. Still, when she became pregnant with me, if her mother hadn't offered to help raise me, would she have ended the pregnancy? I wonder if by the time her mother died and she realized she'd be on her own, it may have been too late.

Sometimes I think an abortion might have been best. Don't get me wrong. I'm glad to be alive and for the opportunities I've had, but it still breaks my heart to recognize how unprepared my mother was, maybe even constitutionally ill-equipped to be a mother in any genuine way. If having me was the "best thing" she ever did, I wonder, for whose sake was it best?

I have to conclude that it was for hers. She wanted me to love her. She wanted someone in her life who'd be hers exclusively, to fulfill her. And I became that person, with or without my consent. There have been times, I have to be honest, when I've been mad at her for having birthed me. I didn't ask for all this. I didn't ask for this trauma, and for the struggle to earn enough to pay for the tons of therapy I've needed to heal these wounds. I didn't ask for these complicated relationships.

What I have are trust issues and an attraction to emotionally unavailable partners. That, combined with a fear of intimacy that compels me to push away the men who might have the capacity to commit to me in a real and sustainable way, makes for romantic problems. My relationships have been mirrors of how I felt about myself. I've only been treated as well as I thought I deserved.

One skill a child learns from having alcoholic or drug-dependent parents is to anticipate the needs of those around them. I learned to take care of everyone and make them happy, you before me at all costs, in an unconscious effort to control my environment or to feel needed so to feel worthy, and that doesn't translate into an authentic and truthful relationship.

I miss my mother all the time, not that she ever made my life any easier—but I would definitely love and appreciate the joy she used to bring. If there's one thing I've learned, it's that finding someone who emits such pure and unabashed joy like my mom did is really hard to come by. Her joy is what I miss the most. Ironically, it's what used to annoy me about her, and now I'd give anything for just a moment of it once more, that sparkle in her eye over the smallest thing.

I sometimes long for a family member with whom I could talk about my mom. I'm in awe of my friends who have siblings and family who've known them their whole lives. What must that feel like? Sure, the beauty of my position is that I get to choose my family. I have friends with very complicated families who wish for the luxury I have, of being able to curate their chosen families. We all tend to wish for whatever it is we don't have. So I have to remind myself to appreciate the peaceful home I've created, a sanctuary where chaos is not welcome.

Today, I'm trying to be my own family to myself, and I get a little bluesy sometimes, but for the most part I don't really get sad at holidays anymore. I revel in the gift of either being alone or going on a trip with a boyfriend or other friends who aren't spending time with their families. My dad and I gave up sharing the holidays a few years ago. He drives me nuts. Over the years, I've grown out of the idealized version of him I created when I was younger, the version I needed him to be back then. As an adult, I see and accept him for exactly who he is, and I've formed my own opinions about who I want to be. For example, he believes in brutal honesty and tough love. I used to think that was the way to live. But I now believe that honesty without kindness can be cruel; I prefer gentle love these days.

He and I have come to accept that we don't have to force traditional ways of being together during the holidays just because that's what everyone else does. We didn't spend the first eighteen years of holidays together, so doing it now feels forced and uncomfortable, not very authentic. He spends them with his friends and I with mine. Everyone's happy.

Being a human is complicated, no matter your circumstances. My gifts and privileges are not lost on me. I thank my angels every single day for the life I have.

◇◇

One of the ways I knew to fill the hole in my heart after my mother's death was to be of service to women. I met my now dear friend and partner-in-good, Barrett, and his wife, Rachel, who had been living in Ethiopia for a year because of her service there as a social worker. When we met he told me he'd noticed how many women had to turn to survival sex to provide for themselves and their children. He wondered if I'd be on board to help find ways to create jobs so they could provide for themselves in a more sustainable way. Weaving on looms was an ancient tradition in Ethiopia, but was predominantly an occupation for men. "Let's help resource and facilitate a program for women to learn how to make scarves!" we decided, at first calling our efforts LiveFashionABLE. (Now it's simply ABLE, working to move the fashion industry forward by creating fair employment to women who make our clothes.)

We partnered with a local nonprofit that offered six months of rehabilitation to women who wanted to leave the commercial sex industry, and for those wanting to weave scarves, they also needed hands-on training. One morning, when I was visiting the women in this program, I sat in on one of the counseling sessions, and I noticed the women spoke mostly of the shame they carried and how they wanted more than anything for their children to never know what work they had done to earn a living. They cried, deeply ashamed and pained by their pasts. This was the moment where it became very clear exactly why I was here with them.

"Can I share my story with you?" I asked.

They all nodded.

Through an interpreter, I told them of my mother's work and, though not comparable—my mother choosing to dance on a pole isn't the same as survival sex—still, I appreciated that she'd done whatever she could to keep a roof over our heads. I told them how proud I would have been had she taken the opportunity they were now taking, of learning a new skill set to earn a living.

"You are survivors. You are strong and working to make better lives. Your babies are going to be so proud of you!"

By the end, we were all in a puddle of tears, holding hands, crying, kissing each other's faces, sharing stories of loss and love despite the fact that we didn't even speak the same language.

Today, ABLE, in partnerships around the world and in their own backyard of Nashville, Tennessee, works with women who have overcome extraordinary circumstances to make a sustainable living.

◇◇

Over the years, I've also gained deeper empathy for my mom and myself and a more profound understanding of the constraints many women face due to our culture. While my mother had many privileges as a white woman with beauty, she failed to take advantage of opportunities that must have been presented to her. She could have but didn't take any opportunities to better her life or fight for her independence because she wasn't willing to work past all the fears, insecurities, and pain passed down to her from her mother and her mother's mother, and so on. And so I guess my assignment here is to break that pattern. It's heavy work but someone's gotta do it. I believe that's why I'm not a mother yet. I'm just scratching the surface of ready. How ironic. Just as I'm feeling emotionally and mentally fit for the privilege, I might just be out of time. She also faced some of the same constrictions I did, trying to navigate a world in which men tend to hold the power. As I walked through my own challenges into empowered adulthood, I developed a new understanding for some of the issues she might have faced.

◇◇

Sometime after Mom died, I met Harvey Weinstein at an industry party. His eyes followed me all around the room after we'd spoken briefly, so I wasn't surprised when my agent Tracy told me the following day that he wanted to meet with me. The location was set for his hotel room but something instinctive in me said that meeting him in a hotel room, after the energy I felt from him the night before, was not a good idea. Somehow, I had the balls to request that the meeting take place in the restaurant instead and for an assistant to be present. There was something about the slimy way he made me feel that first night that gave me the courage, plus maybe my lack of self-esteem told me he couldn't possibly want to meet with me for professional reasons. If there's one thing I've learned in my life, it's to trust my instincts that warn me about potentially difficult situations.

When we sat down to lunch, he bullshitted me for five minutes about movies I would be right for, then asked the assistant to excuse us. My stomach turned to lead when she walked away. I knew exactly why he was excusing her. *Here it comes*, I thought.

"Now, I know you were feeling what I was feeling when we met last night," he said. He gave me the eye.

"I'm not sure what you're talking about." I acted clueless.

We both played our roles until his voice became a little condescending.

"Listen, I'm just going to cut to the chase. You can have a very wonderful life. You can fly anywhere in the world you want to go on private jets. You can go on all the shopping sprees you want, and you can have a lot of fun. *We* can have a lot of fun. *If* you want to be my girlfriend."

My face worked through the options he was presenting, making it appear I was seriously considering his offer and having a hard time deciding. God forbid, as a woman, I act anything but thrilled by this big, powerful man's attentions.

I imagine he became impatient waiting for my response because he then added the phrase that became my out. "Or we can just keep this professional," he said.

Oh, thank God! An escape hatch.

"I need to think for a moment," I said. "Oh gosh. Wow. What a compliment!"

He waited.

"Unfortunately," I said, "sadly, I think we should probably just keep it professional."

"Okay."

I was relieved he didn't push me further. I was sweating from nerves and wanted to get away from him. I got up to leave and thanked him for lunch.

"I trust you won't tell Tracy about this," he said.

"Of course not. Oh my God, please. I'm so flattered, and thank you for even taking the time to meet with me."

The minute I was safely back in my car, I called Tracy. We marveled at his audacity, and she reinforced my instinct not to offend him; together we laughed and thought this was just part and parcel with slimy ol' Harvey.

Later, though, when all the #MeToo details emerged, I realized I'd been complicit in protecting him. He obviously knew he'd acted wrongly or he wouldn't have asked me not to tell anyone. I was also complicit in making him feel okay about the gross proposition he'd made. At the time, the only safe route I saw was to say I was flattered.

I know there are women who gratefully accepted that proposition. There was no way I was the first girl he proposed that idea to, and he must have known the odds were in his favor because he was so confident and casual about it. I was just one of many, and maybe one of many who said, "No, thank you." Perhaps there were even those who had the fearlessness to rebuff his overtures with more disdain and condemnation. I hope so.

Women are often taught to never offend or upset a man when declining his advances. We're taught men have fragile egos, and when you simply say no without dancing around to make him feel you're honored by his invitation, you run the risk of him lashing out at you. We do what we must to escape without harm. My heart breaks for the women and girls who either didn't have the experience to survive those moments unscathed or who weren't heeded when they said no.

I'm sure my mother would have a lot to say about these kinds of situations.

◇◇

Another time, I was on a set for a TV series waiting for the next shot to be set up when I felt a sudden rush of fire to my rear end. Someone had smacked me so hard it took my breath away. I turned around to see the male director of photography, laughing and waving a hundred-dollar bill at the crew, all of whom were in hysterics. Clearly, there'd been a bet.

I was in such shock, I didn't know what to do. In true me fashion, I needed to make everything okay, and because I wanted to be the cool girl, I went along with it. I rubbed my behind and complained about how much it hurt.

"You asshole!" I laughed, making light of the situation.

At home later that night I told another cast member what had happened. From their shock and disgust I realized how not okay the situation was. I finally felt safe enough to get really fucking angry.

The next day, once the cast and crew were ready for the first take of the day, I walked in front of the cameras and asked the director of photography to approach. A semicircle of people gathered, wondering what I was going to say. As he sauntered toward me, fury coursed through my body. Once he got close, I slapped him across his face as hard as I possibly could.

"Never disrespect me or another woman on this set," I said, my voice a calm rumble.

The crew applauded and I whipped around to face them. "Nope! You don't get to applaud now. You were all laughing yesterday. You paid him to do it! This goes for all of you, too."

He held a hand to his reddening cheek and lowered his head. "I'm so sorry," he said.

"I'm glad," I replied. "Now, let's have a great day."

That should have been it, as far as I was concerned. Eventually, though, word got to the producers who told me they planned to fire him.

"Please don't," I said. "He just moved here, and he has a little girl who just started school. I took care of it."

They fired him anyway.

At the time I believed I had to fight my own battles and never considered reporting him. I didn't think he needed to be fired; that wasn't even a thought in my head. I decided that hitting him as hard as he hit me made things even. I suppose you can take the girl out of Albuquerque but you can't take the Albuquerque out of the girl. I wouldn't do it this way again—violence is not the way to solve conflicts, I fully understand—but at the time, I made my point crystal clear and felt proud that I stuck up for myself. After that, everyone on set knew that kind of behavior was not funny and would not be tolerated.

As women, though, I gotta say, we get tired of having to demand common decency.

◇◇

Then there was the sex tape Rudy had recorded when I was a teenager. When I first moved into the world of acting, I had concerns and reached out to him. "Can you please destroy that tape and any photos?"

"Of course." He sounded so sweet. "I'm married now and settled down. I don't want that stuff haunting me, either. And while I have you on the line, can I just say I'm so sorry for how I treated you?"

"That's okay," I said, not wanting to get into it. I didn't know if he was sincere and didn't care to find out. "I just want to make sure those pictures are gone."

"They are," Rudy assured me. "Destroyed."

◇◇

"Mink, are you sitting down right now?"

I didn't think anyone actually said that in real life, but about a decade after my conversation with Rudy, those were the words my publicist used.

"I'm really sorry to ask you this, but is there a chance there's a sex tape of you in the world?"

"Yes, there is." So much for Rudy's heartfelt apology.

"It's okay. No judgment here. But the person you made that tape with is shopping it right now."

It was one of those moments where everything started to move in slow motion, the room throbbing. My stomach knotted and I was certain I was about to throw up. My whole world seemed about to collapse.

The tape I'd made with Rudy was in no way a cute sex tape. This was my child abuse on display. I'd worked so hard to escape that role I'd found myself trapped in, and now, the idea that it could be broadcast to the entire world made me feel like I was going to die.

"I was a minor," I said to her. "I was a kid."

"Don't worry. We're going to hire the most powerful entertainment attorney to handle it."

◇◇

"I just want to tell you all your options," that attorney said when he called. "One of them is that you could make a lot of money from this."

Was he crazy? I was so offended. I hung up and called my publicist back. "I don't want to work with him. How dare he!"

"Minka. Minka," she said, trying to calm me. "He's just a lawyer doing his job. There are people who are very famous now and have made a lot of money as a result of this kind of situation; some people choose to capitalize on it. He's not going to talk you into anything. He'll do whatever you want. It's okay."

I called him back and told him I was seventeen at the time and no, I did not want this to get out under any circumstances. I didn't want to make money off it. I didn't want to gain attention. I wanted it to go away. And I wanted to fucking kill Rudy.

"Okay, the fact you were only seventeen is good. Let me get to work."

He let all the media outlets who'd been interested in buying the tape know that it was technically child pornography and if they published it, we would come after them. He was able to use the music playing in the video to establish my age at the time. Next, he went to Rudy and explained that if he proceeded with the sale of the tape, we'd sue him for everything he was worth. Finally, he negotiated with Rudy and we were able to get the tape from him. Rudy signed a release saying he'd turned over every copy.

And for that release, I had to pay him fifty thousand dollars.

∞

These are the kinds of pressures women deal with now, in the twenty-first century, and they were even worse when my mom was raising me, back in the eighties. To be clear, we were both women with immense privilege, both pretty and white, characteristics that alone opened doors for us, as awful as that is. My mother had many opportunities to get her life together and to make more responsible choices, yet she didn't.

And many women, especially women of color and specifically Black and Native women or transwomen, have to work twice, three, ten times as hard as white cis women and still don't receive the same assistance or opportunities. Women have *never* enjoyed the fruits of equality or equity in the history of humankind and it continues to shape the paths available to us.

CHAPTER TWENTY

A Reckoning

"Want to try a rage room?" Conor asked.

"A what?" I said.

"It's this place where you smash plates and dishes and whatever you feel like breaking to let out your pain and anger."

One of my dearest friends was staying with me, helping me over the worst breakup of my life, and she kept coming up with any crazy thing she could think of for us to do that might help.

We were in the living room of the little house I'd bought for myself in L.A. a few years earlier and I was still in my pajamas and robe despite the late afternoon hour. I hadn't left the house in days and was a mess, coming to terms with the fact that the life I'd been building had just come to an abrupt halt.

Despite Conor's suggestion, I didn't feel the kind of rage or violence needed to smash plates. I would have preferred to climb into bed and just never get up again.

"I don't think so," I said, watching her make me another cup of herbal tea and try to get me to eat something nutritious. I had no appetite, and everything inside me felt dead after the miscarriage.

I was not only grieving the loss of the child who'd left me a week earlier but the loss of the relationship I'd been building with the baby's father.

Part of the problem was, of course, on me. He and I had been together a couple of years and we'd decided to build a family together. This was the first time in my life I'd felt ready to embark on this long-held dream. I was so thrilled when we conceived. We worked hard for this pregnancy, harvesting and implanting the embryo. Despite daily painful injections of progesterone because my hormone levels were low, things were going really well. We heard the heartbeat and planned the nursery. I imagined the kind of mother I was going to be and thought of all the things I'd give this child that I had never had. I'd never wanted anything more in my life than to be this little boy's mommy.

And then I lost the baby. I was crushed.

The old patterns that had long tangled me up immediately reappeared. I was absolutely devastated by the miscarriage. But with my mind, body, and spirit in shock, I played down how much the loss hurt me. My partner was working and I didn't want to burden him with all the overwhelming feelings inside me, the existential aching that seemed to be made of my very DNA. My body had stunningly and suddenly failed me, freezing all the plans we'd been making, as well as icing over my access to any genuine emotions. It was just too much to bear. I'd waited so long for this moment and now it was over. They say there's a ten percent chance of miscarriage with IVF. I became that statistic, and immediately my survival mechanism emerged front and center.

Downplay the pain! I'm fine! See, everyone? I'm fine! I got this. Nothing to see here. No one has to worry about me!

I went so far as to make grotesque dead-baby jokes.

Again, I was in shock. I wasn't thinking clearly but just trying to survive the pain and rush past it. The day after the miscarriage, I was cleaning the house and moving furniture. Moving furniture!

I saw no need to take time to process the loss and just powered my way forward. To sit and feel the pain, I feared, would break me.

I've come to realize I have an exceedingly high tolerance for pain, emotional and otherwise. In bad relationships, there are times when I have either stayed or gone back. "Things weren't all that bad," I'd say. "There's still so much potential!" Then, when it didn't work out, I'd assume responsibility for the demise of the relationship and tell myself that if only I showed up better and loved well enough, I would eventually receive the love I was giving. Silly, naive girl. This was a malfunction in my thinking. Being accountable and self-aware for one's side of the story is one thing, but too often I brushed under the rug *their* side of things, ignoring all the red flags flying in my face for the sake of proving that I could still make this work. When you grow up the way I did, you lack a sense of self worth that insists you deserve healthy love.

Recently, I was talking with a friend and complimenting them on not putting up with as much shit as I have in my life.

"It's not that I'm any better," my friend said. "You just have a higher pain threshold than I do."

That woke me up to pay closer attention to when my nervous system becomes activated around certain people and to honor my body for doing its job, asking me to pay attention. I'm learning to care for myself instead of tending to others first. At the time of the miscarriage, though, I didn't yet know that.

I proceeded with my subconscious plan, making light of what was happening. I convinced myself that then maybe we'd be able to move past this loss without being destroyed by it. I hoped we'd continue with our plans for the future.

If that was my thinking, it backfired.

∞

"You're acting like everything's fine," he said a few days later. "How am I supposed to fully grieve this loss if it's like nothing to you? We just lost a baby, Minka. This was *our baby*. This was going to be *our future*." It went in one ear and out the other.

I had thought all the same things but had zero access to my vulnerability or feelings. In trying to make sure I wasn't a burden to him, I'd given the impression I didn't care as much as he did. Instead of mourning *with* him, I assumed the role of making everything okay *for* him so he could feel better. Here was my old classic codependent behavior, sneaking back in. I would put him and his needs before mine at all costs, even when he didn't ask me to.

It wasn't healthy, and in all the hurt and confusion that followed that miscarriage, we broke up, cutting short all we'd built together.

∞

Throughout my career, I've been inextricably linked to whomever I'm dating. I have had some incredible relationships and have learned so much from them. Some of those men became very good and dear friends, still active in my life now. Others helped me learn how trauma showed up to help me break patterns, and others still only seemed to trigger more pain. Each time, though, I learned something about the parts of me that needed healing. And if I didn't learn a particular lesson, I needn't worry. The next relationship would be the same story. This repeated pattern showed me where I needed to grow. Alain de Botton says, "We blame our lovers, not our views of love." I've also heard that maturity doesn't come with age, it comes with acceptance of responsibility. Another quote really resonated with me when I read, "Whatever isn't claimed as our own is projected."

What I learned was that I needed to stop focusing on what I perceived were my partners' flaws and begin asking myself why I kept attracting and allowing men in my life who weren't capable of caring for me in the ways I needed as a result of their own unhealed childhood wounds—in ways we all deserve: consistent, predictable, and emotionally available. I was drawn to men that I decided lacked something I thought I could offer or teach them.

I couldn't.

◇◇

I was on my own, and now, surrounded by my closest friends, in the comfort and safety of their compassion and tenderness, reality was sinking in. With no one else for me to care for, thereby distracting myself by tending to their needs, my defenses crumbled and my heart dissolved into a million tiny pieces. In the span of three weeks, I had lost everything that mattered to me.

What got me through that time was the women in my life: the one who showed up at my door with a suitcase in hand, and the one with kids who couldn't move in with me but who'd drop off food and call every single day, multiple times a day. The ones who checked in every other day. They listened to me yell at him and fall apart, over and over again with the patience of saints. I'm talking about you, Conor. Khatira. You, too, Vanessa. Annie. Sandey. Fef. The fact that I had such fiercely loyal friends who loved me so much made me think I'd done something right in my life. I will never forget the way these women showed up. With so many incredible friends, old and new, holding space for me, I discovered who my family was.

If I can give one piece of advice to young ladies reading this, it would be to always and consistently invest in your friendships with humililty, love, and intention. I'm not always the best at this, but I've finally found my circle of women who see me and understand me. They know my heart and show me grace when I need it. As a result, they've inspired me to be the best friend I can possibly be for them, too. My sisterhood means the world to me and I cherish them with every fiber of my being. Men will come and they will go, but it is the women in your lives who'll always be there.

∞

After that breakup, I underwent a series of ketamine treatments. What did I have to lose? I could no longer deny that I was the common denominator in all my relationships nor how my old patterns kept wreaking havoc on my love life and would continue to do so if I didn't find a way to heal the little girl inside me who felt so unworthy of love. It was clear talk therapy had only gotten me so far.

After years of discussing my backstory with therapists, I found myself in what I called "awareness hell." I was acutely conscious of all the patterns and unhealthy choices I made with men, but I didn't know how to unravel those wires. I was still attracted to chaos and found ways to re-create it because it felt safe and familiar. Anytime I was triggered, I was acting as if the event in my childhood was happening right now. It will never cease to amaze me that we re-create the environments we grew up in because it's what we know. We go where it's familiar, even if it hurts.

For me, talk therapy only scratched the surface because it only dealt with the conscious level of my mind. If Freud was right about love and psychotherapy being the only two things that truly change you, I was ready to explore the latter in a much deeper way.

I needed to pave new neural pathways. It was time to attempt to heal old wounds. There were only so many times I could tell myself I needed to re-parent and love my inner child before I realized talking about these things wasn't making any difference at all.

Under a psychiatrist's guidance, I would take the psychedelic over a course of eight sessions and see if I could break free of the mindset that had kept me stuck, or at least come to a different understanding of how I sabotaged myself when it came to relationships. This type of therapy is said to be useful for childhood trauma, and over time, I came to understand why and how it's so effective.

As a scrub nurse, I knew the important role played by the anesthesiologist. If you have a cancerous tumor and the surgeon wants to take it out so you can heal, the surgery is only possible because the anesthesiologist finds a way around all your natural defense mechanisms. No one is going to sit still and let a surgeon excise a piece of their body willingly without anesthesia. We will all fight to keep that surgeon's hands off our bodies, to keep from feeling that pain.

That's what my subconscious had been doing whenever I tried to work through the trauma memories of my past. Even when I knew that revisiting the tough moments would be helpful, my subconscious refused and blocked all those efforts. No matter how willing I was to face the music, my subconscious would take over and suppress it and tell me everything was fine. It was just too painful to admit otherwise.

Our mind and body are built to protect us from pain, and in order to survive difficult experiences, our brain stores those painful memories deep down in the abyss of our psyches, so hidden we might think they aren't of any concern.

So the ketamine, I came to understand, would be the anesthesia. It would lower my natural defenses so I could finally get into the places that hurt and try to heal them.

Before taking the drug, I laid out my intentions for the session: I was seeking healing of whatever was stopping me from fully being present in my relationships and in my life. With the psychiatrist keeping watch, I allowed the drug to dissolve under my tongue for thirteen minutes so it could enter my bloodstream sublingually—this is much quicker than just swallowing the medicine and having it enter through the belly.

I had assumed the session would take me back to my youngest years, where the earliest trauma and lack of object permanence was instilled. Where the insecure attachment was formed as a result of neglectful parenting. But it didn't. I was surprised to find myself transported to my sixteen-year-old self, back in that little house I'd shared with Rudy and his dad and brother in Albuquerque. I watched scenes with Rudy unfold, like I was watching a movie, smelling the shag carpet, hearing his voice, and feeling the panic in my chest trying to keep on his good side.

For the first time ever, though, I saw myself from the outside. There she was, just a young teen, alone in the world, cooking and cleaning, working hard to pull her weight and not ask for anything from anyone, staying with a man who didn't want her there, and yet, she had nowhere else to go. The more she maneuvered to get the love and compassion she craved, the more her desires were thwarted. For an hour or more, I watched this movie of my earlier life and I wept deep, chest-shattering sobs for that girl. I felt an empathy for her I'd never before experienced. She was so young.

In the integration session with the doctor the following day, when we went through what had come up while under the effects of ketamine to unpack what had happened, I realized I had been operating in my adult relationships like that scared sixteen-year-old girl. I had decided at some point, unbeknownst to my conscious mind, that men are not to be trusted and always must be kept at arm's length. I had one foot out the door, ready to leave at a moment's notice. I would allow no one to get close enough to hurt me, and if they did, I'd either sabotage or run. My hypervigilance was always on the lookout for any sign that I was unsafe. And if you look, you will surely find. So any hint of danger would be the confirmation bias I was looking for to let me know it was time to run.

The hour I spent crying for that little girl was so healing and that new knowledge changed everything. Now, little by little, that little girl is learning to relax and trust me. She'd always been the one in the driver's seat, leading the way, making the plans; she was used to doing that. But now, finally, with the help of a coach, I'm working to show her that the adult me, the mature me, is ready to take over and make the decisions. She can let go now; she doesn't need to be in charge any longer.

Over time, my hope is that she will come to trust that we are safe, I can handle things, and I can do so without operating from a place of fear of abandonment or panic. All these years, she'd felt the need to steer the bus, having to prove herself to everybody and to be likable—and, by all means, to be the one to run away before the person she cared about could run away from her. But now, at long last, I get to be the one in the driver's seat.

Epilogue

Before I tried the ketamine route, I utilized just about everything I could get my hands on to heal myself and to move toward wholeness, every one of which played an important role in my journey. I did EMDR therapy and equine therapy. I attended Al-Anon meetings, did a Hoffman Process retreat, and took ayahuasca. I'm currently working with an attachment theory coach, which has been illuminating. It's very difficult to talk your way into healing. Working with someone who provides purpose-driven action helps me identify and address my own red flags and unhealthy patterns, and how to undo all the ways I associate chaos with love. We create new ways of moving through life and relationships and ways to react to my triggers. New levels of self-awareness allow me to notice the triggers and choose my reactions, untangling the mess these protective mechanisms make. Triggers will always be a part of my life, but I can choose how I respond to those triggers. Which for me, at this point, is everything. The business of healing long-standing trauma is a constant process, and I'm always looking for the next step. Most important, though, was learning that I couldn't blame anyone or anything outside of myself for the cycles I kept finding myself mired in. It took a long time to finally stop focusing on what was outside of me and focus instead on my inner self and those elements of my life I could personally change.

◇◇

I was still grieving the miscarriage, home with Conor caring for me, when she came up with yet another harebrained idea.

"Want to try pole dancing?"

Without hesitation, I said yes. If she'd asked me if I wanted to stand on my head while being fed candy corn, I would have agreed to that, too. Anything that might help. Just to do something. Get me out of the house. Maybe I could take one tiny step away from this depression that was weighing me down.

The dance studio was in Hollywood, an easy roll down the street from where I lived. Conor drove because I was still too much of a mess to be trusted behind the wheel. She'd scheduled a private session for the two of us and her friend Grace. Once in the studio, we bought the stripper heels needed to navigate the pole. I never realized how instrumental that particular footwear is to this style of dance. We'd brought our own heels to the session, thinking it wouldn't matter, but we were sorely mistaken. Street shoes were not allowed.

The babies I bought were nine inches tall including the platform, and I could hardly walk in them. We looked like newborn colts trying to understand how their legs work. But that was part of the deal. Before we even got to the pole, we'd have to master the challenge of walking across the studio floor.

Conor and Grace giggled as they tried to walk seductively but I was still too much in a funk to get into the spirit. Deep down, though, something was slowly coming alive in me, a new kind of curiosity. Once I started to get the hang of it, I came to appreciate just how powerful, feminine, and sexy walking in these heels made me feel—albeit a bit clumsy.

The instructors were lovely, all either retired or active strippers, and they knew how to move beautifully and suggestively and encouraged us to do the same.

"This is a space to celebrate us as beautiful women in whatever form we take." Constance took us through the first class. "No matter how broken, how chubby, how awkward we might feel in these shoes, whether we have cellulite or less than perfect bodies, none of that matters. Just the love and celebration of our beautiful selves."

Music throbbed overhead and a disco ball flashed sparkles across our bodies and faces. My friends were stunningly gorgeous as I watched them in the mirrors that surrounded us while they followed the moves Constance demonstrated. Soon, I got into the groove, staring at myself in the mirror, shimmying my shoulders, swaying my hips, letting my arms undulate around me, circling my pole. For that moment, I wasn't thinking about my sadness, about having lost my baby and my partner. I was not in my head at all but completely in my body, glorying in the way it moved and danced.

◇◇

Sometime earlier, my therapist had pointed out that I presented myself so conservatively; I wore mostly baggy, demure clothing. "You know," he said, "you're acting like a stripper's daughter."

"What?" I was furious. How dare he! "That's not true," I said, telling him all the reasons why. I had made so many choices to be sure I was never seen that way.

He listened patiently as I made my case before responding. "You're working far too hard to prove to everyone you're not a stripper's daughter. Your pendulum has swung so far to one side that you're not living as Minka. You're living as the girl trying to prove she's not her mother."

His words stuck with me. He literally gave me homework—to wear thigh-high boots and a miniskirt—which I never did. That kind of flaunting my body felt way too uncomfortable but I got his point. The seed had been planted and I was trying to give myself permission to lighten up. (This therapist was so much better than the one who'd told me to call my mother out in such a horrible way.)

∞

But now, strutting across the wood floor in nine-inch heels, wearing an outfit so skimpy I'd be afraid to be seen on Venice Beach in it, everything shifted into focus. I saw myself clearly for the first time. I was powerful, and it was okay to celebrate my femininity, my sexuality, my sensuousness. I was doing this, not as a form of survival at age seventeen, nor for any reason or person, but for the sheer love and conscious exploration of myself. My joy was driven by my own internal feelings of fulfillment. I didn't need anyone to see or approve of me to gain from it.

I felt Conor staring at me. When I looked over at her, she was crying. I recognized the tears she shed, relief to see her friend finally start to come back to life. She'd been with me for weeks, watching me dissolve into a shell of my former self. She now saw what was happening inside me: the smile, the pride, the color returning to my face, the joy in my eyes. I was falling in love with myself.

After that, I became obsessed with that feeling of empowerment, of loving myself, of allowing myself to be sexy and sensual. I took private pole dancing lessons twice a week. Just for the fun of it, just for me and my friends, and for a few months those became the best hours of my day, the time I would look forward to and that would inspire me to get out of bed every day. It was as if my mom, in another universe, had orchestrated all of this. The women who taught me to pole dance loved what they did; they loved their bodies and what they were capable of. They told stories of how their stripper community had saved their lives during their hardest times. They didn't hide their sensuality, nor were they ashamed of it. They were athletic and moved so gracefully. Watching them on the pole blew my mind: They could do things I never imagined possible. The power, the strength, the beauty, the elegance. I was in awe.

In one way or another, those women, stand-ins for my mother, breathed life back into me.

It's kind of ironic, but a side product of this pole dancing was that I came to love and appreciate my mom in a whole new way. This was medicine, the way ketamine also became my healer. In my classes, I was baring my soul, all but naked, fumbling through the moves, having a hard time picking up the choreography but no longer fighting against the shadow side of my past.

I was no longer judgmental or ashamed to be a stripper's daughter. This was my life. This was me, and I gloried in all of it. As a result I walk a little taller today. I'm proud of me and all I've survived.

Why should we suppress or hide our sexuality? It is our super-power as women. It's in all of us no matter our shape, size, or color, dimples or no dimples. Belly or no belly.

I can see why embodying this power can be scary to so many. A woman fully awake to herself is a formidable creature. Just imagine what we'd all be capable of if we allowed ourselves access to our divine goddess power.

Taking those classes and embracing that side of myself, a side I'd long kept locked away, my relationship with my mother grew so much deeper and stronger. The more I healed my wounds and the more forgiveness I developed for her, the more compassion I found for both of us—and the more sadness I felt for how soon she was taken from me.

Now that I'm capable of having a real woman-to-woman con-versation with her, I wish she were here. I think I would now know how to communicate honestly with her, without scaring or intimidating her or being mean to or impatient with her, as I often was during her lifetime.

I have so much more empathy and grace for her than I ever had when she was living. The ideas of forgiveness and compassion were not foreign concepts to me back then. I did my best on her dying days to tell her how much I forgave her and to give her credit. She did many things right.

Still, I would have loved to know her on a human level and to ask her more meaningful questions—as a woman, and not as a scared, resentful little girl who wished she had a better mommy.

Sometimes I have conversations with her, after pole dancing class, say, or driving around, or simply taking a walk. I summon her spirit and ask her the questions I never got to in life.

What was that like for you, raising me?

What were your struggles?

Now that I'm grown, I can handle the answers. You don't have to hide anything from me anymore.

Go ahead, Momma. Tell me about your life.

Tell me everything.

Acknowledgments

There are so many people who helped bring this heartfelt project finally to the page, and I owe them each a debt of gratitude.

First to my mother: I'm so grateful to you for loving me the best way you knew how and for doing the best you could with the tools you had. I am so relieved you are free from all the pain and heartache in this physical form. I feel more connected to you now than I ever did when we were young and just trying to survive. Thank you for looking over me and guiding me. Thank you for sending me flamingos just when I need them to let me know you're here. I feel you with me every single day. And to Rick, my biological father, for planting the seed and providing me the opportunity to leave Albuquerque to start a bigger life. Our relationship is not without its bumps, but I will forever be indebted to you for setting me on this path toward freedom.

Thank you to my many therapists along the way and especially to Dr. Crausman, who helped me see the courage and resilience I'd shown by working at the peep show, rather than the shame I thought I deserved.

My beloved girlfriends (you know who you are) who have been telling me for ten years to write this book: I cherish your loyalty and everlasting support. Thank you, also, to all my ex-boyfriends for the indelible lessons. Each of you was a teacher and I've grown so much as a result of our time. No failures, only lessons and growth.

Thank you to my former manager, Todd Diener, who believed in this project, who insisted I write it, and who reassured me it was worth sharing this story with the world. I am grateful.

Peter Berg always encouraged me to write. Every time we spoke, he asked the same question: "Have you written today?" I'd shake my head. One day, he finally yelled at me: "Wake the fuck up at five every morning and write for twenty minutes. Before you know it, you'll have ninety pages." He was right, and here we are.

Thank you also to the countless people who listened to my story as I practiced sharing and building up the courage to own my truth little by little. I so needed your positive and nonjudgmental responses. Thank you, my beloved Claudia Peña, for the time and love given to pouring over my words and insisting and reassuring me I'm on the right path.

Thank you to Albert Lee, my book agent, for believing in my story, and to all the wonderful folks at Henry Holt, especially editor extraordinaire Serena Jones and superwoman backup Anita Sheih, for your amazing attention to my words.

And to Bernadette Murphy, who spent countless hours with me, holding my hand through the entire process, reading, editing, and rearranging words to help me make it all make sense: thank you.

ABOUT THE AUTHOR

Minka Kelly has portrayed a variety of roles across film and television. She first won the hearts of audiences in her starring role as Lyla Garrity on NBC's Emmy Award–winning show *Friday Night Lights*. Her other credits include NBC's *Parenthood*, HBO's *Euphoria, Man Seeking Woman*, JJ Abrams's *Almost Human*, DC Comics' *Titans*, and the films *The Butler* and *500 Days of Summer*. She works closely with ABLE, a lifestyle brand focused on ending generational poverty by assisting women who have overcome extraordinary circumstances. She currently resides in Los Angeles.